ON THE ROAD AGAIN

On The Road Again

15 HITMAKERS OF THE FIFTIES TELL THEIR OWN AMAZING STORIES

Dave Nicolson

MUSIC MENTOR BOOKS
York, England

© 2005 Dave Nicolson. All rights reserved. First edition.

The right of Dave Nicolson to be identified as Author of this Work has been asserted in accordance with the UK *Copyright, Designs and Patents Act 1988.*

Every effort has been made to trace the copyright holders of material used in this volume. Should there be any omissions in this respect, we apologise and shall be pleased to make the appropriate acknowledgments in future printings.

A full list of illustrations and photo credits appears on page 203. The trademarks Abbott, ABC-Paramount, Brunswick, Cameo, Canadian-American, Capitol, Decca, Dot, Liberty, London, Mercury, MGM, Okie, Oriole, Parlophone, Philips, Swan and Wing appear by kind permission of the owners.

All rights reserved. No part of this publication may be reproduced, stored in a retrieval system or transmitted in any form by any means, electronic, mechanical, reprographic, recording or otherwise without prior written permission from the publisher.

This book is sold subject to the conditions that it shall not, by way of trade or otherwise, be lent, resold, hired out or otherwise circulated without the publisher's prior consent in any form of binding or cover other than that in which it is published and without a similar condition including this condition being imposed on the subsequent purchaser.

Whilst every effort has been made to ensure the correctness of information included in this book, the publisher makes no representation — either express or implied — as to its accuracy and cannot accept any legal responsibility for any errors or omissions or consequences arising therefrom.

British Library Cataloguing-in-Publication Data
A catalogue record for this book is available from the British Library.

ISBN 0-9519888-9-1

Published worldwide by Music Mentor Books *(Proprietor: G.R. Groom-White)*
69 Station Road, Upper Poppleton, York YO26 6PZ, North Yorkshire, England.
Telephone/Fax: +44 (0)1904 330308   *email:* music.mentor@lineone.net

Cover by It's Great To Be Rich, York.

Printed and bound in Great Britain by Antony Rowe Ltd, Eastbourne, East Sussex

For Bruno

Foreword

Hello, Marvin Rainwater here. I am delighted to do the 'liner notes' for this book. Having started singing at the age of fifteen, I am now well into my seventh decade in the business and still enjoying every minute of it. Needless to say, I still have a *Whole Lotta Woman* in my life!

Like all of my fellow artists in this book, I've known all the ups and downs and twists and turns, and a career that's blown *Hot And Cold*, but you won't get a *Boo Hoo* from me. All of the memories are priceless (unless I'm offered a book or movie deal) and I wouldn't trade any of it.

If you have any hits in this business and manage to make and get your share of good money, you are lucky. Most of the artists I know simply live to entertain. Give us an audience and the majority would willingly do their act for nothing (promoters please ignore this statement!).

Dave Nicolson sees our careers as an important part of social history because our music has affected and influenced millions worldwide and continues to do so. Of course, we weren't aware of that back then when we were out there entertaining and hopefully making a living, but when you look back and take stock it does all knit together. I'm very proud to have played even a very small part in that history and to gratefully acknowledge *my* roots and influences in turn.

Most artists give publicity interviews to highlight their latest tour or release, but they don't really welcome personal interviews and I'm no exception. However, Dave is a persistent and painstaking interviewer who is determined to chronicle the lives and times of popular music artists as *they* recall them, and is even prepared to take our selective memories to task in the interests of accuracy!

So, to anyone who ever bought our records, went to our shows and followed our careers: I know that you will be fascinated by this book. You will never get a better bill, and remember, like all of the artists in this book, *I Dig You Baby*!

Marvin Rainwater (Da Rockabilly King)
April 2005
Aitkin, Minnesota

Contents

	Introduction 11
	Acknowledgments 13
1	**Giddy-Up!** *Freddie Bell* 15
2	**Exotic Sounds** *Martin Denny* 25
3	**Steel Magic** *Johnny Farina / Santo & Johnny* 31
4	**Twin Talents** *The Kalin Twins* 37
5	**Rock'n'Roll From Hawaii** *Robin Luke* 53
6	**Mr. Skiffle** *Chas McDevitt* 77
7	**Sea Of Love** *Phil Phillips* 93
8	**Whole Lotta Man** *Marvin Rainwater* 99
9	**Group In A Million** *Herb Reed / The Platters* 111
10	**The Singin' Idol** *Tommy Sands* 123
11	**Rock'n'Roll Is Here To Stay** *Joe Terranova / Danny & The Juniors* 131
12	**Green Light, Red Light** *Mitchell Torok* 141
13	**Bad Boy** *Marty Wilde* 157
14	**The Cool Ghoul** *John Zacherle* 177
	The Interviews 193
	Index 195
	Illustrations and Photo Credits 203

Introduction

After my twenty-year journey with *On The Road* I had no intention of attempting another book of interviews in spite of its warm welcome from pop music fans in many parts of the world. Then, unexpectedly, I found that I had time to fill and decided to have another try at finding those artists whose careers and personal lives had always interested me. It was also a timely opportunity to get to grips with new (to me) technology and the Internet in particular.

When I first started interviewing artists way back in 1981, one of my intended subjects was Sammy Turner. Sadly, all efforts to trace him failed. Therefore, searching the Internet to contact those artists from popular music's past who had interested me came naturally and one of the products is this volume, *On The Road Again*. Unfortunately, not even the thousands of links on the 'net' could locate the *Lavender Blue* man.

For me, choosing artists for interview is nearly entirely subjective and based on memorable recordings that capture mood, time and place of past experiences. Those records are as valid now as they were all those years ago. So, what makes a record memorable? There's no one answer to that, but originality, emotional appeal and airplay are just some of the factors. Some recordings which were massive smash hits in their day are regarded years after with a range of emotions from affection to outright embarrassment — if they are regarded at all.

Many artists can enjoy a string of hits, but not be remembered for anything in particular. Some, like Sinatra, Bennett and Mathis have built up a library catalogue of work which ensures that they are never out of airplay. Artists like Little Richard, Fats Domino and Jerry Lee Lewis, who have never had a *Billboard* No.1 pop hit have become legends. Ironically, singer-songwriter Chuck Berry's only chart-topper from a large quality output is *My Ding-A-Ling*! In my opinion, every one of the fifteen artists in this book, either by accident or design, was involved in the production of great tracks. Often those individual records proved to be far bigger and longer-lasting than their overall career success.

A few of them felt that they were part of creating something special at the time. Others are just surprised and grateful that their work captured public taste — sometimes at the time, sometimes after the passing of time — which ensured them a lasting place in popular music history. To some artists that big success was a blight which obliterated everything before and after, so that they became labelled as 'one hit wonders' when they weren't. To others, having hit records didn't mean a thing. These recordings were made by design and by sheer chance — everywhere from a bathroom to large recording studios. Some of the tracks in this book did make No.1, some did not. Some were lauded in some countries and virtually ignored in others... including their home market. Some were even banned.

Introduction

Like its predecessor, *On The Road*, this book contains interviews with artists who give their own accounts of their work and private lives. If you haven't got the black vinyl any more (shame on you!) then put your tape, CD, DVD or latest technology on and play their recordings as you read these fascinating accounts. And then, when you finish these interviews, play them all again and spare a thought for all the other classic tracks that were surely made but never got to be heard.

Acknowledgments

Thank you to all the artists interviewed for this volume for the pleasure they have given over many years and continue to give, and for the interest, time and patience shown when being interviewed. Special thanks to Marvin Rainwater for providing the *Foreword*.

This book could not have been successfully completed without the generous assistance of promoters, artists' wives and family members, secretaries, fellow writers and fans who facilitated interviews, research and illustrations. My appreciation also to editor and publisher George Groom-White for his commitment and high standards of production, to Verena Groom-White for providing the *Index*, and Paul Barrett for his help with contacts.

Also to Bill Sturrock who for over forty years has shared the good and the bad of live concert performances with unfailing good humour and enthusiasm, and for the life and art of the late Denis McLoughlin.

Dave Nicolson
July 2005

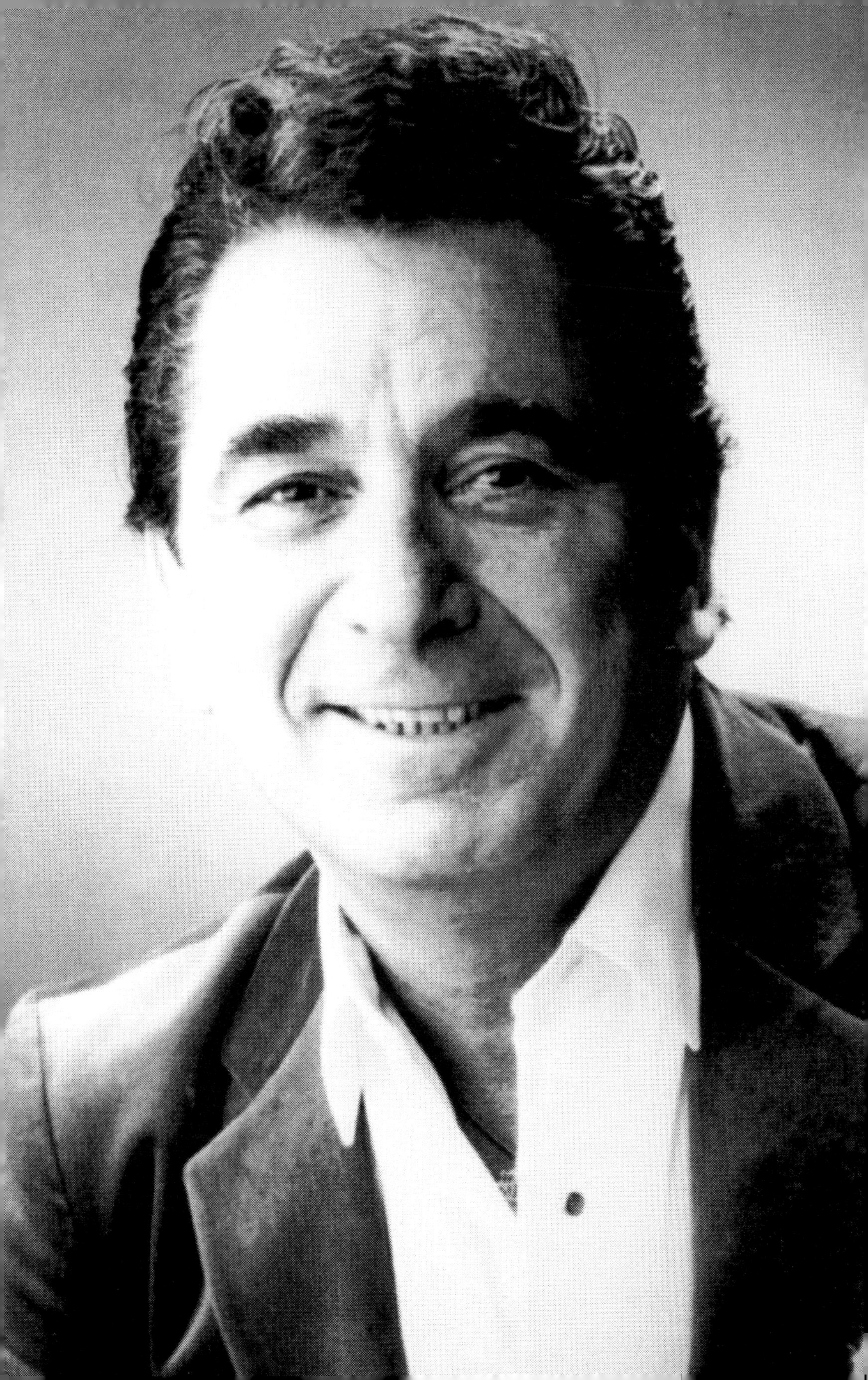

1

GIDDY-UP!
Freddie Bell

A born entertainer and one of the legendary names of the golden age of rock'n'roll, thanks to his classic recording of *Giddy-Up-A Ding Dong,* and a memorable appearance in *Rock Around The Clock*, Freddie Bell developed a very successful Las Vegas lounge act that has kept him in demand with audiences for over half a century. A superb musician and dancer whose dynamic performances at his Sands Hotel 'home' have thrilled millions, he's still rocking and rolling in his seventies.

My date of birth is September 29, 1931 and I was born Ferdinando Dominick Bello in Philadelphia, Pennsylvania. My mother's name was Mary, my dad's name was Andrew. I have two brothers, Carmen and Joseph, and a sister, Nancy. Dad had a meat market and grocery store in South Philadelphia and my mother was a housewife. Later on, after my dad did pretty well, we moved to New Jersey, which was only about thirty minutes away from where our business was. Dad built a home there in Voorhees, New Jersey, which is Cherry Hill. I went through high school — South Philadelphia High School — but I was not a great student; I was a good student. Certain subjects I really enjoyed, but something I didn't enjoy such as algebra or geometry, I was never that good. But I loved to read, and I loved history. That's about it.

At the age my family and I discovered that I was musical *[laughs]*, I guess I was seven years old when I did a show in grade school, *Pinocchio*, and I played the part of Jiminy Cricket. And then after that I became the MC for most of the school shows and activities. I was an impressionist also. When I was thirteen, I was then in junior high school, and Dr. Jacobson, the musical director, said they had two instruments if someone would like to learn. They had a bass violin and a flute, and I chose the bass violin. It was a full bass and being kinda small I couldn't reach it, so I had to stand on a box to play.

There was not so much family talent for music before me, but after me, a lot of the folks in my family. All my nephews have got into the music business. My nephew, Bobby, is a rock singer and works for bands all around the East Coast. My nephew, Binky, my brother Carmen's boy, is a concert bassist who took after the same instrument as I did. His wife is also a

Chapter 1 – Freddie Bell

FREDDIE BELL AND THE BELLBOYS
Exclusive **Mercury** *Recording Artists*

musician, so there is some lineage there. My ma was probably the one that helped push me. Whenever we'd be at any gathering — or anywhere — ma would say: 'Get up and sing.' Or, if somebody else sang, she'd say: 'Get up there and show them how to do it — and dance!' And I *loved* to dance when I was a kid. My mother was probably more encouraging than anyone else.

It's very difficult to say which were my earliest musical influences because I always loved rhythm & blues: I don't know why, but it always got to me. So that's who I used to listen to all the time — such as Wynonie 'Blues' Harris, Arnett Cobb, all the early r&b artists, and that was my influence as far as music. Of course, I loved the male singers like Frank Sinatra and Perry Como, people like that.

As for my first public amateur performance, the first thing I ever did — I told you that I was an impressionist — my first impression in school was Danny Kaye. I *loved* Danny Kaye, and I did all the usual impressions of Jimmy Cagney, Bogart and all that, and, as I told you, I was the school nut in all the shows. I did some talent shows around Philadelphia, but I never did Ted Mack or Arthur Godfrey. As far as what year my talent got spotted, I don't think it *ever* happened really. *[laughter]*

I left school in my twelfth year. What happened was, I got drafted for the service after I left school and was rejected. Then I got married. Then they called me back and I was rejected for a second time. I don't want to go into my ailments. I got rejected from the service at the end of 1951 and I had been working a day job. I worked as a presser in Botiny 500, a clothes factory. So, I quit my job because I thought I was going in the service — I wanted a few months of rock'n'roll. And then I got rejected again and I figured I wanted to do *something*, so I formed a trio in 1951. It was called 'The Three Men Of Rhythm'. How about that originality?!

As far as being a solo performer, professionally, I never was until later in life — after the Bellboys. Within six to eight months I was up to a quintet.

Chapter 1 – Freddie Bell

I didn't have a name for the group. In searching for a name — all the bird names were gone, the Penguins, the Orioles, etc — so my first wife, Olga, said to me: 'Why don't you call it "Freddie Bell & The Bellboys"?' And I thought that was kinda stupid. I said: 'No, I don't think so.' Then we mulled it around and we decided on Freddie Bell & The Bellboys. And that's how the Bellboys came into being.

I didn't start to play trombone until I formed the Bellboys, and the reason was that my manager at that time told me that he'd like to have me out front and moving around, more than playing a full-size bass. At that day, my nickname was 'Freddie Hop'. When I started to front the band, a natural double — they're both bass clef instruments — was a trombone. So, I went out and got a trombone, studied for a short while... not very long, I was never really that good at it — fair, and started to front the Bellboys.

At that time we were working a lot of shows — there were four of us actually — and we were doing a lot of in-show variety show type things. So, we had costumes made which were like the Philip Morris costume — like a bellboy's costume — and we wore those in the show. Then I took the band on the road for 22 weeks and rehearsed every day, started writing, and came along with some of the ideas of what I wanted to do. But before I had my own band, I worked for Ernie Ventura, who was Charlie Ventura the saxophone player's brother, and I was a member of his group for a while. I also played with Richie Salvo's band.

My first recording was a song called *Hound Dog*. No, before that I did a song called *Move Me Baby, Move Me* and another song I wrote called *Cool And Crazy*. I did most of my writing. As a matter of fact, the one thing I liked about recording at that time was the fact that I was doing my own material and I was writing all the songs that were recorded. So, I was on the Teen label, and then at the end of 1952 or beginning of 1953 I was picked up by Mercury.

My first manager was a man named Fred Costa, who was not really the best, but who got me started anyway. He was one of those guys who sent you on the road and you stayed out forever. It wasn't until 1953 that I met Joe Glaser of Associated Booking Corporation, who is the largest single agent in the US, and he became my manager and my agent. I was not under-age, so I didn't need anyone to sign for me, and as far as legal representation to protect my interests, I had none, so therefore I was screwed pretty good.

The original members of the group were: Chick Keeney on drums, Jerry Mayo on trumpet, Jackie Kane on sax, Frankie Brent on bass and Russ Conti on piano. We were aiming at r&b, and the Bellboys were working clubs all over the place, and because of my original record, *Hound Dog*, I became sort-of a large name on *American Bandstand* (both the radio and television shows) — which meant that we were working very good, making pretty good money and not traveling hardly at all. Our style was later called 'rock'n'roll' — it was called 'r&b' at the time. After *Hound Dog,* which became No.1 on *American Bandstand* for sixteen weeks, that sort of kicked us off and we were called to Las Vegas, Nevada in November 1953. We opened the Sands Hotel, and that's where I've performed ever since I have been a Vegas act.

Chapter 1 – Freddie Bell

We were signed as a group — Freddie Bell & The Bellboys — for our first recordings and our recordings were always 'Freddie Bell & The Bellboys'. I was the leader and members were on salary in the beginning. Then we decided on a corporation and I gave each of the boys a portion of my 100%. When we first started, as far as earnings, we weren't making very good money, but then the money climbed and got bigger and bigger. And then we were up to $10,000 a week, which was big money in those days.

Choreography was something I always liked: I always loved to dance. I studied with Georgie Tapps, one of the great tap dancers of all times. I studied with him, but I always loved to dance. I was a dancer from when I was a kid and I did all the choreography for the band. The group's on-stage moves did require a lot of rehearsal for the choreography, but I had all pretty good movers. Probably the worst was Jerry: I had to teach him to dance. And we did a lot of rehearsing and a lot of filming of ourselves to see if the choreography was good.

Elvis would come to Vegas, and I think the first time he worked in Vegas was 1956 at the Frontier Hotel. We were his favorite Las Vegas band and performers, and every night he would come into the Sands' lounge to watch us. And one night he said: 'I love that song you're doing in the show', which was *Hound Dog*. I said: 'Of course,' and I took one of my recordings and gave it to Colonel Parker and he gave it to Elvis to record. I called Bobby Shad, who was my A&R man, and told him that I thought Elvis might record our song and I asked him to re-release my recording so we would pick up the tail sales against the Elvis recording. Well, Mercury Records waited eight or ten weeks, and by that time Elvis had sold six million records. So, there goes another one; that was something I really missed. But Elvis from then on, every time he would see me, would say: 'Do you have a song for me?'

As far as writing *Giddy-Up-A Ding Dong*, what happened was that there was — as a lot of people in England do know — a group in the States called the Treniers. They never called me 'Freddie'. Because my name was Bell, they always called me 'Ding Dong'. And they were responsible for me getting the idea of writing a song called *Giddy-Up-A Ding Dong*. I was into horse racing and *Giddy-Up-A Ding Dong* was a joke about a horse. It was written in 1953 by Peppino Lattanzi and me: we co-wrote all our songs. A friend of years, Pep was a trumpet player and also an arranger for me. He passed on five years ago. It was because of the Treniers that I recorded that song. I didn't think of *Giddy-Up-A Ding Dong* as a rock'n'roll song really because at that time everything was meant for sound and sight: we were not just a band, we were a performing group. *Giddy-Up-A Ding Dong* was recorded in New York City and I think we did, like, ten takes. My producer was Bobby Shad.

The record broke on *American Bandstand* and Alan Freed was the first to pick it up and play it real big. The first time I heard *Giddy-Up-A Ding Dong* playing on the radio was when Bob Horn put it on *American Bandstand*. When it entered the Top 100, I was very excited. I was asked to do little teenage shows in schools, and they would play the record and I would sign autographs for the kids. As far as reaching the US Top Twenty, I would say it took maybe six months. I don't know if it ever got past the Top Twenty, but it did sell about 1½ million records around the world. To promote it, I did guest appearances on a lot of shows. I did the Carson show, I did the Sullivan show. Also, after Dean Martin and Jerry Lewis broke up, I was on the first show, *Colgate Comedy Hour*, when they made up again: we did a thing called *Shake A Hand* which is available somewhere.

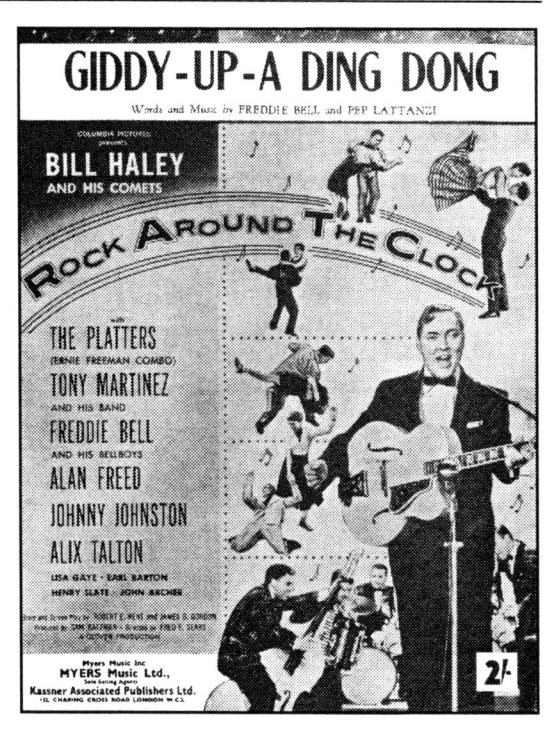

I did not receive a gold disc for a million-plus sales of *Giddy-Up-A Ding Dong*. As far as royalties from Mercury, I really did not make a lot of money with Mercury; but, as most recording artists will tell you, you pay for everything at a recording session, and I never owed Mercury any money — which was pretty good.

I did go out on tour with Irvin Feld, and I also toured Australia [in 1957] with Lee Gordon's tour. With Alan Freed I did the Brooklyn Paramount. I never did any backing for any other groups on these tours. Memories of my touring days were that I had a lot of fun. I was young, having fun. At that time, when we would go on a States tour for Feld, there was, like, eleven bands. As far as traveling overseas, the three of us — the Platters, Bill Haley & His Comets and ourselves — did the Far East, Japan and all those countries. My salary at that time would range from $7,500 to $10,000, which was very, very big money for us at that moment. As far as friendships formed with fellow artists, I've known everyone in the business and have learnt from everyone in the business.

No-one looked after my money properly for me, and I didn't either. As a matter of a fact, I had a business manager who took off with most of it, but I was treated fairly by my managers except for that one. I lived and worked in Las Vegas most of the time, and I did enjoy gaming. And it kept me out of the style that I wanted to live in. The success did affect my first marriage because I was away all the time and subject to temptations and problems. My marriage did not work out at all. With the pressures of traveling and being on the road all the time, and being as susceptible, you can get into all kinds of problems.

How did I cope with girls, drink and drugs? Well, I would say I enjoyed most of them. *[laughs]* Yes, I did get in trouble quite a bit. *[laughs]* I was a kind-of a swinger. What I got out of my tours was seeing new places, meeting new people, and realizing the cultures and the excitement of other countries — which is one of the reasons I love your country, England. As far as working for people around the world, it's amazing to me that music is an equalizer.

I was thrilled by the success of *Giddy-Up-A Ding Dong* in the UK. You asked me about my 1957 UK tour for Harold Davidson, who I really liked very much. He thought I was a wacko, but he was a very nice man. $7,500 plus expenses: that was my price on my tour of England.

The tour was wonderful. I toured with Tommy Steele, who I *really* had fun with, and Chas McDevitt and Nancy Whiskey. I really enjoyed that. When I toured the UK and Europe, there were differences in the audiences. We did the Dominion Theatre in London. It was a large theatre and it was packed. They were very, very good to me, and of course the audience was more on a Tommy Steele kick than they were myself — except when we got to Scotland. As you realize, the Scottish were not really favored about English acts, so I had a much better chance of scoring in Scotland than I did the UK. Doing the shows, we did, like, the Empire circuit and they had comics on the show — it was more a variety show. I liked it very much. I closed the first half and Tommy closed the second half.

Tommy Steele, he was a wonderful man. He had a Cockney accent that I found very, very funny, and every time we would talk I would imitate his accent and he would try to imitate my US accent, and we would laugh all the time. The Steelmen were very, very good musicians and I love Tommy Steele: he's wonderful, a down-to-earth

Chapter 1 – Freddie Bell

A lively performance in *Rock Around The Clock*.

sweetheart guy. I don't know where you got that story about Tommy Steele's poker playing on that tour, but it's true. Tommy loved to play poker and was probably the worst poker player I ever saw in my life! The man would stay with nothing. As a matter of fact, my drummer said he paid all his expenses in the UK off of Tommy Steele.

It was a successful tour and I kept getting offers to tour the UK again, but I never went back. As a matter of fact, I wrote in a magazine at that time: 'I can't wait until I come back to England.' It took me 37 years to do it, but I always loved the UK. As for skiffle music and Chas McDevitt, I loved it. As a matter of fact, I love all kinds of music

The reason that Frankie Brent decided to quit the band after the tour to try his luck in the UK is that everybody has their own aspirations of success: everybody wants to make it on their own, which is the reason most groups don't stay together forever. Frankie wanted to do his own thing and he went back to England. As a matter of fact, he recorded one of my songs, *Rockin' The Polonaise*.

As far as motion pictures, our first film was *Rock Around The Clock*. I was in Las Vegas at the Sands and we flew to Los Angeles for three days to do the film. We spent one day recording, and the next day we were on the set shooting the film with Bill Haley & His Comets and the Platters and so on. In addition to *Rock Around The Clock [1956]*, I also did *Rumble On The Docks [1956]* and *Get Yourself A College Girl [1964]*. They didn't pay well. As a matter of fact, I was very upset at the fact that we didn't get a lot of money to do them films, but in those days exposure was more important to me than salary.

In 1960, after the chart successes stopped, I changed the band. I went to a three-horn band, which gave more of a big band sound, and sorta gave up the rock'n'roll scene. And I became what they call a Las Vegas lounge group, really. More of a variety-type performance rather than a rock'n'roll performance, and to this present day that is what I still do.

I never really accounted or thought about *Giddy-Up-A Ding Dong* being a classic pop record or my place in popular music history, but I think my place is that I enjoyed doing what I did. And I really don't know if I'll have any place *[laughs] anywhere*, but I just enjoyed the business. My favorite artists — there are just so many of them... I love them all. As a matter of fact, I think that *anybody* who gets on a stage and performs deserves some kind of respect.

I think today's music is getting louder and louder. I don't like the heavy metal; I'm not into the heavy metal sound. Today's music industry? You see, we made *records*. In the old days, you had a four-hour session to do four songs, or if you had to stretch you had to pay overtime. But today, the records are produced. I have my friends, Wood Stix, and I go to watch them record, and there's only one guy in the studio at a time making tracks. I enjoyed the old ways of recording 'cause you could have a couple of flaws on the record, which I thought gave it humanity.

If I could go back I don't know if I would do anything differently, because you can't pass post or think back and change things. It's what you do at the time that is relevant to that time. So, I'm really not sorry about whatever happened to me. I am semi-retired now. I enjoy performing, but I don't think I enjoy the business end as much as I did. I never really liked the business end anyway. I still love to perform. I still do shows and go out, but I don't carry a band anymore. I go out and I do shows all over the US and sometimes Europe and the Far East — but not as much as I used to: I don't work full time. I do a lot of nostalgia and festival shows. As a matter of fact, we've got a Hall of Fame in Las Vegas and I'm a member. I thanked them for that. I've never thought of leaving the business. I don't think you *ever* leave the business. Sometimes the business leaves *you,* but you never leave the business.

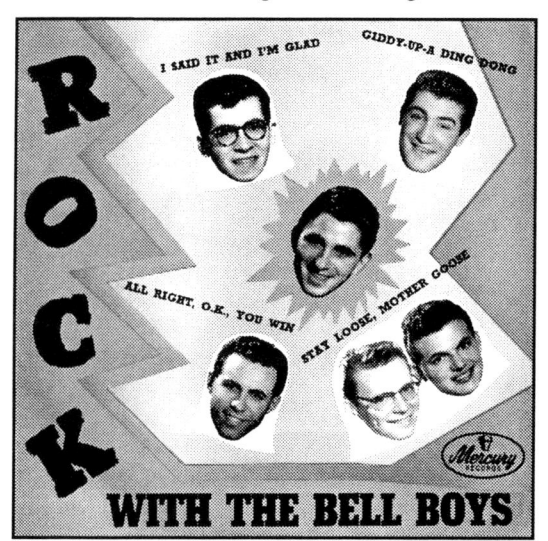

My wife's name is Angela, she's an attorney, and I have a son named Jonathan. I also have three children on the East Coast and two in California. I've been married four times: twice to the same woman.

The lowest spot in my music career was, I think, right before 1960 when I couldn't decide what I wanted to do: whether I wanted to stay in rock'n'roll or change my style.

Chapter 1 – Freddie Bell

The highest spot in my musical career and my life is any time that I'm happy. Really, there are no high spots with me: there are good spots and bad spots. I have a devout, religious feeling for the Maker. I do not follow the religious dogma of the church, but I do have a great feeling for religion — actually, all religions.

Outside of showbusiness, I enjoy playing golf. I enjoy sports. I enjoy being a spectator at the football games. I enjoy watching other people get energetic. As far as planning for the future, I have no plans whatsoever, because when you get to be 72 years old you don't plan any long vacations, but I do hope to be in England in March. I thank you.

To Dave
Aloha
Martin Denny

2

EXOTIC SOUNDS
Martin Denny

One of the music industry's great innovators, Martin Denny, pianist, composer and arranger supreme, 'King of Exotica' and unwitting icon of tiki culture brought the atmosphere of Polynesia into millions of homes across the world through such groundbreaking recordings as *Quiet Village* and *The Enchanted Sea*. The sultry poses of beautiful model Sandy Warner on the sleeves of his Liberty albums enhanced the marketing of a dream, but the music stood — and continues to stand — on its own merits. A living embodiment of the relaxed Hawaiian lifestyle he portrayed in sound, Denny continued performing and recording into his nineties.

I was born on April 10, 1911 in New York City. Though I was playing piano professionally at age fifteen, having studied under Lester Spitz and Isadore Gorn, my real career began at age twenty when I went to South America. The 4½ years spent there touring with the Don Dean Orchestra contributed quite a bit to my sound, which is best described as a fusion between the South Pacific, the Orient, Latin America, American jazz and classical. I was in the US Air Force after Pearl Harbor and, after discharge from the services, I settled in Los Angeles where I studied piano, composition and orchestration at the Los Angeles Conservatory of Music. In 1954, I came to Hawaii under contract to Don The Beachcomber, a Honolulu club, and over the years I have performed in every major hotel in Hawaii.

When I first came over, I was playing strictly jazz as solo, got a trio, added a fourth and eventually a fifth. All the groups were mine: I employed the others and gave them their starts. Harvey Ragsdale formed his own orchestra after; Julius Wechter brought my sound to Herb Alpert and eventually formed his own Baja Marimba Band; and Arthur Lyman branched out on his own. Original band members were Lyman and John Kramer, then I added Augie Colon when I opened the Shell Bar at the Hilton Hawaiian Village in 1956. It was there the 'exotic sounds' originated. In short, I was influenced by my Latin background and adding Augie, who did bird calls, added a whole new dimension to my sound. Rehearsals were at various places: studios, our place, wherever we were performing.

There was certainly no influence by the Tarzan jungle character popular in the Thirties and Forties, and I was not influenced by Rodgers &

Chapter 2 – Martin Denny

Left to right: Julius Wechter, Harvey Ragsdale, Martin Denny, Augie Colon and Frank Kim at the Waikiki Shell, 1950s.

Hammerstein's musical, *South Pacific,* which was based on James A. Michener's book, *Tales Of the South Pacific.* James Michener is a friend of mine, and my daughter Christina thinks the influence was the other way round! I read all of his books, and he wrote the liner notes for one of my albums. But I did end up using quite a few of the instruments that were in the movie. Other people who have contributed liner notes for my albums include Walter Winchell, Louella Parsons, Les Baxter, Ferdie Grofe and John Sturges.

Si Waronker, president of Liberty Records approached me to make records. *'Exotica',* my first album, was recorded in mono during 1956 at Webley Edwards' studio in Honolulu. Webley was the originator of the show *Hawaii Calls.* Stereo, then the emerging thing, helped to expand my music when we re-did *'Exotica'* in 1957, but by then Julius had replaced Arthur. I chose my own arrangements and editing of the albums, and did it on a budget of $850! We did three sessions in one, and I had to plead with the engineer to give me an additional half-hour. But they sold each LP at a retail price of $4.50, so they made out okay. It took maybe a week to pull it all together.

It was Liberty's idea to release a single, and in 1957 we released my first one, *Quiet Village,* which was a track from the 1956 *'Exotica'* album. Les Baxter wrote *Quiet Village* — it was from his album, *'Le Sacre du Sauvage',* on the Capitol label. It was unusual, and inspired me to add the bird calls and frogs. When *Quiet Village* was recorded for the *'Exotica'* album in 1956, there were very few takes and the recording engineer was Bob Lang. When it was re-done in stereo in Liberty's Hollywood Studios during 1957, the engineer was Ted Keep.

The record 'slept' for some time, but thanks to exposure by a disc jockey in Detroit it took off, and I was elated when it was a big hit in 1959. It was very exciting for me, as I was topping all the main artists in the country — including Frank Sinatra. Of course, I traveled all over to promote it, and did the shows of Johnny Carson, Dinah Shore, *Hawaii Calls*, *Stars Of Jazz* and Bob Crosby to name a few. All sounds were always made the same for recordings as live performances — oral bird calls and various instruments.

'Exotica' sold 400,000 on its release and I got a silver record for it in 1957. I received a gold record for one million sales of the original mono version of *Quiet Village*. There was pressure on me to do *Yellow Bird* as the follow up single to *Quiet Village*. I didn't do it and it went to Arthur Lyman. *The Enchanted Sea,* written by Frank Metis and Randy Starr, was my arrangement again. Si visited me in Honolulu and I took him to our saltwater splash pool on the ocean. Si said that would be his next project — the enchanted sea. It was another hit. Singles were always taken from the content of the albums I did. Si Waronker was the producer for my first 8-10 albums, then there were various A&R people over the years.

I did meet Sandy Warner, the model who was featured on most of the Liberty albums — but not until later, during one of my performances in Waikiki. She introduced herself when she was on her honeymoon. Her poses helped sell the albums — they were a great attraction and I have no quarrel with that. Liberty paid me my record royalties in full and I have my own Exotica Music Publishing Company, which is administered through the Songwriters' Guild Of America.

My new-found fame enabled me to buy my first home in Hawaii, where we resided for 32 years. The first royalty check was used as the down-payment. The downside was the traveling, as we had to be away from family several months at a time. This was difficult for private life as well as members of the group. I never owned a hotel or a nightclub, but turned down a number of offers.

I certainly don't think living in Hawaii limited my career — if anything, it enhanced it! Tiki parties — held with tikis and torches in people's backyards — on the mainland were big, and my music fitted right in. I would define a 'tiki' as an aboriginal idol, but I never really thought of them as gods or graven images of mythical gods of Polynesia. We had a tiki once in our back yard. It was made out of some organic pressed pieces of wood and looked like a bad dude with a mean expression. Other than that, I never even owned a tiki, but I got into masks for a while and have some of them. I remember when I played in the International Marketplace and there were tikis all over around Duke's.

Tiki has also become a cult. I think that I got associated with that Polynesian atmosphere and it stuck. I have been associated with tiki, and people use my music for it, but it is not something that I started or set out to establish. In the beginning, it was more the fantasy of paradise that my music took people away to. Now, with nostalgia and retro, the younger generation is into it in a different way. Here in the islands I am considered 'The King of Exotica' and, with the new craze, people now consider me as an icon for the tiki culture. It is not what I identified myself with, but a label that was assigned to me by fans.

However, I was never limited to the islands, as I am known and have traveled all over the world. I opened the Waikiki Shell and, in 1990, did two tours in Japan and was popular with a young crowd: it was standing room only. When Electric Light Yellow Magic Orchestra took *Firecrackers* and recorded it, it hit the top charts in Japan for four months and then enjoyed big success in Canada. I did a lot of college dates and opened many hotels and rooms in the islands as the feature attraction. In 1985 I performed in London, although it wasn't a scheduled performance. I was a guest with my brother on an insurance convention tour and was at Lady Astor's mansion, where I was asked to perform. They told me that they already had a piano set up for me and expected it. I was thrilled. Yes, I have been all over. We lived in Beverly Hills for three years, too.

The military also helped spread my sound. They would hear me and take it around the world and share it. *'Exotica'* went under the North Pole and the crew of the *SS Nautilus* sent me a letter and a copy of the record — it's here, framed. I have recorded over thirty-five LPs, and over twelve CDs are on the market now. Recent movies like *Joe's Apartment* and *Confessions Of A Dangerous Mind* used my music and fourteen of my pieces were utilized in the soundtrack of *Breakfast Of Champions* starring Bruce Willis and Nick Nolte, produced by David Blocker. Recently, Jennifer Lopez recorded my *Firecrackers* into her own version and my music was played at the Super Bowl. I have three Lifetime Achievement awards, and as recently as last month received another honor: 'Rotary Treasure'. The Mayor of Honolulu declared 'Martin Denny Day' on July 22, 2000.

As to whether I think of myself as a Hawaiian or an American, well, Hawaii is part of the United States, so the two are the same. But yes, I am very affected by culture and definitely an American, and a Hawaiian resident — a *long* resident here for almost fifty years. Though not by blood, I am called a 'kamaina', which is someone who has been in Hawaii for many years — an old timer to the islands — and is accepted by the locals. I am recognized for my contribution to the island and received a Na Hoku for Lifetime Achievement.

I have one child, Christina, who manages my affairs. She has gone on tour with me before to dance and done quite a bit of singing, but has never recorded. I do not consider myself a religious man, but Christina accepted Christ in 1982. I am not a Buddhist and wasn't aware that my music 'indicates a Buddhist approach to all creatures'. I believe music is universal. As far as creatures are concerned, I have a silver toy poodle, Tita, who is my baby. My long life I put down in part to my genes, abstinence of liquor or smoking (although I drank until 1976), keeping the mind active and belonging to organizations. I used to be physically active, alternating days of swimming and walking. I hiked Diamond Head on my eightieth birthday and continued into my eighties. My three claims to fame are a gold record, a hole-in-one, and catching a 184 lb marlin.

If I could re-do things in the past, I would have continued my exotic sounds rather than being put into a jazz category, being that the early part of my recordings were the most creative. I would like my work to be remembered as a unique sound — an identity — attributed to Martin Denny. It's romantic and adventurous.

If I have an enduring appeal, I am proud of it and put it down to having created a unique sound. My own favorite artists are Gershwin, Ferdie Grofe (who was Christina's godfather and our good friend), Rodgers & Hammerstein, Cole Porter, Vladamir Horowitz, Arthur Rubinstein and Chopin. There are so many of them, but Gershwin is tops. Apart from my own music, my choice of recording other people's material would be the music of Les Baxter. I find today's record industry and how it's run disappointing, also the type of music being produced — rap and hard rock for instance.

The outlook is promising. My things are getting exposure globally as a result of the tiki culture. A new release, called *Baked Alaska,* through EMI Records by Collectors' Choice Catalogue, is expected in July. It was recorded live for the armed services at an Air Force base in Alaska in the 1960s. There are two other CDs in the works, but not scheduled yet for release: *The Intimate Martin Denny* (with a picture of my late wife and I on the cover in a piano keyboard frame and dedicated to her), and *Dining With Martin Denny*, which was recorded live while I played at the Mauna Lani Bay Resort on the Big Island of Hawaii. I played four years on Maui at the Westin Wailea Beach Hotel and two years on Hawaii at the Mauna Lani in the Eighties. I performed today for the Widows Of Veterans and on Father's Day was playing for a hospice. A large performance with the band is in the planning stages for this year. In April we packed a club out with standing room only and had people fly in from the mainland and Japan to see us play. The Fire Marshall was not pleased with us for breaking the code — so many people.

At present, Christina and I are working on my memoirs — to have them published while health holds out — at 92!

After suffering failing health for some time, Martin Denny died peacefully in his sleep on 2 March 2005, aged 93.

STEEL GUITAR HALL OF FAME

...NTO & JOHNNY FARINA
...1959 THIS DUO RECORDED STEEL'S
... GOLD RECORD, WHILE INTRODUCING
... INSTRUMENT TO THE ROCK 'N' ROLL
... HEARD IN COUNTLESS MOVIES
... COMMERCIALS, IT HAS BEEN STEEL'S
... GRAMMY WINNER (1999), THE
... RECORDED, AND THE ALL-TIME
... POPULAR INSTRUMENTAL, "SLEEP
...K". THE BROTHERS ACHIEVED INTER-
...IONAL STARDOM, RELEASED OVER 40
...UMS, AND HAD #1 HITS IN MEXICO
... ITALY. THEIR MUSIC EXPANDED THE
...CIATION FOR THE STEEL GUITAR.
...JOHNNY

3

STEEL MAGIC
Johnny Farina / Santo & Johnny

Sleep Walk is arguably the most haunting pop instrumental ever made. The timeless magic of its pulsating background beat and gliding steel guitar melody line has endured for over forty years, inspiring countless cover versions, but the original recording by the song's composers, two young guitar-playing brothers named Santo and Johnny Farina, has never been surpassed. Santo retired from the business some thirty years ago, but Johnny has continued recording and playing his steel guitar for appreciative audiences around the world.

I was born Johnny Farina on April 30, 1941 in Brooklyn, New York. My father was a baker and mother a housewife. I have one brother, Santo, who was born on October 24, 1937. I have no sister: the 'Ann Farina' who is on the composer's credit for *Sleep Walk* was Santo's wife. When I was growing up, we moved several times to different locations within Brooklyn and then moved to Long Island when I was eighteen. I went to Catholic grammar school and on to public school for junior high and high school before I quit at the age of sixteen. My favorite subject was History, but I wasn't a good student: music was all I wanted to do. I loved music and don't know what else I would have done if I hadn't gone into showbusiness.

Growing up, I was influenced by all the sounds that came out of the big old radio and listened to many different types of music. Frank Sinatra, Sammy Davis, Dean Martin, Perry Como, Bing Crosby and Frankie Laine were my favorite artists. I am a self-taught steel guitar and rhythm guitar player and started to play when I was about nine years old. My brother, who also plays steel guitar, did not teach me. At the outset, we both shared the same instrument and both learned steel. Later on, I started to learn rhythm guitar. My instruments were Fender and Gibson. We were encouraged at home because dad wanted Santo and I to play steel guitar after hearing it played while stationed with the army in Texas and Oklahoma.

I first performed in school concerts, and later on Santo and I played at family parties while we were in our teens. Santo and I are brothers, so I guess we always had our act going, and always used only our first names, Santo & Johnny. Santo and I never appeared on any amateur talent shows. We started making money in our early teens playing our music, so that to us meant we had turned professional. I can't remember where our professional debut took place or how much we got paid. It was probably in Brooklyn, New

Chapter 3 – Johnny Farina / Santo & Johnny

York for not much money. At first our parents weren't too happy about us embarking on a showbusiness career, but they went along with it and were proud after we became famous.

It was just magic how *Sleep Walk* came to be written: we just came home from a gig one night and just started jamming, searching for something new to add to our original songs. We just went with our feelings and we would both inject different ideas until it sounded right to both of us. Santo and I wrote all the songs. Santo's wife, Ann — the third 'Farina' credited for our songs — was not involved. Both of us chose the title *Sleep Walk,* which is two separate words. Lyrics were later written for *Sleep Walk,* but not by us.

Sleep Walk was first recorded in 1958, at home, on our own

Chapter 3 – Johnny Farina / Santo & Johnny

equipment, which was a Webcor reel-to-reel tape recorder that our dad bought us around 1956 so we could hear what we sounded like. I wanted to become famous, so I talked Santo into cutting some demos with me and I shopped them around for 1½ years till I got a publishing company, Trinity Music, interested in listening to *Sleep Walk*. They were totally taken by our song and our sound.

I don't remember exactly how many takes were required for the 1959 studio version, which we recorded at Trinity Music in Manhattan, New York; I would say a couple. The only other musicians involved were a bass player and a drummer whose names I can't remember. Neither can I remember who produced or engineered the record. *Sleep Walk* was our first record release and it was released by Canadian–American, who leased the track from Trinity.

When I first heard *Sleep Walk* played on the radio I was in Coney Island, a seaside area in Brooklyn, New York. I heard it over a kiddies' ride PA. I was happy and couldn't believe it. Although I can't remember where I was or what I was doing on the occasions when *Sleep Walk* entered the Top 100 and then went to No.1, I do remember the feeling: it was just *great!*

We promoted *Sleep Walk* on the Dick Clark *American Bandstand* show, but we weren't allowed to play live as they were not geared for it. Actually, our grandmother loved Perry Como, so when we were offered to appear on either the *Perry Como Show* or the *Ed Sullivan Show*, we chose Perry Como's show to please grandma. Perry treated us great: he was a great man and a great talent. It was on his show that we first met Caterina Valente, who recorded *Sleep Walk* in German and French.

I can't remember who promoted our first tour, but it was in the Midwest, with Jimmy Clanton, the Bell Notes and the Crests, etc. I don't remember what we got paid for these tours, but for the times I guess it was the right number. We never felt at a disadvantage on these tours because we were an instrumental duo. I thought we were very special because of our unique sound. We were the only ones to use the steel for rock'n'roll, and we saw the reaction of all our fans. Although we were young, we didn't find it hard to avoid trouble with female fans, drugs and drink. We were from Brooklyn and 'street smart', and we knew not to get into trouble. Although I was single, Santo was married, but I didn't see any problem.

On these tours, Johnny Maestro of the Crests and I became best friends, and that's how it will always be. The black acts knew how to handle themselves and public hostility in certain parts of the States, and took it as part of the times. I did some touring with

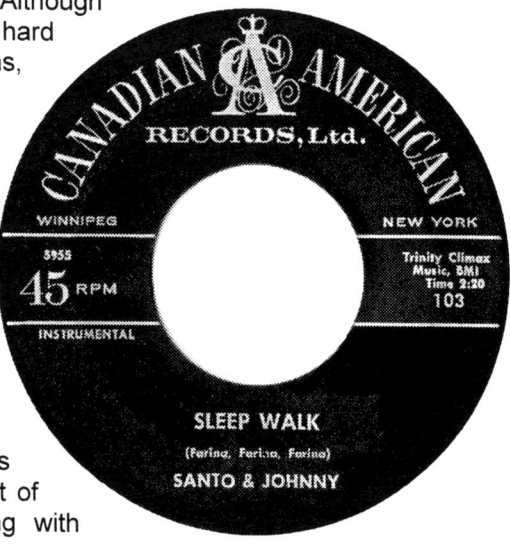

Duane Eddy. I liked him a lot and respected his guitar-work. As artists, these tours gave us fame, excitement and money — all three. My funny memories are of the tour buses that were always breaking down and were always too hot in summer or too cold in winter. They had no toilets — we had to pee out the door as the bus slowed down — and hard seats, but we always had fun. So much different than today's buses.

I am very thankful for *Sleep Walk* and I never felt any competition from any of the artists recording my song: I was very pleased with the large number of cover versions. I held on to my share of the publishing rights, but we don't own our masters yet.

Santo and I kept watch over our incoming finances and we had good people who advised us. Ed Burton was the name of our manager. He also became a good friend, but passed away many years ago. However, there *were* tensions between Santo and myself as brothers and artists — we were no different to the Everlys or the James Brothers — and they were not resolved. I don't know what Santo is doing now and have no comments to make on why we broke up or when we last spoke.

There wasn't much pressure on us to come up with a follow-up record as we were already in shape with *Tear Drop* and others: we never stopped writing. *Tear Drop* was the follow-up, and we decided. Our label, Canadian–American, believed in us all the way and it was a good relationship. The success never changed me, except now I was able to share my wealth with my family and friends, and that made me happy. There were many records after *Tear Drop*, but honestly I never kept track of how they did in the charts.

From 1959 to the early Seventies, Santo & Johnny performed as a duo. During that time we had many years of hits in Italy and Mexico. After that, when Santo ceased to perform in the Seventies, I went solo and recorded as a solo artist immediately after we parted. Today, I am still doing the same things: I play, write, record, perform at rock'n'roll shows, casinos, clubs and theaters, and I put out my first solo CD, *Pure Steel (Volume 1)*, in 1994. I use a back-up band: guitar, bass, drums and keyboard. I don't find any difficulties getting bookings with promoters as one half of a famous duo. At first, they weren't quite sure until they heard me again.

The lowest spot in my career and life, I guess, has to be after the break-up with my brother, and the highest spot happened on August 31, 2002 when we were inducted into the International Steel Guitar Hall of Fame. Santo was not with me that night. I went and performed solo.

If I could go back in time would I do anything differently? No, I don't think so. I believe in God and treat people good and help if I can. No, I never wish that I had been a singer-guitarist. I once sang on a demo, but never had any desire to push my singing. I felt the steel had its own voice and I sing through my steel. That's my voice, and it's unlike anybody else's.

Which instrumental, other than *Sleep Walk,* would I like to have composed? It has to be *Ebb Tide.* I did record it and I did a great job on it. Not bragging, just fact.

My wife Rose and I have been married for forty years. We have two children — a boy and a girl — and three grandchildren. Our son plays cello and bass. I have no comment to make about Santo's marriage and children.

As I've mentioned, today I am still performing, writing and recording. I'm now working on a Christmas CD and recently finished something that's new in my career — I wrote a movie script. I like nostalgia shows and perform at many of them. They mean that I get to keep in touch with my friends and meet the many fans who cherish Santo & Johnny. I have no problem in playing *Sleep Walk* for over forty years. It's a song that just has the magic and each performance of *Sleep Walk* always feels fresh to me.

It's hard to say how I value my place in pop music history with such a classic record. It's just a powerful piece of music that will never age. It made its statement in 1959, and since then it has never stopped its popularity and it fits into any time from 1959 to 2003 and beyond. It is *pure magic.* I will send you a story about *Sleep Walk* where the writer says *Sleep Walk* is part of our collective being — it's in our DNA.

Hal

Herb

4

TWIN TALENTS
The Kalin Twins

Inspired by their idol, Johnnie Ray, Hal and Herbie Kalin are natural entertainers. They launched their career in fine style with *When*, a worldwide smash in 1958, and followed up strongly with *Forget Me Not*, *It's Only The Beginning* and *Sweet Sugar Lips*. Sadly, their somewhat square image and poor management rendered them unable to compete with the teen idols of the day, and they quit music in the mid-Sixties to take up careers in the Washington, DC court service. Both are now retired, but still ready and willing to perform at the drop of a hat.

We were born Harold Ross Kalin (Hal) and Herbert Harry Kalin (Herb) on February 16, 1934 in Port Jervis, New York (where New York, New Jersey and Pennsylvania meet). Hal is the elder twin by fifteen minutes. We both detest our real names. Father was Robert Ross Kalin and mother was Sylvia Marie (*née* Barber). The name 'Kalin' is most likely Swiss or German. Our great grandfather, Gustav Kalin, came to America from Stuttgart, Germany in 1857. His parents lived at that time in Switzerland, and it is believed that he was born and raised there.

There was an older brother Charles ('Chuck'), born in 1931, who died of a heart ailment at age 43, and we have a younger brother, John ('Jack') who was born in 1939. Jack was a sax player in our band for several years in the Sixties. Father was a cab driver in early life and owner of a gas station later. Mother held several jobs, such as book-keeper, salesperson, etc in various Port Jervis businesses. Our parents divorced when we were about age six and then mother married William DeWitt, our stepfather. We lived with our mother in Port Jervis until 1952, when we were eighteen.

Neither of us took music lessons. However, we learned enough on our own to back ourselves in rehearsals, etc (Herb on piano, Hal on guitar), but we never became proficient enough to play our instruments on stage or in our act. As far as we can determine, we have no ancestors who were in the music business. Our mother always wanted to be an actress; however, she did not pursue it. The most influential artist for both of us was Johnnie Ray. We were also influenced by Tony Bennett, Frankie Laine, Nat 'King' Cole and a whole host of 'pop' artists before rock'n'roll. After our own hit, and after we worked with the rock'n'roll acts of the late Fifties, our major influences were

Chapter 4 – The Kalin Twins

probably Fats Domino, the Everly Brothers and Bobby Darin, all of whom were close friends of ours.

Our first known performance was at a firehouse Christmas party when we were five or six years old. Following that, we appeared in typical school shows. Our mother and other family members were not really aware that we liked to sing. I don't recall any family member ever seeing us perform until after we had hit it big. In 1952, as high school seniors, we appeared in a 'Senior Minstrel'. The cast was in blackface, however, we were not. With two friends we did an impersonation of the Four Aces, and Herb did an impersonation of Johnnie Ray. We only sang once or twice as a duo while in school and usually sang with others as part of a quartet. We did not even think about being a duo until we had been singing professionally as singles for a number of years. When rock'n'roll became popular, we felt we could best express that music with a two-part harmony sound.

While in high school, there was no television and we never appeared on any radio talent shows. Port Jervis is a small town and there was little opportunity for a career in showbusiness. In the summer of 1952, after graduating from high school, Herb worked in a few bars in the Port Jervis area doing a Johnnie Ray impersonation act. In October, Herb left home for Miami to look for fame and fortune in showbusiness and Hal joined the Air Force.

Had we stayed in Port Jervis we would undoubtedly have ended up as life-long factory workers. Other than singing, we both wanted to be baseball players — though we were not all that good at it — and we liked the newspaper business and cartooning, however, we never really looked into it.

When Hal was in the Air Force from 1952 to 1956, we kept in touch by exchanging tape recordings of songs we were working on. Hal was in Japan and sang at the Officers' Clubs on base and in a few local clubs wherever he was stationed using the name 'Mickey Ladd', and Herb was singing in the Club Players club in Washington, DC using the stage name of 'Buddie Ladd' during most of that period. Herb chose the name 'Buddie Ladd' because the group on most Johnnie Ray records was the Buddy Cole Quintet and 'Ladd' because the vocal group on those Ray records was the Four Lads. 'Buddie' was spelled using 'ie' because Johnnie Ray spelled his name with 'ie'.

We appeared as the Ladd Twins once or twice at the Club Players club just prior to our writing a couple of songs and making our one and only demo in September 1957 with *The Spider And The Fly* b/w *The Beggar Of Love*. We wrote 'The Ladd Twins' on the demo. At this time, Herb worked as a salesman at Stewart's Men Shop and Hal — believe it or not — worked for the Western Union Telegraph Company where, as part of his job, he was required to deliver singing birthday telegrams! In October '57, we made our first visit to New York to take our demo around the record companies personally. We were turned down by many, many labels, most of whom would not even listen to it.

We came back to DC sometime in November. We were broke, and our auto broke down on the way, which necessitated hitch-hiking home. While Herb was working in the Washington clothing store, he met the daughter of another clothing salesman. This woman knew a songwriter named Clint Ballard Jr. and agreed to introduce him to us. We met him and

Chapter 4 – The Kalin Twins

he agreed to take the demo to Jack Pleis of Decca Records in New York. Jack said he heard some promise in our style and asked us to take a live audition. After returning to New York for a successful audition, we were signed to the label in November as 'The Ladd Twins'. Then, we decided that, if we were ever to become famous, we would rather use 'Kalin' than 'Ladd', so we asked Decca to change it. They suggested 'The Ka*y*lin Twins', so that there would be no question of the pronunciation. We vetoed that, pointing out that Kalin was not pronounced as rhyming with 'Kayling' (the 'Kal' rhymes with 'bail', not a long A). We note with some humor through the years that in Britain we are usually introduced as 'The *Kylin* Twins' — that's the British pronunciation of the American long A. Anyway, Decca finally agreed to 'The Kalin Twins' in early December 1957 and our very first professional appearance as the Kalin Twins took place at the Club Players club in Washington on New Year's Eve 1957.

For the first Decca recording session in December '57, we recorded *Jumpin' Jack*, *Walkin' To School* and *The Spider And The Fly*. Decca released our first record, *Jumpin' Jack* (one of Clint Ballard's songs) and *Walkin' To School* (one of our original songs) in January 1958. *The Beggar Of Love* was never re-recorded and, in fact, we have misplaced the original demo. Therefore, there is no version of that song available anywhere. In fact, we cannot even recall the lyrics.

Clint Ballard asked us to sign him as our manager if Jack Pleis gave us a recording contract, so when we got the Decca contract we signed with him. He was a very likeable person, however, we felt he was too deeply involved with songwriting to spend adequate time managing our career. We knew nothing about the ins and outs of big time showbusiness and Clint probably knew less than we did.

We are both songwriters and generally agreed on material to record. We wrote several songs at a time and generally knew which ones were the most commercial. For our second release, *Three O'Clock Thrill* was picked by Clint Ballard Jr, the song having been written by a couple of his songwriting pals. We felt it was a bit too much teeny-boppish, but we saw the possibility of success and agreed to record it. We also picked a ballad of ours, *Tag-A-Long,* for the second song but we could not find a suitable third song to record (most Decca sessions recorded three songs at a time). It was about 2:00 am and we were dead tired, sitting by ourselves in Jack Pleis' office in New York, going over a stack of several hundred demos sent in by songwriters. Wearily, we agreed that the next song we heard we would record, regardless of how good or bad it was. Herb reached over his head and blindly pulled a demo from a stack on a shelf. It was a demo of a song called *When*, sung by a guy named Paul Evans.

It was a corny, country & western version using only a guitar — but a promise was a promise. We wrote Jack Pleis a note and told him we wanted to include *When* in the session. During the next day or so we played the song over and over and came up with a catchy harmony arrangement. Jack had the idea of adding a clicking sound and a rock'n'roll sax. *When* was recorded in Studio A at the Decca Building in New York City. The vocal back-up was the Ray Charles Singers — not the black Ray Charles — and the musicians were all studio musicians whose names are unknown to us. Jack Pleis did the musical arrangements and the producer was Marv Holzman.

We thought immediately after the session that *When* might be a hit, but Decca and Clint Ballard did not agree. For several weeks they promoted *Three O'Clock Thrill* as the 'A' side. Behind their backs, we kept asking deejays to play *When*. We went on promotion trips to all the major US cities, and every time we'd leave an area we would notice that *When* had hit the local charts in that city. In time, it started showing up on charts all over America and eventually the rest of the world.

Neither of us can remember first hearing *When* on the radio. We had already had a local two-sided hit in the Washington/Baltimore area with our first Decca release — our song *Walkin' To School* was a hit in DC, and Clint's

Chapter 4 – The Kalin Twins

Magazine interview, 1958.

song, *Jumpin' Jack,* was a hit in Baltimore — and we were used to hearing our records. You can imagine the battles with Clint on that first record since he was the writer of one side!

Clint Ballard only wrote that song for us. After that, we had little contact with him. We did not ask him to write songs for us and he did not submit anything to us. Usually, we would only see him when we visited New York. He did, however, go with us on our trip to England — at our expense. As we mentioned earlier, Clint was completely wrapped up in his own songwriting career and had neither the talent nor the time to devote to us. He really never managed us: his contract — and 15% — was really a pay-off for having introduced us to Jack Pleis. The only time he ever saw us perform was during the UK tour of 1958. He did not see us perform prior to that or after that.

The time *When* entered the US Top Ten, we were appearing at the famous Apollo Theater in Harlem, New York and were the only white act on the bill. Etta James, on the show with us, came into our dressing room to announce that she had just seen on TV that *When* had hit the Top Ten. Frankly, we couldn't believe it. A dream of a lifetime had actually come true! It was too much to take in all at once. We knew the record was getting airplay all over the country, but to believe that it was actually one of the top-selling records was unbelievable.

We toured to promote *When.* Usually we traveled alone, and in each city we would meet with the local Decca distributor, who would bring us

Chapter 4 – The Kalin Twins

around to meet the local disc jockeys. Other artists were doing the same thing, and as a result we got to meet many of the top stars while waiting for an interview at a radio station in one town or another. We met Frankie Avalon, Connie Francis, Fats Domino and many more while on these promotion trips. The friendships that were lasting were made while appearing on the road, performing with other artists. Our booking agency put together traveling roadshows of several artists in one package, and we would be with stars such as Frankie Avalon or the Platters, for example, twenty-four hours a day.

We would travel by bus and, because of the tremendously fast-paced scheduling, the acts would usually check into a hotel every other night. We would run out on stage — not even knowing where we were — to sing our songs, and then jump back into the bus for the long haul to the next city. As a result, we got to know intimately many, many stars like Bill Haley, the Everly Brothers, Fabian, Chuck Berry, Bo Diddley and so on. We have more or less lost contact with most of them, but a few friendships still last. Frankie Avalon is a close friend, and Cliff Richard is still a pal — we went through the same bus routine with Cliff in England as we did with the American stars in the US.

Our appearances on big television shows weren't for the express purpose of promoting a record. However, the appearances certainly helped in making our songs more popular. Dick Clark asked us to appear every time we released a new record, but there were other times that we did major TV shows that had nothing to do with record promotion — Ed Sullivan, Patti Page, Lonnie Donegan, etc — shows that asked us to appear simply because we were the 'in thing' at the time.

In September 1958, we were doing the *Dick Clark Show* — a live, New York TV variety show on Saturday nights, not *American Bandstand*. We had just released our third record, *Forget Me Not*, and had done it on the show that night. As we left the studio to head for the airport to go to England for the first time, someone showed us a copy of *Melody Maker* that showed that *When* was No.1 in England. We were thrilled of course, since we had battled the Top Ten in the US for weeks and were not able to hit the top spot in *Billboard* (it had hit No.1 in a few other trade papers, but *Billboard* was the authority in the US).

Chapter 4 – The Kalin Twins

When we came to Britain in 1958 for the Grade Agency, we appeared from Monday, September 22 for two weeks at the Prince of Wales Theatre in London (with Jimmy Jewel and Ben Warris, the Mudlarks and violinist Florian Zabach) before doing a tour of the cities from Sunday, October 5. We were originally to co-headline with the British singer Michael Holliday, but when he became ill his place was taken by the comedy duo Jewel & Warris.

At the Prince of Wales Theatre, the British press tried right away to start a feud between the Mudlarks, the main support act, and us. However, we liked them so much — and we assume they liked us too — that we laughed at the press clippings that tried to make us enemies. *Melody Maker*, for instance, would say something like: *'The Kalin Twins Have Never Heard Of The Mudlarks'*, but we would then hold a press conference and heap praise on them, saying they were one of our favorite groups. Eventually, the headlines changed to: *'Kalin Twins Dig The Mudlarks'*. And when we got to know them, we really did 'dig' them. We had little or no contact with Jewel & Warris. We met them, and there is a photo of us shaking hands in our dressing room, but other than that one meeting we never saw them again. We could hear them on stage from our dressing room, but that was the extent of our relationship. The Mudlarks closed the first half and Jewel & Warris came on just before we did.

The highlight of our London stay was our appearance on *Sunday Night At The London Palladium* on September 28, but we nearly took the decision not to appear! Paul Robeson, the controversial black American singer, sports figure and communist sympathizer, was also appearing and he had already renounced his American citizenship as a protest about his country's racist policies. His stance had not offended us, but we thought that we would get some massive publicity, to give our career a tremendous boost, if we pulled out of the show at the last possible minute and cited him and his renunciation as the reason. Our imagination ran wild as we envisioned the world press hanging on our every word as we read a prepared statement outlining our patriotism and anti-communism. Looking back, we aren't proud of our thinking back then, and thankfully, when he came to see us backstage with his genuine warmth and gentle, smiling face, we abandoned our crass publicity plan completely. We never told Clint or Decca what we were planning to do.

In our one-night appearance tour of the cities, there was a different bill to the Prince of Wales one. For those twelve one-night stands we appeared with trumpeter Eddie Calvert, the Most Brothers, the Londonaires, Tony Marsh and a

43

seventeen year old Cliff Richard with the Drifters. We were the headliners, Eddie Calvert was the guest artist and closed the first half of the show, and Cliff and his group came on before our final spot. This was the only time in his career that Cliff did not headline a show. Being pop artists, we were aware of Eddie Calvert. He was one of those genuine people, as is Cliff, who became instant friends.

Each night, Bert, the driver of our tour bus, would drive us to a top hotel in the particular city we were appearing, but the band members had no such arrangement. They were left to their own devices in coming up with 'digs' for the night. If none could be found, they would be forced to sleep in the bus. To this day, we don't know if the hotels ever found out how we solved the problem. One by one, the musicians would sneak into our rooms, which were usually mammoth first class suites of several ante-rooms. Seldom did a sofa or an extra bed go empty.

We laugh about that tour now with Cliff, since he became such a superstar. In fact, he asked us to come over and appear with him at Wembley Stadium in 1989 to celebrate his thirty years as a star. We joke with him that he was trying to get revenge by finally appearing on a show with us in which *he* was the headliner. He is an exceptionally talented person and a guy we happily call our friend. In addition to Cliff, we also consider the Drifters — or Shadows as they call themselves today — to be good friends. However, it is difficult to consider someone a personal friend when we don't see each other all that often.

We never had *any* contact with Decca or Brunswick in the UK during that tour and we never noticed any particular publicity generated by them. Since we did not manage our own financial arrangements, it is difficult to recall what we got paid for the two weeks at the Prince of Wales and the one-nighters, but it seems that the contract called for £1,200 per week and we may have received an extra bonus for the Palladium appearance.

To us, it was a business. We enjoyed the attention of course, but we never took advantage of girls. Drugs and drink were never a part of our career. We were never offered drugs and we didn't drink, except socially (kind-of square, we know). Herb was married in 1955 to Jonnie (*née* Kelly) and had a two year old daughter, Suzan. His wife traveled with us when she could and they had a stable relationship. The fact that Herb was married didn't affect our relationship — on tour or off — at all. Hal had no particular love affairs during that period.

As twins we had very few conflicts. Hal favored country music and Herb leaned more toward pop music. We argue about the same as any other brothers, but have had no major arguments in our personal or showbusiness lives. The longest period we have not communicated after an argument is less than one hour! We don't have any increased degree of telepathy because we are twins. At least, we are not aware of it. However, since we do think the same, and have a shared upbringing, we generally can pick up signals from each other that others may not notice, which leads outsiders to believe it is mental telepathy. As a result, we find it quite easy, especially on stage while singing, to co-ordinate the phrasing, etc. You could say we think as one insofar as performing is concerned.

We don't think our success changed our relationships with family and friends. Both family and friends supported us and we got along the same after our success as we did before. We always had our own friends as well as friends in common. I would that think that we are generally good mixers — but not the loud, typical showbusiness types. Usually, we like the same type of people. We value honesty and sincerity. We usually 'put up' with phonies, and make friends with those artists who are genuine. That's also true in our personal circle of non-showbusiness friends as well.

We never considered ourselves as rock'n'rollers. Even *When* was more middle-of-the-road. We saw ourselves as pop artists and we really wanted to appeal to the older folks. Two Johnnie Rays was what we always wanted to be. Decca Records altered our birth year from 1934 to 1939 in some of the publicity. They, unlike us, were aiming at the kid market. We both detest our real names and during the first couple of years of our career (1958-60), we used 'Herbie' and 'Harold', but since then we've been using 'Herb' and 'Hal'. We thought about our image often, but apparently didn't see it the way others do. We have never heard that clicking the claves onstage for *When* did not endear us to the fans. No-one has ever mentioned it.

We wanted to take some time before releasing a follow-up to *When*, however, we were swamped with bookings and getting time to come to New York to record was difficult. We did not like *Forget Me Not,* but Decca were thrilled with it. Actually, though it got little or no airplay in England, it hit No.12 in the US and sold around half a million. It was a 'hit' by all standards, however, deejays never play it today. It's a forgotten oldie. We agree that our British visit, which took place in the same month that *Forget Me Not* was released in the US, probably hampered it to some extent. Had we been home to promote it, it may have moved a couple of notches up the charts, but we were satisfied with its success. Oddly enough, we never saw one disc jockey in England. We also hadn't the time to listen to the radio and therefore had no way of knowing whether *Forget Me Not* was a hit or not. When we got home, we were pleasantly surprised to see that it was No.12 in *Billboard*.

After *Forget Me Not*, we had a semi-hit called *It's Only The Beginning* and then a chartmaker, but not a hit, with *Sweet Sugar Lips*. Then we began

Chapter 4 – The Kalin Twins

to have more time to write songs and to record. However, although the records were getting better and better — at least in our opinion — we could not get disc jockeys to give us any airplay. Each time we'd record what we felt could well be a hit (for example *One More Time* or *Trouble*), we were totally frustrated by never hearing it on the radio. If they don't hear it, they won't buy it.

It was not the practise in the US for labels to have their own radio shows to promote their records and, in fact, it was illegal. However, the illegal practice of payola *did* take place, especially with the smaller labels. To our knowledge, Decca never paid a penny to anyone to get their records played. Neither did we, or any of our managers or agents. We were getting regular national airplay on *American Bandstand* from Dick Clark until he asked us to record a song in which he had a financial interest — he owned the publishing rights. Decca refused to allow us to record it, stating that it would be considered a form of payola. We called Dick Clark and told him that we were not going to record the song, and from that day on we stopped getting airplay on his show. He claimed that it was because we had no more hits, but we have always said that without airplay no-one would have a hit.

From 1958 to 1960 we were poorly managed. We probably earned somewhere in the neighborhood of $500,000 a year for the first couple of years, then a gradual decline until we left the business. Though half a million sounds like a tremendous amount, we gave Clint Ballard 15% and another 10% went to local booking agents. Then we had to pay all expenses, such as air fare, hotels, etc. Finally, what was left had to be split between the two of us... not to mention Uncle Sam's cut. We sent Clint his commission on a regular basis and eventually, in 1962, asked him to step aside for a new manager, Don Seat. He agreed, and we have not seen him in over forty years. Don Seat was a great manager. He kept us working at top salaries all over the world. We traveled with Conway Twitty a great deal, including a booking in Australia. He also managed Jerry Lee Lewis.

We recorded for Decca until 1962 or 1963. Half of the Decca records were cut in New York and half in Nashville, Tennessee. We always used studio musicians hired to play for the session and some of them were well known in their own right. Boots Randolph played sax and trombone, Floyd

Cramer played piano, Billy Grammer played guitar, etc. Around forty sides were recorded altogether, thirty of which are on the Bear Family CD released in Germany.

Decca has always been fair to us and the parting was amicable. Decca was sold to MCA, which releases some of our records, and to this day we get royalty checks every six months.

We've never thought about trying for ownership of our Decca masters: we guess they'd be better equipped for distribution. Later, we recorded for a few smaller labels and made three or four records, but we were never able to get enough radio play to have a hit. Those releases were as follows: Amy Records (1960s): *Thinkin' About You Baby* b/w *Sometimes It Comes*; Magnum (1970s): *Silver Seagull* b/w *The Giveaway*; October (1980s): *American Eagle* b/w *When (Disco Version)*.

No, we didn't feel that we had lost our direction. We've always performed with the same general direction, that of being good pop singers, trying to be a notch above the many good-looking rockers who obviously had no talent. The British Invasion had nothing to do with our decision to end full-time traveling. In fact, our sound is not all that different from the Beatles. It was the constant traveling on the road, the inability for Herb to see the children on a regular basis, and Hal's desire to get married that led to our decision. There were no financial problems. We were still able to command a fairly high price (around $3,000 a week) and still receiving royalty checks.

The time we decided to quit full time showbusiness and go 'off the road' was 1966. Hal got married to Marion (*née* Kerr) in 1967 and immediately took a job at the Superior Court of the District of Columbia, in Washington, as a bailiff and a clerk of the court. He took courses part-time and received his Associate of Arts — the equivalent of a degree — from Trinity College in 1975. Herb went to Maryland University and, after getting his BA degree in Psychology in 1971, took a job at the same court as a probation officer in 1972. We were both straight-A students graduating with High Honors.

Both of us had ended up living in Washington, DC. When Herb was on the road trying to make it in showbusiness, he ran out of money in Baltimore and had only enough money to buy a bus ticket to Washington, DC. He got a job in a club and

Chapter 4 – The Kalin Twins

The Kalin Twins — Eighties style.

Chapter 4 – The Kalin Twins

eventually got married, had children and simply stayed there. When Hal got out of the service he came to DC and, after scoring with *When*, we never made an effort to leave the area, except to take bookings on the road.

There were only a few months in 1966 when we weren't performing, and we began taking bookings in the DC area almost immediately. Although we took occasional bookings outside the area, we never really did go back on the road. From 1966 until today, we have primarily appeared in nightclubs and a variety of one-nighters generally in the DC–Maryland–Virginia area and always as a duo. Neither of us have taken any single bookings, however, we both occasionally will get up and sing by ourselves if we are a guest in a karaoke bar. Also, on very rare times we have done guest spots as the Kalin Twins while in a karaoke bar.

We rarely did any 'oldies' shows after 1966. We did one or two in the Washington area and one in North Carolina about ten years ago. Once in a while we did one-nighters for civic organizations that were holding what they called an 'oldies' night, meaning that the theme of the evening was the Fifties. However, we were the only act on the bill — as opposed to 'oldies packages' that usually have about ten acts from the Fifties on, all appearing together. Those are fun to do, but don't offer much money since there are so many acts to be paid.

We usually try to do our recorded songs as close as possible to the original recording. Some artists get bored with their own hits and they slowly evolve into something not recognizable. Before appearing, we listen to our records to refresh our memories as to the phrasing and tone of the original. We owe that to the listener. They didn't buy a jazzy version — they bought the original sound.

Sometimes we worked fairly regularly (perhaps forty weekend bookings a year), and at times we'd go several months between bookings. We have never totally given up and still work part-time, but we no longer dream of a comeback — too many years have gone by. In recent years, we have begun to go back to our first love, doing Johnnie Ray tributes as a major part of our act. We even did a one-nighter in London in 2000 for the Johnnie Ray International Fan Club. One-nighters these days pay around $500 to $1,000, but money has never been a factor in deciding to take a booking. Most club owners don't realize that *we* would pay *them* to sing there.

We did have responsible jobs in the DC Superior Court, but we just put in the time until we retired within a few months of each other in 1992. Neither of us have regretted it. They weren't bad jobs, but it wasn't showbusiness. We never talked about our past career with colleagues. Occasionally, someone would find out and were amazed that 'Mr. Kalin' was once a rock'n'roll star. We were both happy, however, that we did the right thing to leave full-time showbusiness when we did, as there was nothing to be gained by staying until we could not make a living and there was nowhere to go but oblivion. Now, we are free to take bookings wherever and whenever we choose. However, we don't work all that much any more. But we love the freedom and the time to write songs, work on our autobiography and communicate with people.

The invitation to appear at Wembley, London with Cliff Richard in

Chapter 4 – The Kalin Twins

June 1989 for his thirty-year celebration came about when Hal met a fellow in a bar who knew someone in Cliff's band. The fellow asked if he could let the friend know that we were still in showbusiness. Hal agreed, and soon thereafter we got a call from Cliff asking us if we could come over and appear with him. We loved Wembley and the feeling of being stars again. Cliff wanted to pay us but we refused. We did it for old times' sake and because we were friends.

On the personal side, Herb and Jonnie divorced in 1985. Herb's second marriage in 1993 was to Charlotte (*née* Post), who took her life in 1995. He has two daughters, Suzan Lynn and Kelly Lee, and two sons, Buddy Ladd Kalin and Jonathan Ray Kalin (Johnnie Ray Kalin), who are both police officers. Buddy sings occasionally in nightclubs, but not on a full-time basis. Herb chose 'Buddy' which, while still a nickname, is not quite as informal as 'Buddie'. Also, 'Buddie' seems to be a bit effeminate. Okay for showbiz, but not for a cop. Jonathan does not use 'Johnnie Ray', as we began to call him when he was a child. He likes 'J.R.' Both sons like their names. Hal and Marion are technically still married, though separated since around 1987. They have no children. However, Hal is like a second father to Herb's children, and a second grandfather to the grandchildren. Neither of us are really religious men. Herb supposes there is an answer to life somewhere, but he hasn't found it in organized religion, and Hal is more of an agnostic than an atheist.

For Herb, the highest spot of his entertainment career was the day Jack Pleis offered us a recording contract with Decca Records. The lowest spot was seeing Johnnie Ray on the street in Asbury Park, New Jersey — a summer resort — the day he was terminated from the Sand Dunes club (for

Chapter 4 – The Kalin Twins

failing to draw a crowd), which was directly across the street from where we were working, packing them in at the Lincoln Hotel. It was the summer of 1962. With Hal, his highest spot was walking out on stage at the London Palladium, and the lowest was deciding to quit the business in 1966.

In our lives, Herb's highest spot was meeting Johnnie Ray for the first time in Miami in 1953, and the death of his wife, Charlotte, in 1995 was the lowest. The day he got out of the Air Force, after counting the days for four years, was Hal's high spot, and his lowest was the day he foolishly joined the Air Force and realized that he had four years of agony to go.

For both of us our favorite artist was Johnnie Ray. Also high on the list are Frankie Laine, Kay Starr, Etta James and Tony Bennett. We always wanted to have a hit ballad — a song that could become a standard such as *As Time Goes By*, and one of our favorite songs of all time is *Rags To Riches* by Tony Bennett. What do we think of today's music? Do they still call it 'music'?

Looking back, we would probably not have done anything differently. We are fairly happy people — as happy as 69 year olds who want to be 39 can be. Hopefully, the future holds a few more bookings, singing for people who remember us. It's always nice to hear someone say that we made their day by bringing back a few happy memories.

It does irritate us when most people who have ever heard of us know us only for that one song, *When*. If *When* had been a Top Twenty hit or less, then *Forget Me Not* would be seen as a huge success. If our chartmakers were in reverse — *Sweet Sugar Lips*, then *It's Only The Beginning*, and finally *Forget Me Not* and *When* — we'd be thought of much differently.

Showbusiness success and longevity are not usually related to talent. Luck is probably more important. In the long run, it probably doesn't really matter though. Many people devote their lives to showbusiness and come out of it totally unknown. We should be happy for all our experiences in showbusiness — memories that few people have.

According to the royalties we have thus far received, the total worldwide sales of *When* is roughly three and a half million. Unfortunately, we have yet to receive a gold record from Decca. For several years they maintained that the US sales were slightly under a million and therefore we could not receive the gold record until US sales actually reached a million. We had our managers and other interested people negotiate with Decca for years and, just when it looked as though they were going to issue us the gold record, Decca sold out to MCA. We have not bothered asking MCA about it. Too many years have gone by now, and most people think we have the gold record anyway. We're too old now to fight the system.

We were pleased recently to hear that Eric Clapton had publicly stated that he found our music 'incredible' and that we influenced his later work. The Rolling Stones, on the liner notes of an earlier LP, also talked about how we influenced their career. It is these kinds of tributes that make it all worthwhile. That's what the evolution of music is all about — passing the torch to the next generation who will influence yet another star of the future.

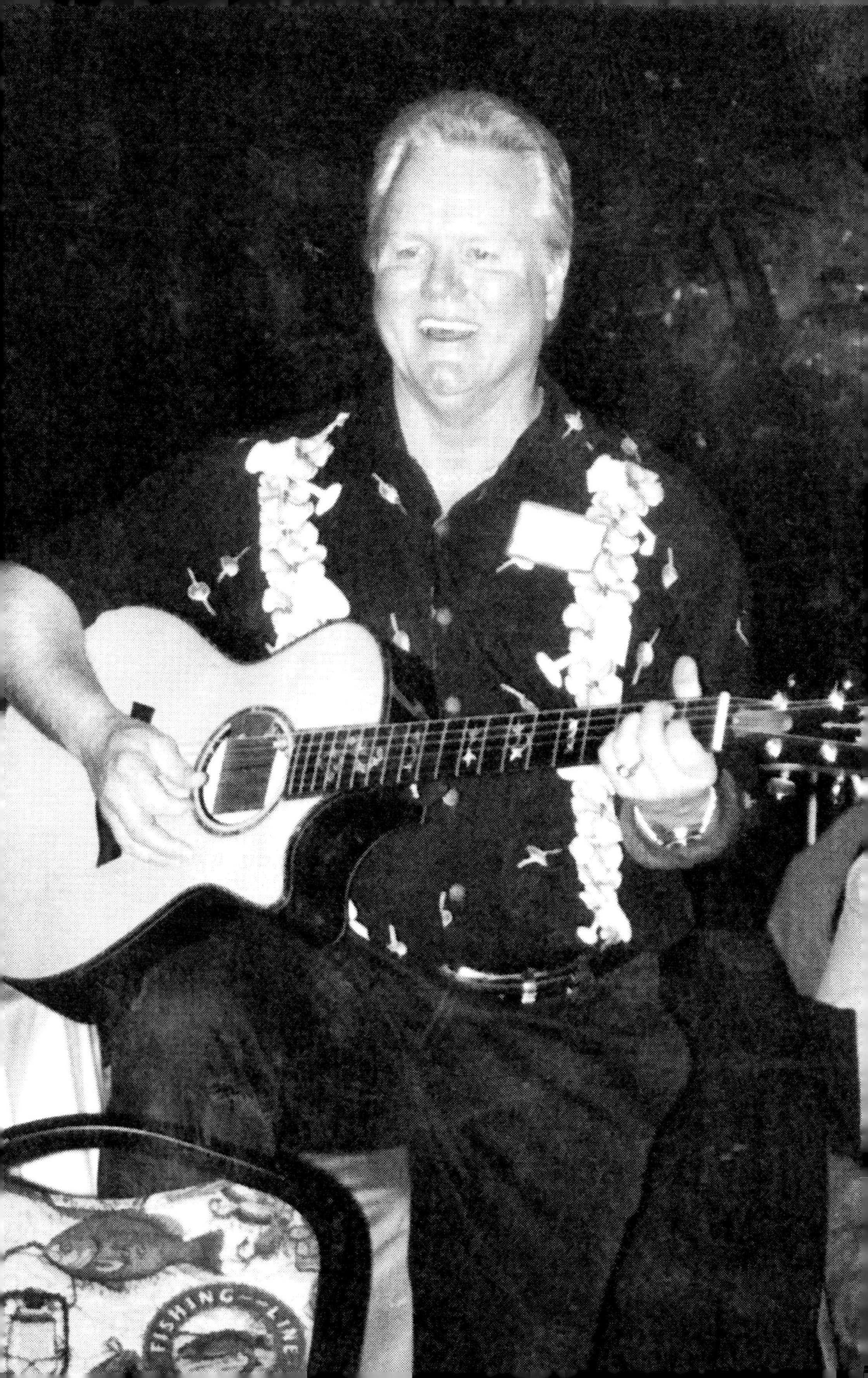
FISHING LINE

5

ROCK'N'ROLL FROM HAWAII
Robin Luke

Composer and performer of the enduring rock'n'roll classic, *Susie Darlin'*, Robin Luke had it all. A fine guitarist with teen-idol good looks and a promising vocal talent, he was also a first-class student. When the big hits failed to materialise, he simply pursued his education and became a respected academic. Today, he still performs for pleasure.

I was born March 20, 1942 in Los Angeles and am proud to say that I am approaching the magic years — the golden years. *[laughs]* My proper name is Robert Henry Luke, but my real name is Robin Luke: that's the name my mother called me about a day after I was born and I've been 'Robin' all my life. Mother was Patricia (*née* Bulloch), born in Belfast, Northern Ireland, and father was Robert Henry Luke (I actually was a 'Jr' until he passed away about twenty years ago). I have no brothers and only one sister, Susie and that's *Susie Darlin'* — *and* we'll get into that I'm sure.

Dad worked for Douglas Aircraft Company and was with them for over forty years. He was born in 1918 and died at age 58. When he died, he was a director for the company. Mother was in the movie business as a retoucher at the Samuel Goldwyn Studios. Her father — my grandfather — was, of course, from Ireland and he became head of the still department at the same film studios, taking all the photographs of the stars in those days. And his son, Malcolm Bulloch, became the head of the still photography department at Paramount Pictures for many, many years. Coincidentally, he took all of the pictures of Elvis in all those movies: he was the one who took all those beautiful 8x10 photos. Indeed, I remember when I was with Elvis when he was in Hawaii on the set of *Blue Hawaii* and my uncle was over there taking still pictures.

Because of my dad's job, we moved about every two to three years at the minimum. One of the places I lived at the longest was College Park, Georgia, just outside of Atlanta. I lived there from about 1948 to 1954. I lived in Hawaii for eleven years from 1954 through to 1965.

I went to public schools until I got into the Seventh Grade, and then I went to Punahou Academy located on the island of Oahu, where we lived in the township of Aina Haina from 1954 until 1959. Founded in 1841 by missionaries to Hawaii, Punahou is a very proper private college preparatory

Chapter 5 – Robin Luke

school through high school, which would be through the Twelfth Grade in the American system. It is very famous for producing outstanding individuals, and I was lucky to attend. It was the hardest school I attended — including college and graduate school for my PhD.

Graduating from Punahou in 1959, I went to college at Pepperdine University, California but would go back to Hawaii, of course, where my folks lived until about 1965, for all the summer breaks and every other vacation I could squeeze in. In 1964, I graduated from Pepperdine University with a Bachelor of Science degree in Psychology. I also received a Bachelor of Science degree in Biology & Chemistry and then moved to Missouri to acquire a Master's in Business Administration — a MBA — and then a PhD in Business with an emphasis in Marketing in 1974.

So, yes, I did go to school! And I was a good student, thanks to some very caring parents. The fact that my parents never went to college made them feel that it was an extremely important thing to do. I had no chance: they were committed to me going to college, and that really had a lot to do with me giving up my profession, so to speak. I announced my retirement from recording just at the very beginning of 1964, when I had done my last song, and it was probably fortuitous 'cause just a few months later the Beatles came along and they'd probably have killed me dead otherwise. In '64 I took off and went into the graduate programs.

Really, I have no idea what would have happened if I had remained in showbusiness. I would probably have exhausted my 'entertainment abilities' and then entered the production, producing and executive management phase of the recording industry or related industries.

I have a wonderful story to tell you — it brings back great emotion to me. My mother was an accomplished musician on the clarinet and the violin, but because of my dad's business we had to move from one location to another. He was a service rep for most of his life for Douglas, and so he would represent the company with particular airlines, which meant that we would usually move every year or two to these airline bases known as 'fixed base operations' or FBOs.

When I was five years old, they gave me a ukelele, a little plastic one — an Arthur Godfrey brand. Within about three or four months I was playing every Walt Disney song that I could ever think of and every Mother Goose rhyme that I could sing, and they were impressed by that. And so, my mother realized back in 1948 that a guitar might be an appropriate instrument. Because we traveled so much, a piano was simply too heavy to carry and a trumpet was a bit too loud in some of the motels and hotels in those days, so my mother decided on a guitar.

After asking around many times for who was the best guitar player, one name kept coming up and that was Perry Bechtel, who was in Atlanta. She finally had a meeting with him and asked him if he would teach her son to play the guitar. At that point, he tried to impress upon her that he'd never taught any child in his life from the beginning.

But my mother was Irish and, as a result, she insisted. And, I think, simply to get rid of her, he said if she would go home and dress me up and have me practise, he would audition me a week from that date. That's all she needed for some opportunity! She came home, told me I had to practise, and I practised like crazy. She bought me my first suit — it was a little Glen Plaid suit — and I have a marvelous photo there with my guitar... but I'm getting ahead of myself.

She did not have a car at the time — only my dad did — so the next week she took the bus, with me (and my ukelele) in tow, back downtown to the only major music studio in Atlanta, Georgia. I can picture this: me sitting there at five to five and a half years old with my little plastic ukelele, playing all of these nursery rhymes and Walt Disney songs with Perry Bechtel looking on and my mother beaming proudly. *[laughs]* To make a long story short, at the end of my audition he turned to my mother and said: 'Mrs. Luke, I *will* teach your son to play the guitar.'

I had five years of very serious studio work with him. He was an old-timer and insisted that I learn to read music and run scales. In fact, I think I ran scales for the first two years before he ever taught me a real song. However, because of his very formalized training, when I finally got into the business, I started doing studio work — because by that time I was probably one of the very few musicians that really understood the classic learning system of instrumentation and music theory. But I did have his pleasure from 1948 to 1954 and he taught me a great deal.

Perry Bechtel is very, very famous. As a sense of history, he was Eddie Peabody's partner on the Orpheum circuit, and at that time, of course, back in the early Twenties, Eddie Peabody was an accomplished banjoist, as was Perry Bechtel: they played together. What's curious is that he moved on. In about 1928 or so, everyone dropped their banjos and picked up guitars, and so did Perry. He became an accomplished orchestral musician and played orchestral guitar for some of the major bands of all time. He retired in Atlanta, Georgia and started giving clinics, and he was trying to tell my mother that now he gave these clinics to people who came and stayed with him, or in a hotel, for up to a month and charged them a very handsome amount of money.

In 1928, Perry was sponsored by both the Martin guitar company and the Gibson guitar company. He was at Martin at this time and he was a plectrum banjoist — which is the four-string variety — and, of course, because he played that style, if you ever listen. He had some albums out and so, of course, did Eddie Peabody. There was a lot of very fast strumming and they'd play octaves, which is jumping from the first fret to the thirteenth fret, a great deal. It was very difficult to do that with a guitar, because in those days a guitar had what they called a twelve-fret neck: the guitar literally met the neck at the twelfth fret. He went to Martin & Co. and said: 'Can't you make one with *fourteen* frets before it hits the guitar's body?' They said: 'Well, we'll try,' and they came out with a guitar called the OM-28 Model. And I'll tell you, Dave, the OM-28 (of course it was called the 'OM-28' because it was 1928) became a renaissance instrument. Because of that he is widely recognized for reinventing the guitar, and today every guitar has fourteen frets. In fact, you have to make a very special order to get a twelve-fret neck. So there's a little trivia for you, and it tells you a great deal about his contribution to the musical instrument.

Early musical influences? Well, because I was in College Park,

Chapter 5 – Robin Luke

Georgia, and because I was playing the guitar, the only artists who really played it at that time, in the late Forties, were the country singers, so I was listening to people like Eddy Arnold. Particularly, I can remember how I met him. The first week or two that we were in Atlanta, Georgia, we stayed at the Henry Grady Hotel and Eddy Arnold was playing there. These were in the days when you had sort of dinner-theater. You would go down to the main salon and eat dinner while someone was up on stage playing, and it was Eddy Arnold at that time with his Tennessee Plowboys. But I remember his Cadillac out front and a little teeny teardrop trailer that held their instruments.

Now, you gotta remember I was only five years old then, but I was really taken with him singing *Bouquet of Roses* and songs like *Molly Darling*. I *loved* it! Now, I'm only five years old and my parents used to leave me behind the stage while they would go somewhere — perhaps to the bar or the lounge — and I would watch him night after night singing, sitting behind the stage, just transfixed. And I think it was that love of his singing and the instruments that led my mother to run downtown and start that guitar search after she got me the ukelele. So, yes, country music meant a lot to me and I can still find myself turning on country stations when nobody's looking. [laughs]

I started singing and playing from the moment I got my instrument. I did a lot of things in school and won little awards for amateur shows and things. Of course, my family encouraged me, and whenever guests would come over it would be: 'Robin, get out your guitar and sing' — because, from what they tell me, I was a natural and had a good sense of rhythm. My first amateur public performance was certainly in school performances and plays. I never sang in a group; I always sang solo. When I got older, I certainly spent a lot of time listening to Rick Nelson, Buddy Holly, Elvis and those types of singers. Curiously, Rick became a pretty good friend of mine, but that's another story.

In Georgia, I was an Eagle Scout and when we moved to Hawaii I wanted to continue my scouting. Then I found out that, unfortunately, in the Hawaiian Islands, only people who were cissies were scouts and real cool guys were on surfboards, so of course I bought a surfboard. When I went to the beach, I found that a lot of the beach boys — now, we are not talking about *the* Beach Boys, we are talking about *real* beach boys — after they'd swim and surf would get musical instruments, from ukeleles to guitars to whatever, and play on the beach and I used to play with them a great deal. I loved their musicianship and learned a lot of their Hawaiian styling, and I think *Susie Darlin'* — if you listen to it — reflects a lot of the Hawaiian chordal structures. And if you listen *real* closely to *Susie Darlin'*, I'm playing the ukelele in the background along with several guitarists.

I wrote *Susie Darlin'* when I was about fourteen and a half. It wasn't inspired by any particular girl. Believe it or not, my recollection is that a melody line which had a semi-Hawaiian chalypso[*] beat kept going through my mind, whether I was surfing, studying in class or playing my guitar. When I decided to put words to the music, it just flowed out of my head easily in a

---

[*] A cross between the cha cha and the calypso.

matter of hours. When I got to the chorus, I decided to put a girl's name in and thought: 'Why not put my sister's name in?' Susie was a very popular name at that time, and using her name wouldn't get me into any trouble with all the other girls at Punahou. I thought it was the safe thing to do, and it certainly was! This song's first title was *All Night Long* — since that phrase was mentioned six times, it seemed a natural title. It was only when we went to copyright and put it out that we found out that another song had been named *All Night Long*. I struggled with another title and the only thing that seemed to work was *Susie Darlin'* — and the rest is history.

So, that's really how I started to write. I wrote some other songs and then, when I was a junior in high school, I sang the song at a variety show. These variety shows were *big*. You've got to remember that Hawaii was not yet a state and we had the annual *Punahou Carnival*, and people from all over the island would come, enjoy the rides and then also go the variety show, which was put on by students of the Academy. That year, it was me with a very good friend named Dick Ednie — he was playing the gut-bucket, which is an interesting instrument with a big tub with a string and a stick on the end of that. I think you've probably seen those before. We sat up there, the two of us, and sang *Susie Darlin'* along with a couple of other songs. There was a guy in the audience and he came down. His name was Kimo McVay. He was interested if I wanted to make a record of that and took it to a man named Bob Bertram, who owned a small company called Bertram International which manufactured hula records primarily for tourists.

We recorded *Susie Darlin'* for Bertram International in a bedroom on a portable tape recorder, and the echo was literally the bathroom with a speaker at one end, a microphone at the other, and a flip-switch which would throw it. And, if you listen to *Susie Darlin'*, the third *'Oh, Susie darlin' '* we forgot to flip the switch and so there is no echo — there's another little bit of trivia for you. It took us about two months to record that, because we had about seven or

Robin welcomes the Everly Brothers and Don's wife, Sue, to Hawaii.

eight overdubs, and the type of Ampex machine it was, it was 'all or none'. In other words, you would record track-on-track, sound-on-sound, and if you made a mistake then you had to start all over at the beginning. There was a large hospital next to this apartment, and there were several times when we had it just about perfect and come about the sixth or seventh overdub all of a sudden you would hear 'wooooooooooooooooooh' — an ambulance would go flying by and we'd have to start all over!

I played a majority of the instruments on the session, although Bob Bertram did some percussion *[laughs]*: he was the 'drums'. The drums were a set of brushes hitting a Capitol Records cardboard box. I remember that pretty well. Also, the percussion sticks that you hear going clickety-click-click were a Sheaffer pen in a pocket being hit by two sticks. So, it was a sort-of 'you make it up as you go along' affair. We also had some other guys playing bass, 'cause I didn't play bass at the time.

Susie Darlin' was brought out in the summer of 1958. I can't remember where I was — except in Hawaii — when I first heard *Susie Darlin'* played on the radio, but I will tell you that Tom Moffatt was largely responsible for making it a hit. Tom, who was the No.1 deejay, played it every fifteen or twenty minutes for about six months.

The song was No.1 in Hawaii for six months as all my friends bought it. You only had to sell 600 copies a week to get No.1 there, but six months was a long time. Then, after the six months, what happened was that a honeymooning couple, Dottie and Art Freeman from Dot Records in Hollywood, heard it and took it back to Randy Wood, the president of Dot Records. He liked it, bought the master from Bertram International — I don't know what he paid — put it out, and the rest is history. My parents had to sign contracts for me because of my age.

When I was in the Islands, I did appear on some television shows and did a lot of other types of shows after *Susie Darlin'* became a hit. There was a rock'n'roll show there that was very, very large. A man named Ralph Yempuku owned the Honolulu Civic Auditorium, which had a lot of fights and wrestling matches. Every month his promoter, Earl Finch (a former carnival organizer who was most often seen with his hat and cigar *à la* Elvis' Tom Parker), would bring over the Top Ten talent from America. It was really interesting because I would meet these people on my own ground. Tom Moffatt (who is now a very, very successful long-time promoter in the Hawaiian Islands) being the No.1 deejay, as I have mentioned, was the master of ceremonies for all of these shows. We kinda grew up together, and he and I would go out to all the airplanes and meet all these stars as they came in for the *Show Of Stars*.

I remember, for example, when the Everly Brothers, who'd had two No.1 records with their songs: *Wake Up Little Susie [1957]* and *All I Have To Do Is Dream [1958]*, were going to be the No.1 act at one of the shows. They walked off a prop airplane — probably a DC-6 — and as they were coming down the ramp I threw leis over their necks and shook their hands. Well, they arrived a little late and as we were trying to get them to the car, Don Everly was all business. He was very, very serious and saying: 'We have to get to the show. I have to do a sound check. We have to do that because when we finish the show we have to make sure and...'

Tom Moffatt jumped in and said: 'Don, I'm sorry, but you aren't finishing the show, *Susie Darlin'* is No.1 here in the Hawaiian Islands.'

He said: '*Susie Darlin'*!? Who's that by?'

Tom said: 'Well, that's by Robin Luke.'

And Don said: 'Well, who the *hell* is Robin Luke!?'

And I said: 'I am', as I was right next to him.

Interesting what went on in those days. When *Susie Darlin'* first entered the US chart in the summer of 1958, I was in Hawaii between my junior and senior year of high school. Curiously, there were petty jealousies between students that went to private schools and those who went to public schools (I attended Punahou Academy, which was private). Sometimes, this got down to name-calling and there were some well known derogatory slang expressions for different ethnicities among Japanese, Caucasian, Korean, Portugese, Samoan, Malay, Filipino, etc. There were several times when we were forced off the road by a gang of guys from another high school that wanted a piece of me because their girlfriends liked my records. Fortunately, I rode around with the Ednie boys, George and Dick, who weighed well over two hundred pounds, and they relished the opportunity to set these guys straight — usually straight down the asphalt! Looking back, I can see that I really owe these guys.

All of the hoopla was casually received by me, my parents and friends, because Hawaii was a US territory out in the middle of the Pacific Ocean. Therefore, we treated the US almost like you would treat another country. Of course, I had already made my first trip to the States with my dad

Chapter 5 – Robin Luke

on promotion tour number one. We went to Philadelphia for the first Dick Clark show, then Washington, Baltimore, Allentown and other car stops to visit deejays and do record hops for the deejays.

In those days, deejays had a great deal of power. They could make or break your song by playing or not playing it on the radio. They made substantial quantities of cash by holding weekly record hops at a local building, school or theater. They would be up on the stage and spin stacks of wax while the kids danced. These hops were really a lot of harmless fun and provided a safe and clean opportunity for teenagers to meet people and dance their legs off doing the bop! On occasion, the deejay would ask a recording artist to join him on stage. They would introduce the new song (or old one usually first) and the artist would lip-sync the record by miming the words (I always did it with my guitar). It was common practise and would be preceded or followed with an autograph session where the kids would get your autograph on a picture or a record.

Susie Darlin' took off the week after I appeared at these stops. One of the interesting things — and why it became so notorious — was how long it stayed on the charts. I believe it came on the *Cash Box* charts at No.58, took months to get into the Top Five, and then went *slowly* down. Almost a year took place before it dropped off the charts. This is why it sold 2½ million copies. It was really a sort-of 'sleeper' in a way. It didn't go up and down right away; it started on one side of the country and then moved around and just kept selling. As a result, it was a very major seller.

It also connected internationally but, due to the times, was not purchased all at the same time. Months went by between it being a hit in Europe and Japan and Australia. We had to make four additional records that we called 'the island records' that were released primarily in the Hawaiian Islands, on the Bertram International label, while *Susie Darlin'* was still going up the charts elsewhere on Dot. By the way, the original light blue-labelled Bertram International recordings are *very* valuable. I have seen *Susie Darlin'* records with the original record sleeve go for $1,000-plus! The *extremely* rare EP has gone for much more! Just think: I had a box of five hundred of those I gave away to friends. That box today would be worth over half a million US dollars!

As I have told you, *Susie Darlin'* was my sister — her name was Susie Luke. Now, of course, she is married and her name is Susie Robison. She lives in Columbia, Missouri. She loved the song... she was only five and a half years old when it came out. I can remember one time I sang *Susie Darlin'* along with other songs with the Honolulu Symphony Orchestra at the Waikiki Shell, which is at the foot of the Diamond Head crater on Waikiki Beach. It was very formal: I had a white tuxedo on and, of course, the finale was singing *Susie Darlin'*. They put Susie up on stage in a real pretty little dress and had her sitting there looking at me. Directly after the show the media came up and started to interview Susie, who was becoming quite a pro at this by this time at five and a half. They said: 'Well, what do you think of your brother's success?' She looked up and said: '*Susie Darlin'*, that's me — I'm famous!' And we all just roared with laughter.

On *Susie Darlin'* I gave all of the publishing

Robin and sister Susie.

to Bob Bertram and he published my first songs on Congressional Music (ASCAP). This was his company. I did not realize the advantage to publishing your own songs until later, but after that I did set up my own company, Roblu Music, and started getting my own royalties. ASCAP has done a good job giving me my share of the writer's rights to those early songs, including *Susie Darlin'*, but it would be right to assume that the Bertram family has not been fair with the distribution of publishing royalties.

I was on the *Dick Clark Show* thirteen times and somewhere in the middle of all that I was asked to be on the Como show. The *Perry Como Show* was in August of '58. He was terrific and took a particular interest in me because I reminded him of his son, Ronnie. So, he spent a little bit of time with me and we had a very nice relationship on the show. I sang *Susie Darlin'*, *I Still Get Jealous* and *Five Minutes More*. The last two songs were written by Jule Styne and he was honored on the show. I later made a recording of *Five Minutes More* because of the demand for it after singing it on the *Perry Como Show*. I did get a fee for the show: I think it was $2,000, which was a whole lotta money in those days, and at the same time I had to fly from Hawaii and back, and so that sucked up a good part of it. It was certainly a lotta money: it was enough to buy a car, and almost a Corvette, back then.

I really didn't do a great deal of promoting on my songs. I didn't do

Chapter 5 – Robin Luke

one-night stands, but I would take off some weekends and do a big show or I'd go to New York. Usually, what we did when we did the Dick Clark shows, we would arrive in Philadelphia, do a Philly show and then spend three or four days zooming around radio stations, record hops, etc. We'd then finish with a Saturday night Dick Clark *Beechnut* show and leave the next morning for back to Hawaii or to L.A. to go back to school.

I've no idea what I got paid for appearances, they were always different. I usually traveled alone: on the very first tour my dad went with me, but after that I did it by myself. I was only about sixteen at the time so it was sort-of amazing, as I'd never let my own kids do it. I didn't do any of the Dick Clark tours, although I did some of the shows like the Hollywood Bowl and others. There were many offers to go overseas, but college kept me from nearly everything but occasional weekend sorties. However, I did tour outside the US: I was in Canada and Australia.

After one of the many Dick Clark shows I was on, a fan brought me something a little different from the ordinary stuffed tiger (my nickname in high school) or cheesecake (my favorite dessert). She brought me an *alligator!* Well, of course, I had to get it home to Hawaii. In those days, a flight to Hawaii included a long-propeller airplane, often with a stop in Chicago and either San Francisco or Los Angeles before crossing the Pacific to Hawaii. I asked one of the prop men to find me something to carry Ally the alligator in, and he produced a 35 mm motion picture reel canister that was about 1½ feet in diameter and about three inches thick. He punched pinholes on the top for air and Ally had a home.

I carried it with me all the way and literally smuggled it into Hawaii, which was — and is — very strict about what comes in and out of the state. After about a week in the bathtub at my house, with no-one easily able to bathe (the alligator was about twelve inches long and ferocious: he would literally jump up one foot in the air to snatch a piece of meat hanging by a string and swing wildly until you let him have it), my parents insisted that we part company with the beast.

It just so happened that I was leaving that weekend on a Hawaii tour with Frankie Avalon and others, with the first stop on the island of Kauai. We arrived in Kauai, unloaded our gear and headed for the Koko Palms Hotel, owned by the Fernandes family, which was the nicest hotel on the island at that time. Late that night, Frankie and I sneaked down to the hotel moat — a canal that they had carved out of the earth where they had their luaus and had outrigger canoes floating. I opened the canister and out popped Ally. He took a look at Frankie — and a couple of other entertainers — for a second and headed straight for the water. There's more...

Years later, my mom mailed me a newspaper article from Hawaii (they were still living there) with the startling headline: *'8 Foot 400 Pound Alligator Found On Kauai'*. It had lived a satisfying life by the Koko Palms in an estuary that upstream had the beautiful waterfall that is seen in the Elvis movie, *Blue Hawaii*. I bet Elvis would have never jumped in if he knew that about a hundred feet away was something that could have made minced meat out of him!

Of course, if the authorities ever come after me about this I'll say that I

Chapter 5 – Robin Luke

made all this up. I hope Frankie can agree with me... There's your scoop! I have no idea what happened to the alligator.

Memories? Well, I've got so many I could bore you and I just don't have time. *[laughs]* You're gonna need to get this, but I'll give you two stories from my touring days.

Story One: In 1960 I went to Australia for Lee Gordon Productions. We toured for two weeks: Sydney, Melbourne, Hobart and Tasmania. The package was called *The Johnny Cash Show* and the other artists were Gene Vincent, Jim Morrison (I do have a picture of him but can't really tell if he is *the* Jim Morrison or not — perhaps he was a local entertainer), the Playmates, Bobby Day and Col Joye & The Joys. The show in Tasmania was held in an enormous building that was made out of wood. We were there in their winter and it was *cold!* If you take a look at a world map, you will notice that the next piece of land south of Tasmania is Antarctica! It was an old building and we could see the snow through the cracks of the building.

I took my trusty Gibson ES-175D guitar on the trip, Johnny Cash had a Martin D-28 and Gene Vincent had borrowed Bonnie Guitar's very valuable Gretsch White Falcon — a totally white arch-top acoustic-electric with gold parts, and tuning knobs with rubies on each knob, honest! The guitar cost $2,000 in 1960 and, as such, was one of the most expensive guitars available.

I came off stage after my encore and met Johnny as he was about to go on stage to finish the show. We were anxious to get back to the hotel and so we had arranged to meet together immediately after he finished. I would have his guitar case opened so he could case his instrument, and we would run down a very long ramp to a limo that was waiting for us street-side.

Gene had experienced a serious motorcycle accident just before the tour and, frankly, should not have made the trip. He had a hard body cast that ran around his waist and went all the way to the foot of one leg. Since it was hard plaster, the only way he could move was to swing his leg in an arc in a very awkward fashion. Gene was on his way down in the business and he really needed the money the tour would bring him — probably to pay for his injury, among other bills. My song was No.1 in Australia at the time of the tour and I was paid a whopping $2,000 for the two week tour, which was a lot of money. I am sure that Gene got significantly less.

Well, as Johnny finished his performance and jogged off stage toward me, Gene and I could hear that well-recognized sound of fans breaking through the lines of guards and rushing the stage. We could hear thumps and bumps as people rushed the stage and were attempting to get to us all. Johnny said: 'Let's get out of here!' and with that he swung his guitar into the case, locked it, and began to run toward the limo down the long, steep ramp. I followed in hot pursuit with my guitar, and we could both hear Gene attempting to run with his 'peg-legged' cast: clumpity-clumpity-clump! All of a sudden, we heard him scream in terror as he lost his balance and lurched forward, slamming his body on the concrete with his face, hands and shoes following close behind! His guitar case shot out in the air in front of him, like a gymnast in the middle of a tumbling routine, and crashed to the floor.

Johnny and I, seeing and hearing this, ran back to Gene. Johnny (a

Chapter 5 – Robin Luke

big, strong man) scooped him up while I grabbed the handle of the guitar case, and we made it to the limo just as the horde of fans consumed it. The limo driver freaked out and simply closed his eyes and floored the vehicle till it cleared the surrounding mob. I'll never know how many people he ran into or ran over, but soon we were at the front door of our hotel.

The three of us shared the top floor of the hotel in separate rooms. We entered our rooms for the evening and shortly thereafter we heard Gene's anguished cries: 'Oh, God! Oh, God! Oh no!'

As we rushed to enter his room, we found Gene standing over the opened guitar case on the bed. Inside the case were what appeared to be a hundred white pieces of wood, plastic and gold parts. The White Falcon had disintegrated when the case hit the floor. Gene was inconsolable and he wept for what seemed an eternity. The cost of replacing the guitar was significantly more than his compensation for the tour. He had to get Bonnie another, and the new one would never be able to replace the one custom made for her. I don't think Gene ever recovered from the loss. I never heard from him again.

Story Two: Towards the end of this tour, Johnny and I, being the shyest people on the bill, began to naturally spend time together: likes attract. One night, we got back to our hotel very late, well after midnight. I had just pulled the covers over my head when I heard a knock at the door. I was alarmed at hearing the knock, because my parents and others had told me to (1) lock the door of my room, and (2) *never* open the door on one of these tours — for a multitude of reasons, most of which were obvious. I was about to call the front desk for help when a low voice from behind the door said 'This is Johnny' in a timbre and drawl that no one in the world could ever duplicate. When I jumped out of bed to open the door, there was Johnny with his D-28 held at his side. He looked down at me and smiled, saying softly: 'Robin, I just can't seem to get to sleep. Could I come in and play a few songs awhile?'

Now, you have to understand that I learned to play in Georgia from 1948 to 1954 from Perry Bechtel when the flat-top guitar was a country & western instrument — long before rock guitar hit the scene. I therefore found myself listening to a lot of c&w music. When Johnny Cash first hit the charts with *I Walk The Line* on Sun Records, I was a loyal fan for life. I still believe that the Columbia album that was released just before he went on the Australian tour, titled *'The Fabulous Johnny Cash'*, is one of the greatest albums of all time — period.

Johnny came into my room, sat down at my feet while I went under the covers, and started singing: he sang old country songs, gospel tunes and some of his greatest hits while I harmonized along with him. He played while I sang old radio commercials for Tube Rose Snuff (*'If your snuff's too strong, it's wrong, it's wrong / Get Tube Rose, get Tu-u-ube Roooooose!'*) and old Eddy Arnold songs, like *Beautiful Brown Eyes* and *Molly Darling*, that I had learned between the ages of five and thirteen, and the next thing I knew it was morning. Yep, Johnny had sung me to sleep and then quietly shut the door to my room — without locking it! — and had gone to bed. I'll never forget that night. I slept like a baby, and I now realize that this particular night was one of the most special and treasured moments in my life.

Chapter 5 – Robin Luke

I had so many friendships with artists and I still do see, occasionally, a few of them. I can remember, for example, Andy Williams coming to the *Show Of Stars* in Hawaii wearing red suede shoes. He'd just broken up from his brothers, the Williams Brothers, and he had a little song out called *Butterfly,* and I remember him bouncing around. Later, of course, he was one of the biggest things around and got me a few good seats at a time when I appreciated it, and he is still performing just south of me in Branson.

On tour, we would pass around our studio photos and often, in boredom, autograph them for the artists we were traveling with. My mom dutifully kept a great many of these photos, and some of them are unique. A collector of Sam Cooke memorabilia traveled from Los Angeles to Springfield to see a photo that Sam had autographed that said: *'To Robin, a swell guy!'* He broke down in tears, saying that he had never seen the picture before.

While I was an active performer, I can honestly say that there were absolutely no color, race or ethnic barriers in the entertainment business that were brought to my attention. We sang, bathed, relaxed, played, rode on buses, planes, etc. together. We partied, ate and performed together.

Did I have any difficulties avoiding trouble with drugs, drink and girls on tour? You do ask some penetrating questions! I had the good fortune to grow up in a loving family that had good moral values, an appreciation for education and an innate responsibility to pass on to their children the difference between right and wrong. As a result, I was well prepared to respond in a responsible manner to the temptations awaiting me as a 'teenage idol'. Although the magazines referred to me as one, I never felt that I was promoted in that way. By the way, my dad used to refer to me during this time as the 'idle teenager'!

Yes, there were many instances of alcohol and drug use. The drug was primarily marijuana, although I did see a few 'shoot up' backstage during my career. Of course, like most addicts, they would always invite me to join

Chapter 5 – Robin Luke

them. A simple 'No thank you' response always worked for me. My dad had promised me a new car if I didn't drink or smoke until I graduated from high school. This promise was well known among my friends. Therefore, every time I was offered a chance to go astray in high school, my friends would say to the person offering me such a vice: 'Hey, don't offer it to Robin. He's getting a new car if he...' I suggest that, if a parent can afford such a prize, they make this pledge. A result of this promise is that I have *never* smoked anything, except a few hams and turkeys!

At first, like any red-blooded boy, I loved the female attention. Who wouldn't? However, after a time, I started to get uncomfortable. Fans in wolf packs do not act out in normal ways, and they do things they would never do alone. I have had to fight gangs of fans off when they started ripping my clothes off. Believe me, this is not an enjoyable experience, and it makes you somewhat apprehensive about relationships in general. Fortunately, I always had a girlfriend back home where I was just a guy. On the road, I had to be careful. Certain types of girls — you know the kind — were always hanging around. Again, I realized the traps one could fall into associating with them and therefore avoided the temptation, but I do have to tell you about the one time I almost got involved.

It was on the Australia tour. At the request of a local entertainer, Col Joye, I attended a record hop at a record store outside of Sydney. I was in the middle of an autograph session, when I looked up and saw the most beautiful girl I had ever seen in the corner. She appeared to be shy, but I swear that there was a halo-like glow around her face. She had short, naturally blonde hair and looked like she had come right out of one of the teen magazine Breck Shampoo commercials. She had a white-with-pastel-stripes angora sweater on and looked the epitome of what every person would envision as someone who came from an aristocratic background. She was drop-dead perfect! I must have looked at her, star-struck, for several seconds, because she gave me a beautiful shy smile and then moved her eyes down to the floor. Col Joye immediately whispered in my ear: 'Do you like that?' I simply nodded my head and went on autographing. I left the store, but could not forget her face.

After the last evening show that night, Col Joye asked me to come out of my

Chapter 5 – Robin Luke

dressing room — and there she was! Col had managed to get her to meet me after the show! She was as beautiful in speech as she was in person. She did come from a very good professional family, was about to enter the most prestigious school in her country and admitted that, since I was her favorite singer, she just had to see me in person at the record hop, although her parents had forbidden such a thing. She was there that evening at the great risk of upsetting her family.

I asked her if she would have dinner with me. She placed her hand in mine and, just at that moment, a disc jockey from a radio station busted in and said: 'Robin, *Miss Susie Darlin'* is ready for you to have dinner with her!' He began pulling me towards the dining room where a cadre of radio personalities and executives were seated at a very long table. Right in the middle was an empty seat beside the most overstuffed teenager I have ever seen, with a gown that looked like something that had exploded from a chiffon factory, with a crown on her head that said — no joke — *Miss Susie Darlin'!* I turned toward the most perfect girl I had ever seen, and she was gone!

In shock, I sat down and was informed that the station had a *Miss Susie Darlin'* contest, that they had received over three hundred entries, and that this pig was the glorious winner! I was only required to have dinner with her, but that anything I wished to do with her later was all right with her! I actually felt like passing out, but instead providence came to the rescue. While looking in the deejay's eyes, my blood pressure went so high that I had an explosive nosebleed. As I felt the blood begin to shoot out of my right nostril, I simply turned to this puffed-up teen winner and said: 'Excuse me, I apologize for the interruption and inconvenience.'

I was heading for my room when Col Joye appeared from out of nowhere. I was happy to see him, because I hoped that he was going to bring this girl to me again. When I asked him where she was, he simply said: 'She's gone.' I never saw her again, but, as you can see, I still think of her. I can't remember her name and I didn't try to find her. I just spent the evening in my hotel room and didn't return to dine with the competition winner.

Chapter 5 – Robin Luke

I got a lot of things out of being an artist, being a recording star or simply playing music. I may not have mentioned, but I did a lot of studio sessions and did a lot of background for a lot of rockers. I could play the guitar — and still do, every day — and have quite a collection of vintage instruments gathered over the years.

The success affected me and my family in a lot of ways. I learned about the difficulty of business, of people welcoming you on one point and then sort-of stabbing you in the back on another. But I enjoyed the world of business and, of course, ended up getting a PhD in it. It allowed me to grow up very quickly and see the world in a way that I would never have seen it as a young boy growing up in Hawaii. At the same time, there was a lot of pressure to perform — and I don't just mean singing, but to perform *off*stage as well as *on*stage.

There was no pressure to finding a successful follow-up. Quite honestly, I kept writing songs, and many of the songs that I sang were ones that were self-written. Of course, Dick Clark was very good at singing over other people's hits, as you are well aware. I was part of that with two songs that went into the Top Ten: *Everlovin'*, that Rick Nelson recorded, and also *Bad Boy* which Marty Wilde in Britain made a big hit. We put those out and enjoyed the ride up the chart with them.

Chicka Chicka Honey was just a natural follow-up. It was something I wrote and we recorded it in the bedroom. Because there was naturally a period of time when *Susie Darlin'* was dropping down in Hawaii, but just starting up the charts in the rest of the world, we put those songs out — which we called the 'bedroom songs' — just as a sort-of filler until *Susie Darlin'* started to drop down in the US, and then we could do major studio productions in Hollywood.

I have no idea how many records we released, but there is a CD with 31 songs on it, and all songs were released during my active career on Dot Records after the first few. We had some that came out on both because, of course, Bertram International released the local ones and Dot the international ones.

I had a very good relationship with Randy Wood. He was my manager and never took a penny for it, and, because my parents were in Hawaii, he used to make sure that I was in good shape. Of course, he took care of Pat Boone at the time too, so Pat and I spent a great deal of time together. Needless to say, we spent a lot of time in the office and also socially, and I got to know his family quite well at that time. Although Pat was certainly the largest property for Dot at that time — and Randy took advantage of that — I don't think the rest of us lost out because of it. Randy knew from the get-go that I did not want to stay in the world of music all my life. Like Pat, I told him I wanted to go to college, but it was a little bit different as I hadn't even entered college at that time when I first met him. He realized that, number one, you're only a teenager once. And I sure was no Frank Sinatra, so we decided that we'd take it for as long as we could, and at the same time I never stopped going to college. We were very close to Hollywood at Pepperdine.

I did get my royalties from Dot: Randy was very fair to me, and I never had the problems or catastrophes that you heard from other artists. It was very good for me, 'cause it helped pay for my education. Frankly, I still get royalties. Of course, the large majority now are from writing not from singing, but you'd be amazed how many copies Bear Family Records sells and others. I think that *Susie Darlin'* must be on a hundred different CDs at this time. Every month I get a new one, or I'm told about somewhere where it has been recorded. I never owned the masters to my records and today they are owned by the MCA Corporation.

Yes, I did write some songs for other artists and, as you have mentioned, Tommy Roe did record *Susie Darlin'*. I was very pleased when he recorded the song. I enjoyed his version and appreciated the fact that he liked the song enough to record it. It had previously been recorded by Chris Howland and another artist in England; Tommy Kent in Germany *[Polydor]* — what a great version; people in Japan and many other countries. Also, Bobby Vee had many nice things to say about my writing style and certainly performed some of my songs on stage, even if he didn't record them.

I just wasn't smart enough to stay in showbusiness *and* go to graduate school. As I mentioned earlier, I announced that I was going to retire actively from showbusiness and it was fortuitous, because the Beatles came out three to six months later and would have killed me anyway! *[laughs]* But it was a natural progression to go back to graduate school, to enjoy what I had done, and probably put it to an applicative sense as being a business professional and eventually ending up as an academic administrator in universities.

In 1967, I met my future wife, Linda Pratt, and we married on June 28, 1969 before I got my degree. We were married for twenty-eight years and had two children, who are still with me: they are Tiffany, who is now 28, and Bob, who is 22. We lost Linda in an automobile accident on May 29, 1997. My daughter is graduated from the University of Missouri with a degree in Business & Marketing. She is presently employed and married to a wonderful guy named Chris. My son graduated this past summer with a Bachelor of Science in Engineering School & Computer Science and now is getting his Master's: a very sharp kid, we were proud of him. He's going on for a PhD, and he is single.

After losing Linda, I virtually floundered for a year or two and then met a wonderful lady who was named Mary Newberry at the time. I proposed, and we were married on December 29, 2001. Mary has four children: Steve Landis, Jeremy Landis, Ethan Newberry and Rosie Newberry. Ethan is 16 now and Rosie is 14. They are, of course, in the house and they are going to high school. They are wonderful children. I couldn't have had them any better if I'd given birth to them myself. We are enjoying our life. We bought a new house, as I mentioned, and that's why I've been late getting back to you, 'cause we've been going crazy carrying boxes and breaking boxes apart. I really don't sit around these days eating bonbons. I'm a very active employee for Southwest Missouri State University as a professor and head of the Department of Marketing in their Business School.

I really don't need to go back to showbiz although, as you know, there is a spectacular thrill when you are invited to go to these 'oldies but goodies' shows that are major in size. Certainly, now I pick and choose from them and, as you can hear by my venues of Hawaii and Vienna, Austria, I'm pretty fortunate that they pick some pretty neat spots. And it's always a lot more fun to travel with your wife when someone else is paying for it! Today, I look at that as just a wonderful opportunity to see old friends and to be greeted and appreciated by past fans.

I rarely go to nostalgia shows as a spectator, but I sure love to go to shows. I guess most things now are nostalgia, as people have been so long-lasting, singing. I just saw Stephen Bishop, for example, and Charlie Musselwhite last week. They did a wonderful concert here and, boy, that brings back some great blues and rock memories. But, sure, I'm active and go out as much as I can get away with. Also, every time I ever go to a bar or a lounge where there's a group, they get me up on stage to sing a few songs. In fact, on February 1 we're having the first and last *Robin Luke Show* here in Springfield, Missouri. I'll be performing for an hour on stage at the Juanita K. Hammons Center To The Performing Arts, which is the largest concert hall in Springfield, to about 2,500-3,000 people hopefully — although I've never really counted the seats there.

Although I don't actively seek them out, I am in touch with a lot of people in the industry. We do see each other, and occasionally I am called upon to do interviews like this, and the next thing you know it leads to seeing or talking to some 'oldies but goodies' on the phone or in person.

Susie Darlin' was extremely good to me and I have appreciated it more

> **Southwest Missouri State**
> U N I V E R S I T Y
>
> Robert H. Luke, Ph.D.
> Professor and Department Head
> Department of Marketing
> College of Business Administration
>
> 901 South National Avenue
> Springfield, Missouri 65804
>
> (417) 836-5413   Fax: (417) 836-4466
> E-mail: rhl286f@smsu.edu

and more as time has passed by. Due to my line of work, at first when I tried to enter the professoriat it was pretty difficult to be accepted seriously, because every time you're introduced they introduced you as: 'This is Robin Luke, the rock'n'roller.' And in academia that doesn't work too well. What it made me do was frankly work harder, and I published many journal articles and took the position of being a manager of departments. Of course, over time people find out who you really are, and now I *love* to sing *Susie Darlin'* anytime I can get away with it, and basically play now for friends and kids and do whatever I can to keep the good memories alive, and it's just a wonderful, rosy, sweet, fuzzy, warm memory to me.

Does it please me that *Susie Darlin'* is a classic? Absolutely! There is not a week that goes by that my secretary doesn't receive a package in the mail asking for me to autograph something. I always feel honored to oblige these persons, as they usually have a personal reason for their request. They often say it was their favorite song, or that they married their 'Susie Darlin'' while the song was playing. A recent request included the fact that the guy

Chapter 5 – Robin Luke

was very successful and had several restaurants including an 'oldies restaurant' that had a '55 Chevy convertible with the name *'Susie Darlin''* pin-striped on the rear fenders. Now *that's* a commitment!

My own favorite artists? The more you live, the more you realize what you listened to, and clearly Chuck Berry was my seminal rock'n'roll star. When I was in Vienna, we really had a wild guitar war at the end singing *Johnny B. Goode* and, although I'm not Chuck Berry, I can sure have fun singing and screaming it out. Also, Buddy Holly is a very strong influence in my life and, as far as groups go, you never beat the Rolling Stones. If people can't jump up and down listening to the Stones, they don't have any rhythm at all. *[laughs]* I have so many other favorite artists too, that it's almost unfair to mention two or three. But I never consciously copied anyone, and no-one has ever confronted me with trying to copy anybody.

The lowest spot in my music career? *[bursts out laughing]* Well, in my music career, the lowest part was when I was on stage in Hawaii. I remember it well. I had gotten my teeth knocked out in about 1958 playing mountain baseball: I just forgot to catch this end of a log that was the 'ball'. So, I had a temporary bridge in my front three teeth, and at one point on stage I was singing and it got to a break in a song — I think it was an Elvis song — and I threw my guitar to the side and I said this word that began with a 'p', or some popping sound, and I watched the teeth fly right out past the microphone on stage. I don't think I've ever observed such panic in my life, but I did an Elvis gyration, caught the bridge, passed the microphone in mid-air and fell to the stage floor. People started screaming, thinking I was doing some sort of Elvis act, when actually I was sticking my teeth back in my mouth! And that was probably the lowest. Certainly, if I hadn't caught my teeth, it would have been!

Losing Linda in 1997 was the lowest spot in my personal life. I almost lost my mind at that point, 'cause she was clearly extremely important to me and my family — but I've gone through that now and, with the love of people around me and my children and certainly my latest bride, Mary, who is just very, very, important to my life now. I don't know how I could have gotten where I am without her. I love her more every day. She is an absolutely magnificent woman and one of the most caring individuals I have ever known in my life.

The highest spot in my music career? Well, I think just in the continual loving and sharing of that world with others. I guess, clinically, the highest spot was the *Perry Como Show*, as that was the No.1 show with the highest viewership on TV. At the same time, there are high spots along the way that personally meant more. For example, the story I've told you about my friendship with Johnny Cash on that 1960 Australia tour.

Without question, the highest spot in my personal life was the birth of my two children. My son's was more eventful, simply because he was born in our bedroom in the US Virgin Islands in 1980 by mistake! I delivered him with four house guests present — mostly family — in the middle of the night!

Outside of music and my university work, I have always been interested in yacht racing, as I started sailing when I was eight years old. From 1977 to 1984, I was a professor at the University of the Virgin Islands, and I continued my yacht racing there and raced actively throughout the Caribbean. The St. Thomas Yacht Club had seven Olympians when I arrived,

Chapter 5 – Robin Luke

and I learned a great deal from them.

We won many races over a seven-year stay. However, the biggest thrill was winning the CORC (Caribbean Ocean Racing Circuit) Series[*] over a three month period! There were over 140 racing sailboats in the series, including a bunch of maxi-boats — *Kialoa* among them — the most famous racing boat of its kind.

My late wife, Linda, and I started up Island Yachts, a 28-boat yacht charter company made up of racer/cruiser type sailboats in 1977. We were very successful with this concept, and I was very pleased to be invited to Annapolis in October of this year to help the owners, Skip and Andrea King — Skip was our manager — celebrate Island Yachts' 25th anniversary with the media. How time flies!

I continued my racing efforts here in Missouri on Stockton Lake, one of the largest inland lakes according to the number of sailboats (400 plus). My wife and young family (Tiffany was then nine and Bob was five) joined me as crew and we won the most prestigious race, the Governor's Cup, two times. While I did all I could teaching others the art of racing, and sold — at cost — a lot of boats to people with my former yacht company contacts, Stockton Lake just wasn't the same as the USVI and I left racing in 1997.

Here's another story. A few years ago, Perry Leslie was the Director of Golf at Highland Springs Country Club here in Springfield and they were having a PGA tournament. As is the case with most tournaments, they have a celebrity round with some stars. Perry and I were friends, and so he asked me if I would be Glen Campbell's caddy.

As we were walking from the first tee to the first hole along with two thousand spectators, Perry asked: 'Glen, isn't it true that you and Robin Luke go back a long time?' Glen replied: 'We sure do! Robin gave me my first check in Hollywood.'

It was back in about 1959-60 and we were in a recording session. For years I used the Champs as my studio band. You may remember Dave Burgess' group that had Jimmy Seals (Seals & Crofts) on sax, and other talented musicians. Their biggest recording was *Tequila*. Dave came into the vocal booth while the musicians were assembling and the arranger was handing out sheet music for the session songs. He said: 'There's a new kid here that I'm thinking of using for my road band, and I wondered if you would let him play in the session.' (An interesting aside: many bands could get away with having more than one 'band'. Before satellite and TV technology and 'real-TV', no-one really knew who was who. This gave bands the opportunity to have more than one — sometimes several bands — on the road. The 'road band' would split their take with the real band.)

I said: 'Sure, tell him to bring his ax into the studio. As I looked out the window of the vocal booth, I saw a young Glen Campbell with his guitar in his lap flipping the sheet music over and over. I walked from around the booth and whispered in his ear: 'You can't read music, can you?' He looked up as if he was about to melt and replied: 'No sir, I can't.' I suggested to him that I would ask the A&R man to play the original dub recordings a couple of

---

[*] Puerto Rico, US Virgin Islands, British Virgin Islands and Antigua Sailing Week.

72

With golfing buddy, Glen Campbell.

times, so he could get a feel for each song. If he was as good as Dave said, he would be able to fake it. Well, Glen faked it just fine.

Now for the rest of the story. I have already mentioned that on the golf course Glen said: 'Robin gave me my first check in Hollywood.' He then immediately followed up with: 'And look at him now: he's carrying my bags!' The crowd roared!

If I could go back, I don't think that I would do anything differently. It's a good question, and it would take a lot of time to really think about it. I think that you could have always done things better, inside or outside of the recording business, but I think you can go nuts thinking 'what if '. I really feel I was in a position to do it correctly, with some dignity, and also to move through it. One thing I could tell you is that I wish more and more artists would have had something behind them to back them up, because — sort-of like professional sports — there are so many that make it and once they do make it and they get injured, or get old, they're left as fairly lonely people, but if they could possibly have had a better education, and a professional education, then they could move on. I really consider my life as going on upward, certainly not sideways. So, I look at my career, as brief as it was — it was really for me about five years — as being just a wonderful and glorious time to express myself and to learn things in the world of life.

Today, I am consumed with many other interests, including DE events in my Porsche Carrera 4 Cabriolet, collecting vintage guitars and Lionel trains, working at SMSU and in the yard, and enjoying my life, my children, extended family and my wife, Mary. Life is *good!*

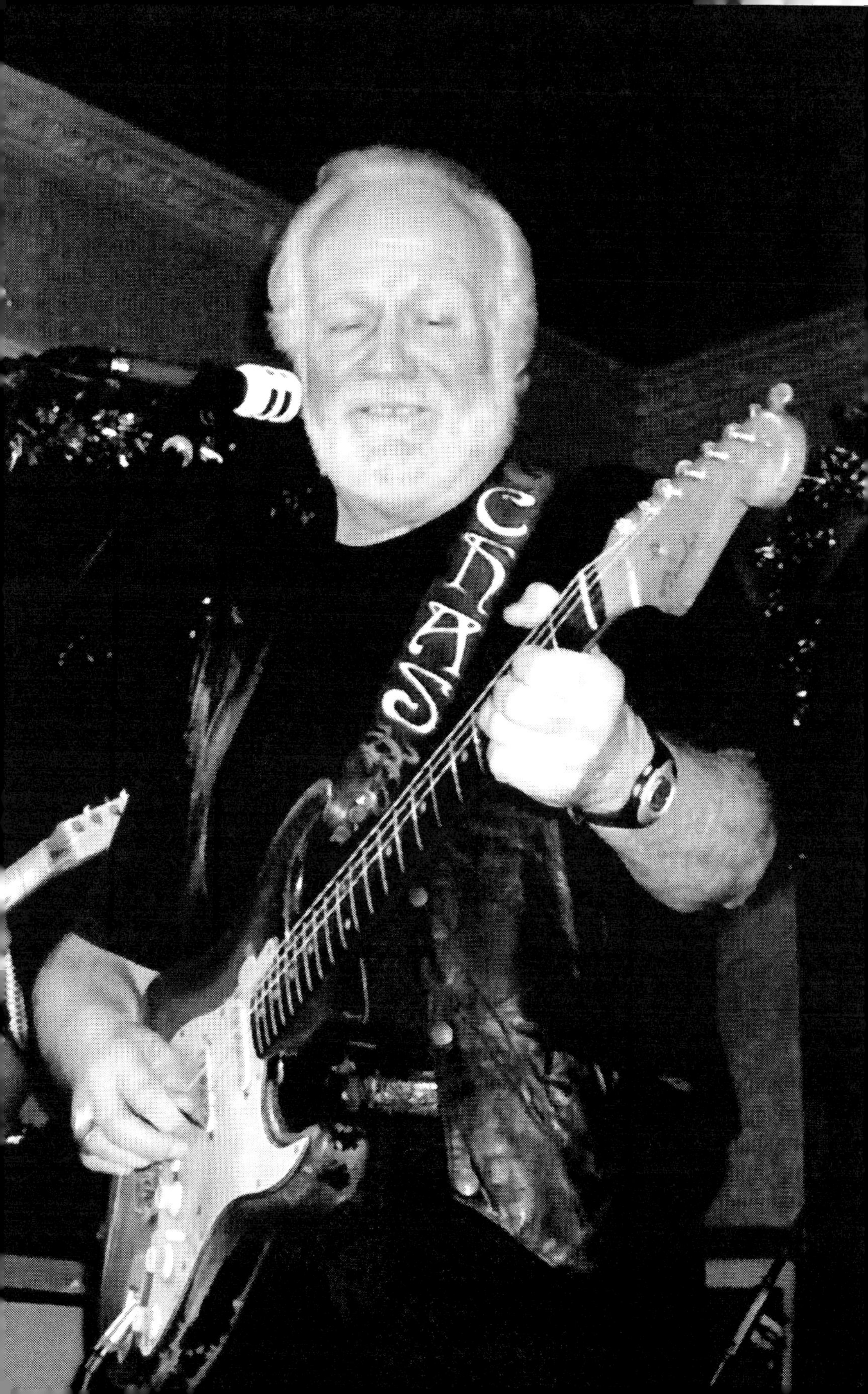
CHAS

6

MR. SKIFFLE
Chas McDevitt

Jazz-inspired musician and singer Chas McDevitt emerged as the leading light of British skiffle after Lonnie Donegan's early exit. His group's rendition of *Freight Train* with Nancy Whiskey on vocals and its whistled accompaniment is one of the most enduring memories of the Fifties — a classic that inspired thousands of would-be imitators as well as bringing sizeable US success. Always happy to move with the times, McDevitt later branched out into folk music and is still very much in demand as a headliner for nostalgia events.

I was born Charles James McDevitt on 4 December 1934 in Glasgow. My father, Charles, was a master tailor and my mother, Leonie Marie Thérèse, who was French, was a housewife. Mother was a nun, a Sister of Charity, who wear those big veils. She was a nursing sister; nursed my father, and got dispensation to renounce her vows and marry him. I have a brother, Paul, who is nine years younger than me. I had a great childhood and was at the same school from the age of six till I was nineteen. I left Glasgow when I was two; moved to Hampstead in London; left there at the beginning of the Second World War, and spent the rest of my childhood in Camberley, Surrey. I attended the Roman Catholic Salesian College in Farnborough, Hampshire for thirteen years, where I got ten GCE 'O' levels and four 'A' levels, which I think was the maximum you could get in those days. In football, I was captain of the house team; played for the school; played for Aldershot Boys; played for Hampshire Boys. I could have played for the English Catholic Schools, but I had just started my illness then.

When I was sixteen, I had pleurisy and a shadow on my lung and was in a sanatorium for nine months; that's when I got interested in the guitar and the banjo. The first instrument I was given was a ukelele and the George Formby influence with ukelele and banjo was always at the back of people's minds. But my musical influences came from the radio, as I used to listen to Josh White and people like that. That was around 1949, and I used to write to all the visiting American artists. The *Melody Maker* was my bible, and any latest releases that came out, I always bought them. Very few radio programmes would play Josh White and the blues; it was mainly the deejays that actually played obscure things, and you would occasionally get an American blues record played. Of course, Josh White had a series on the

Chapter 6 – Chas McDevitt

BBC, and any Americans coming over to this country got on there. He'd sing, like, *House Of the Rising Sun* and *Miss Otis Regrets,* so there was still a lot of blues things — and anything connected with the blues and gospel singing interested me. The blues appealed to me because of its association with jazz, and I loved trad jazz.

I don't know where the interest in jazz came from, but it was probably from the Crane River Jazz Band at the *Festival of Britain* in 1951. They had a big do at the Festival Hall and I was still in hospital and couldn't go, but my friends went. The Crane River Jazz Band were, in my opinion, the stars of that show. I was able to listen to their performance, as a selection of 78 rpm records were issued, which were recorded live at the concert. I eventually played for them years later, but there was only one of the original members left by that time. I'd never heard them on the radio, just by friends' records. But jazz clubs were springing up in this country from about 1948, and they'd be sort-of 'records' jazz clubs, where you would go and play each other's records and play the piano.

There was no particular talent for music in the family. My dad used to enjoy singing in the bath and at family reunions in Glasgow, where they would all sing along by the piano, but I was seldom at those as I was too young. My parents weren't really interested whether I was musical or not. I was taking piano lessons, but I was more keen on playing football than having piano lessons. At school I was thrown out of the choir because I was trying to sing like a gospel singer instead of straight — I was trying to jazz them up a bit. From the time I was sixteen, I was playing banjo. I did read music at first, but not so well now.

By 1952, a few of us had instruments and we used to go to a church hall and rehearse. The brass instrument players were pretty grim; but myself -at least - I'd been borrowing the chord book from the banjo player in the band and learning all the chords for the numbers. We'd never performed publicly except messing around in this church hall. Every Saturday night we'd go to the High Curley Jazz Club, at the White Hart Hotel outside of Blackwater near Camberley, to listen to the local band, the High Curley Stompers. There was a farm in Bagshot, near Camberley, called 'High Curley', and the band was named after it, as it was the home of the piano player. One Saturday, I went down the jazz club and the banjo player said: 'You'll have to play tonight.'

And I said: 'I can't play.'

He said: 'Well, I've broken the vellum in my banjo.'

I said: 'Well, borrow my banjo.'

He said: 'I can't play yours; mine's a tenor and yours is a G, so you'll have to play.'

So, I was thrown in at the deep end, and I played. And, according to the band, I was so much better than the other banjo player that they insisted on having two banjos for a while, and we sort of played in unison — at least, we played the same chords. As they were always short of a bass player, they persuaded the other guy to take up the double bass. I've no idea what I played that night, but the band's signature tune was *Dark Town Strutters' Ball,* so I will have played that. I played with them for two years until I went to London.

Chapter 6 – Chas McDevitt

I made my pro debut on that Saturday night in 1952 with the High Curley Stompers, while still at school, when I sat in for the banjo player at the High Curley Jazz Club. We were earning fifteen bob[*] a night every time we played with the jazz band, but sometimes they just shared out whatever came in at the door and if you got ten bob then that was it. When we started, we'd only play on a Saturday night and perhaps one other night of a week. Fifteen shillings was a big night for us then. I mean the *whole band* used to go out on a big date to the Savoy Ballroom in Southsea, Hampshire. That was a huge place and the Vic Lewis Band would be playing there one night and we'd be there the next night. But we had to belong to the Musicians' Union, and the minimum union rate for the whole band was £15. So that's what we charged, but we were undercut in those days by the local non-union band, which was Bob Potter's. He now owns the Lakeside Complex in Camberley and all those fabulous hotels, and had all those rock groups in the 1960s. But he had his band undercutting us frequently.

My first recording would be when the High Curley Stompers made a soundtrack for a co-production film. It might have been in 1953, when I first got my guitar. I can't remember the details, or what I played, but I know they wanted me to pick guitar over the titles. And so, what I had to do was take the two bass strings off the guitar — remember I'd only just got the guitar — tune it to banjo; play the melody on the banjo; stick the other two strings on, and then mime to what I'd played, so it looked as if I was playing six strings.

My family didn't object to my musical interests. As long as I carried on with my studies there was no problem. In spite of my success with exams they didn't really have high expectations of me. I went through various stages of what I wanted to be. At one stage, when I was much younger, I intended to be a priest. I think a lot of Catholic kids go through that stage. Then, by the time I was in the sixth form, I went for a scholarship — I was going to go to university. I didn't know what I wanted to study, I just wanted to go there for the university life, but I needed a scholarship. As I didn't have Latin I had to have extra lessons and things like that. The lessons took place, but it was the qualification of getting Latin. I mean, I was offered a place at university if I got Latin in the first year, and I thought: 'I'll never do that!' That didn't come off, so I didn't really know what I was going to do.

Having missed nine months in the sanatorium and gone back to do the scholarship, I left college in 1954 when I was nineteen. I finished up going to Unilever in Blackfriars, London, anticipating what I suppose my family hoped would be a career, as they knew some of the directors there, but to me it was a short breach until my music took hold. I started off in the shipping department, and that's where we used to rehearse the skiffle group in the archives at lunchtime. At Unilever I wasn't hoping to be anything particularly; just make some money and, because of the family connections, work my way up.

I didn't serve in the armed forces. I had it deferred, of course, because of my illness and then, when I had my medical at eighteen and a half, they passed me A1. I thought this was wrong and I showed them the

---
[*] 75 pence.

letter from the doctors. Their faces dropped, and they took back the A1 certificate and made me Grade 4. I was still at school then, so I didn't have to go into National Service.

I don't think any talent was ever 'spotted' — it's always been a thing of pushing yourself and pushing other people. But when I had the skiffle group rehearsing in the archives of Unilever House, which was an occasional thing we used to do, I lived in Hampstead at the time and we used to go and rehearse in a couple of pubs. By then, I was also playing banjo with the Crane River Jazz Band — which was really a new band as the only original member was trumpeter Sonny Morris. I used to sing with the band and then in 1955-56 we started featuring the Chas McDevitt Skiffle Group within that jazz band, and at the same time I was playing with the skiffle group in coffee bars. I was also in another group, the St. Louis Trio, which was a spin-off from the Crane River Jazz Band, consisting of Pete Timlett, the piano player from the Crane, Marc Sharratt and myself. When we played with the Crane River, we were featured as the interval band and we used to play regularly at Cy Laurie's Jazz Club in London's Windmill Street. And one day we looked in the *Melody Maker* listings and thought: 'Crikey, we're not there this week, the St. Louis Trio's there' — but that's just the name that the Crane River bandleader had decided to call us! So, I was playing in the Crane River Jazz Band, the St. Louis Trio and the Chas McDevitt Skiffle Group.

At one stage in 1956, I was still at Unilever's and then suddenly I was falling asleep at three o'clock in the afternoon because the jazz band was playing late. My career hadn't developed at Unilever. One day, I was sitting in a row of clerks staring at the back of a bloke's head in front of me. He'd just finished paying off his mortgage and was just about to retire, and I thought: 'God, that'll be me in forty years.' Well, I couldn't stand the thought of it. Even whilst I was there, I took a competitive exam for the Customs & Excise executive grade. I came eleventh out of 165, I think, and I could have gone straight into the executive grade. By then I'd had a relapse of my illness and so I had time off work, and the Customs gave me a year to make up my mind. But, by the end of that year, 1956, we were recording with the group, so I didn't pursue that and left Unilever's.

Having left Unilever's, the band didn't get much work. We were almost starving and we had to pay for a flat in Chelsea in the King's Road — I had moved out of home years before that. My family really didn't know much about my chosen profession, but it didn't cause any rifts. I was playing what became skiffle, at the same time as Donegan started, when with the jazz band we'd had the breakdown group which was banjo, the bass, piano and drums. We played sometimes in the interval, and sometimes as part of a set. We played Josh White numbers, we played blues numbers and twelve bar blues — which was basically skiffle. And you did, in quick rate, 1920s standards, which were always jazz numbers anyway. When my group started, and people like the Vipers, we were much more of a skiffle group than Donegan was — because, if you define skiffle as homemade music, after his first record he stopped using the washboard.

We never had a tea chest for a double bass in the early skiffle group. The City Ramblers used to use a tea chest, and some of the groups I've played with in recent times in Leeds and New Orleans use a tea chest. They were largely for show; because you couldn't easily hump those things around on your back, and they're hard to play, although some people managed to play them very well. A group I played with in Finland, the Werner Brothers, are absolutely fantastic — their tea chest bass player is absolutely amazing. He has a microphone inside.

There was no rivalry with the other skiffle groups. With Donegan, we knew each other, but never worked together until years later, when I used to go out supporting him. And then, when I got the group together — Marc Sharratt, John Paul and Nick Lawrence — in 1984, we went to France and he was there as well. The Vipers' career came to an end in 1957-8, and Bob Cort I never classed as skiffle really. He was like these modern day fabrications. He was an architect — I think, anyway — and had a pub in Leicester. He died years ago.

We were playing in the 2Is in 1956 and we used to guest in a place called the Gyre & Gimble, which was another coffee bar. My washboard player, Marc Sharratt, came back and said that there was this guy with a portable tape recorder — which was unusual in those days — recording these groups and people. There were two of them, Bill Varley and Roy Tuvey, and they'd signed up the Vipers at that time, and Tommy Steele. And I said: 'Well, try and get us in.' We got talking to Bill Varley, and he'd heard us. And luckily, he and Roy Tuvey had this bit of a recording studio, Trio Recordings in Denmark Street, where they made demo records for all the music publishers. That's how they had this portable tape recorder. The first 'proper' recordings we made were demos for Bill Varley on which I sang *Freight Train* and a few other things including a couple of rock'n'roll numbers, I think, including *Giddy-Up-A Ding Dong* and *New Orleans*. We called it *'New Orleans'*, but it was a major key version of *House Of The Rising Sun*.

So, Bill Varley signed us up and became our manager. Roy Tuvey didn't have a great deal to do with it; he was just Varley's partner at that time. He went on to do broadcasting programmes with people like Morris & Mitch.

We didn't have any legal representation with signing contracts. In those days a contract was hardly anything. Whatever I signed with Bill Varley was hardly worth the paper it was written on. They came a cropper with Tommy Steele, because Bill, Tuvey and Geoff Wright had Tommy Steele signed up and they started doing big things for him. And then along comes John Kennedy and Larry Parnes and they were able to take Tommy away from them, because he'd signed underage and they hadn't got a parent's signature. There was a lot of trouble in those days over that.

We entered the Radio Luxembourg talent competition in November-December 1956 and won that four weeks running. We just missed out on the final, when I sang *Freight Train,* but it was a fix anyway. A sort-of 'society'-type evening piano player won it. We still got plenty of coverage, playing in coffee bars and doing this. A folk singer, Nancy Whiskey, was also in that talent competition.

Various skiffle groups like the Vipers had got recording contracts before us, and I said to Bill Varley: 'Do you know what's happening; why's everybody recording but us?' And he sort-of shoved the demos around and

Chapter 6 – Chas McDevitt

Oriole were the only people who took us up. We thought we were on a good thing with them, because they were one of the only companies that had their own pressing plant. Oriole was a privately owned company by a man called Levy, and he had Levy's Sound Studios in New Bond Street where a lot of other people recorded. And, of course, they had their other record label, Embassy, which sold in some shops. There was no audition for Oriole, only on this demo record.

The Chas McDevitt Skiffle Group's first single was going to be a slow version of *Freight Train* sung by myself, but it was never issued. After the demo recording made by Bill Varley, we cut a proper recording at the Oriole Studios. Then Bill Varley suggested that we should be different from other groups by including a girl singer, and reminded us of Nancy Whiskey, the girl who had taken part in the Radio Luxembourg talent competition a few weeks earlier. We'd worked with Nancy before at the Unity Theatre — the communist theatre up in Camden Town — where they put on shows, and met her at skiffle clubs. She was into folk stuff and had already made a few tracks for Topic Records that weren't released until after *Freight Train*, but they were sort-of Irish rebel songs. In the folk clubs she used to sing a Scottish song, *The Calton Weaver*, and the chorus of that is: 'O whiskey, whiskey, Nancy, whiskey / Whiskey, whiskey, Nancy-o' and people used to cry out: 'Sing Nancy Whiskey!' and that's how she got her name. Her real name was Anne Wilson — which upset the Americans when we went over there. The Pogues recorded *Nancy Whiskey* a little while ago.

Bill Varley asked Nancy to join the group; she was reluctant to at first, but she did in the end. Then we re-recorded *Freight Train* with her singing and that was it. We must have recorded it sometime in late December 1956 at Oriole's New Bond Street Sound Studios, because it was released in January 1957, and we did our first variety theatre show at the Metropolitan Theatre in Edgware Road, promoted by Ambrose and Joe Collins — Joan Collins' dad. 'Skiffle' was top of a bill which included Joe Henderson, Digby Wolfe, Larry Grayson and ourselves, and we closed the show. We had never been on a music hall stage in our lives before. They thought they were going to make a fortune, but they didn't. It was a bit too soon as *Freight Train* b/w *The Cotton Song* didn't get into the Hit Parade until April 1957.

I was happy for Nancy Whiskey's version to replace my own; it was different and she had an unusual sound. The re-recording only took about six takes. I think we put the whistling on after about the second one. It was all done 'live', you know; you didn't dub anything on in those days. There was feedback in the middle of the track and the guitars were a bit out of tune, but that's it. We were new and green, that's the thing. In later years, there was a group called Remember This who recorded *Freight Train* in Scandinavia. I remember them telling me they had terrible trouble with copying the hit to try and get the original sound, until they realised that they had to de-tune one of the guitars to make it sound like the original one. *[laughs]*

There was no romantic involvement at all between Nancy Whiskey and myself or any members of the Chas McDevitt Skiffle Group. She was okay, but she didn't really like skiffle anyway. The guy who became her husband, Bobby Kelly, a piano player with the Ken Colyer band, was very jealous of her success — that's my interpretation of things — and he was always the fly in the ointment. She had come down to London from Glasgow with him and people like Jimmie MacGregor. Nancy was a few months younger than me, so she'd be twenty-one when she recorded *Freight Train*. She could be a bit fiery, but there were no tensions between her and the five male members of the group. Nancy was a brash Glaswegian, but she was always good fun. As I say, it was him saying to her all the time: 'You should be on your own,' and all that sort of thing.

It was because of him that she left, because she became pregnant. And she announced to the press that she was going to marry this guy, and his wife said: 'How can she marry him, he's still married to me!' So that's when the big scandal came out. He did become her husband later on and she had the baby — a daughter, Yancey, named after Jimmy Yancey the blues piano player. I don't know whether it was his way of trying to get her away from the group or what, but he really ruined things for her by that. I think she was as happy as she could be with the group, but she was only with the us for less than six months out of the eight as we weren't working all that time.

If you look at the picture of the group on the front of the 1956-57 sheet music for *Freight Train,* which was taken before the record made the charts, it is a composite. There are four people looking in one direction and two looking straight at the camera. Those two, John Paul, the double bass player at the back, and Marc Sharratt, the washboard player at the front, were stuck

---

CHRISTMAS GREETINGS

to all of you who helped make 1958 a wonderful year for me — may 1959 be as bright for you

NANCY WHISKEY

Direction: SONNY ZAHL, KAVANAGH PRODUCTIONS, 201 Regent St., London, W.1

Chapter 6 – Chas McDevitt

in afterwards. Marc took the first picture of the four of us — myself, Nancy, the blond Marlon Brando lookalike guy is Alex Whitehouse, and the dark curly one is Dennis Carter — so, he couldn't be in the picture, and John Paul, the bass player, wasn't there. I took Marc's picture and he probably took John Paul's, and they were both stuck on together. The guitar I'm playing in that photograph was my first Hofner and soon after that I got a Martin Dreadnaught D-18.

We were in the UK when *Freight Train* hit the charts. Everybody else was getting into the charts, and we were so convinced our record should be a hit anyway that we had moaned to Bill Varley to tell Oriole to get their finger out and get promoting the record, because we were getting plays and onto television, but nothing was happening. What was happening was that Oriole were so busy making money pressing records for other people, they were neglecting ours and hardly advertised it. So, we really had a go at them, and from that moment it started to move. Then a Canadian deejay, Gerry Myers, picked it up and played a lot of it. They heard it in New York, and that's how it became a hit in the States.

I think *Freight Train* got into the American charts in June 1957, as we did the *Ed Sullivan Show* in the July. So, Chic Records, who issued it in America, probably released it in May. Nancy went over on her own, with Bill Varley, for a few days to start with for a big record convention in Chicago to promote it. And then it started to move, and so the three of us — Marc Sharratt, myself and Nancy — went over to do the *Ed Sullivan Show*. We had to use three American musicians because of the Musicians' Union ban. It depends on what music papers you read, but in some charts, like *Billboard*, *Freight Train* got to No.4, but they had different ways of calculating. Some of them would calculate on the number of plays on jukeboxes; some would calculate on the number of plays on the radio; and some of them were sales. But in the *Cash Box*, which is the one they seem to use now, it only ever reached about No.40 or something like that. We never got a gold record, but it certainly sold over a million in the States alone. You could tell by the record sales and the royalties that were due but we never received. Chic Records was named after the guy who ran it, Chic Thompson from Thomasville,

Georgia.

The Rusty Draper version of *Freight Train* was just a straight copy, but we never met him. He was on the *Ed Sullivan Show* doing *Freight Train* and we weren't due to appear for another fortnight on the same show. And the record company persuaded this PR woman, Lauri Ames, to take up our cause, and she got Ed Sullivan to announce after Rusty Draper's performance that the people who made the original record would be on next week. So they brought the show forward and gave us a plug immediately after his record! The week we did it, we were on with the Everly Brothers and they did *Bye Bye Love*. The Everlys were very friendly and very taken with our American musicians: Hank Garland on lead guitar, Bill Mure on guitar and Sandy Block on bass. We didn't know who the hell these Yanks were who were playing for us, but they were really smitten by them. To us they were just session musicians, but to the Everlys they were stars in their own right.

We didn't have the chance to do any other shows, but *Ed Sullivan* was the big one; Donegan didn't do the *Sullivan Show*. We were due to go on tour with Alan Freed. However, all hell broke loose with the agency, and we had to get back to England for a tour of Moss Empires with Terry Dene anyway, but we could have stayed a few days longer. We went and met him and all the stars of the *Summer Festival* at New York's Paramount Theatre: the Everly Brothers, the Kalin Twins, the Moonglows, the Cadillacs, Screamin' Jay Hawkins, Big Joe Turner, Chuck Berry, Teddy Randazzo, Ruth Brown, LaVern Baker, a woman trombonist — I forget her name — and then, on stage, the Alan Freed Big Band with Sam 'The Man' Taylor and Al Sears on sax. Paul Anka was a late addition; he came on in short trousers. He was only fifteen, so they were either trousers or summer shorts. We also did a show at Palisades Park, which is a bit like Battersea Park. The Americans didn't really know what skiffle was, and *Freight Train* was just another record, but sufficiently different though. It was well played, and on television we saw Spike Jones And His City Slickers play it as a skit. They came on dressed as Chinese coolies and sang: '*Fleight train, fleight train*' etc. It's one I've always wanted to get hold of, and it must be available on tape somewhere.

Although we got the Oriole record royalties all right — one sixth of one penny each — and PRS royalties, no US royalties were received from Chic Records. Even our Ed Sullivan TV fee went up in smoke when Chic Records disappeared over there. They had one more hit record, by a country singer, after *Freight Train* and then

> THE CURRENT SKIFFLE
> **HIT!**
> **Chas. McDevitt**
> **Skiffle Group**
> with
> **Nancy Whiskey**
> **'FREIGHT TRAIN'**
> (CB.1352)
>
> ORIOLE

they just disappeared. When Chic Thompson took us over there, he started claiming all the hotel accommodation, etc, against our royalties. I remember signing the back of the cheque — which was for $1,000 I think — when we got paid for the Sullivan show, thinking I was going to get the cash for it from Lauri Ames, who had us under her wing to get us into there. She just pocketed the money as expenses for her part!

As soon as we came back to the UK from America we chose the new group line up, as John Paul, Alex Whitehouse and Dennis Carter didn't want to give up their day jobs and become fully professional. They were replaced by Lennie Harrison (bass), Bill Bramwell (guitar), and then Tony Kohn (vocals/guitar). With this change, the electric guitar came in.

The main A&R person at Oriole was a man called Jack Baverstock, and he really knew nothing about skiffle. I mean, *nobody* did in that profession. They left it to us, and we had a free hand in doing what we wanted — totally — with everything we ever did. In the music, we didn't try to play like anybody; we just played and reflected in the music the contents of the band. If you listen to the Embassy records, they're a little different because we've got Jimmie MacGregor playing mandolin with us. His harmonies are slightly different, so that gave a different tinge to our music. And then when the bass player changed and we had Bill Bramwell on lead guitar, the style again changed; and of course, with his lead-playing and scat singing, it became very jazzy. At the same time Tony Kohn came in and he had a sort of deep bluesy voice, so the style changed again.

In the UK, we'd already put a record out as the follow-up to *Freight Train*. This was *New Orleans* b/w *Worried Man*, which was recorded at the same time as *Freight Train*. Now, *Worried Man* wasn't going to be the 'B' side; *Banana Boat Song* was going to be the 'B' side, but by then there were so many versions of *Banana Boat Song* on the market that we put that one out on Embassy Records, and used one of the Embassy tracks on the Oriole record. But that record sank without trace, as, of course, the public had been familiar with Nancy singing the lead voice. So, when a second record came out without Nancy on it, the record company had a lean time promoting it. We didn't put her on all the records, as when we did a stage show she only came on and sang two numbers; the group did everything else. When we did the first record session with her at the end of 1956, we did four songs, and she sang one of them. So we used two of the tracks for the first release and two for the second. Obviously, with the success of *Freight Train,* Oriole had come alive to us and Jack Baverstock was keen to get our records out.

After that, Nancy made *Green Back Dollar* b/w *I'm Satisfied* with us. I think we recorded *Green Back Dollar* just after we came back from the States. We used to do it as a slow East Virginia blues, and in fact we sang that at the Royal Festival Hall in the big skiffle concert in April 1957. On the bill were Johnny Duncan, Ray Bush & The Avon Cities Jazz Band & Skiffle Group, Bob Cort, Dickie Bishop and ourselves. Our manager, Bill Varley, recorded everything we did and he recorded those tracks. The first number was *Cotton Song* and he didn't get the machine working immediately, so the opening chorus is missing. We found the tapes a little while ago — there were about four or five tracks and they were put out as a mini-LP by Rollercoaster Records. Following *Green Back Dollar,* there were a couple by the other guys in the group and myself, and then the next one was *Face In The Rain.*

When we came back from promoting *Freight Train* in America, Oriole presented us with a couple of tracks they wanted us to record, and one of them was *Face In The Rain*, which we'd brought back from America. And that again was something completely different to what we'd normally done; it was more commercial. The publishers Pan-Musik, who later became part of Kassner Music, had a lot of say in these things, and I should imagine that the record company had something to do with that, because Pan-Musik had a lot of stuff out on Oriole. *Johnny-O* was again another Pan-Musik song they suggested, and that was Nancy's last record with the group. Now, we didn't promote that or push it at all, as she had left by then and Shirley Douglas' *Across The Bridge* was released virtually at the same time. So, as far as change was concerned, it just changed because of content of the musicians and the songs we chose. If you listen to *Face In The Rain* and *Across The Bridge*, that's not really skiffle. I mean, skiffle line-up, skiffle instruments, but it's hardly what the original skiffle sounded like. So, we were changing anyway.

Our appearance in the movie *The Tommy Steele Story* in 1957 came about through our music publishers Pan-Musik. Gerry Benson who ran Pan-Musik together with another guy, Oliver Ward, had something to do with films and they wrote us into that. Our appearance was recorded as a segment and filmed at Shepperton or somewhere like that. We'd never ever mimed to the record before — as is evident by the screen shot. Nancy managed okay with the lyrics, but my whistling in the back on the record is different to my whistling on the screen. It was awkward, particularly when the

```
GOLDEN DISC
JOHNNY-O
with NANCY WHISKEY
from the film "THE GOLDEN DISC"
B/W
BAD MAN STACK-O-LEE
with
CHAS. McDEVITT and HIS SKIFFLE GROUP
on ORIOLE CB 1403

PAN-MUSIC LTD.  :    Song Copies Available
        EVELYN HOUSE, 62, OXFORD STREET,
              LONDON, W.1. MUS 0597/8
```

producer said: 'It doesn't look as if you're whistling, so put something into it! So, I started shaking my head and looked very camp. It's embarrassing. I cringe every time I see it.

In the end, Nancy got fed up with doing the same sort of skiffle stuff. She wanted to go solo and be a folk singer, I think. And when she eventually went solo and tried it doing folk songs, she sank without trace. She was really 'hand on the ear' folk almost — where they're singing to themselves like A.L. Lloyd and people like that. Popular enough in the folk clubs, but it wasn't a good career move to concentrate on that. The parting was friendly enough. She didn't work for months after she left us because of the baby, but we resented her leaving the group like that, because at that stage we were just about taking off. We knew that she was going to leave as we started our ten-week tour of the Moss Empires, so we were auditioning girls all the time. She left on 31 August 1957 at the end of our last week in Newcastle, where the Railroaders — Hank Marvin and Bruce Welch — came to see us. We didn't have any contact with Nancy until she started to work again after the baby was born, and we did a show at Finsbury Park Empire with Marty Wilde around 1958-59. Marty was top of the bill, and I was on with my group and she was on with her group, the Teetotallers. That's the only time I ever remember working with her again.

Shirley Douglas took Nancy's place and her first date with us was 11 September 1957. She was recommended by a guy called Paul Andrews, a singer who had used Bill Varley's studio and was quite familiar with us. He got Shirley to sing live down the phone to Bill Varley, and Bill Varley suggested that she come over from Northern Ireland. So, she flew over to Manchester and in a theatre there she sang for us. We thought she was pretty good. I mean, girls used to queue up at the stage door to audition, but half of them couldn't sing.

To make a further decision — I think it was a week later, or whenever it was — we were in Liverpool, and she flew over again; and I think that's when we decided she was going to be with the group. The first date she did with us was a live BBC television show with Michael Holliday called *Now, The Hop Fields* or something like that. At the same time she did a date with us on the Isle of Wight as well, with Michael Holliday again. On that date something happened that I'll never forget.

On the Isle of Wight we did two shows: an afternoon show and an evening show. One was in Ryde and one was in Shanklin, or something like that; either side of the island. We went over by the ferry. Michael Holliday was top of the bill, and he said to me: 'Look, I'll go top of the bill at the first theatre, and you can top the bill in the second theatre.' I said: 'Oh, that's great.' So we did that. Of course, we finished the second show, went to catch the ferry and it was long gone. He knew that the ferry was leaving early — that's why he wanted to do the first spot! We were lumbered then; the whole group with all our gear on the dockside. Bill Varley had to commission a fishing smack, and we all piled in this thing with sails and a motor. It was a stormy night — it was belting down — and we went back across the Channel to Portsmouth like that, and it was absolutely murder. I remember Shirley had a brand new pink furry coat on, and she wouldn't come under the tarpaulin

A Merry Christmas

★

CHAS. McDEVITT
and
SHIRLEY DOUGLAS

★

A Happy New Year

with me. I kept dry under the tarpaulin, but she just got soaking wet. Bill Bramwell had his hand round the mast and a bottle of gin or rum. It was absolute chaos, but that was all down to Michael Holliday. We were gullible; we thought: 'Close the show; that's a good idea', never thinking that would happen.

When you saw us with the Treniers in 1958, Tony Kohn was with us and recorded *Sporting Life* with us, and then Bill Bramwell, who was on lead guitar, he got to sing *My Old Man* usually. It was still skiffly, and then eventually, when Tony Kohn and Bill Bramwell left, it became 'The Chas McDevitt Freight Train Boys'. By then Shirley was on bass guitar; Red Reece was on drums — he played with Georgie Fame. Then, when the pianist, Roy Powell, left, we had Les Bennett *[guitar]* with us for a very short while before he went to Donegan.

Then, when the guys were on holiday once, I was asked to do a show and I said: 'I can't, the guys are away.' So they said: 'Well, use a backing group.' So, Shirley and I did it together, and we suddenly realised that we could work together without the group. Shirley and I married in 1959. In 1960, we became a folk duo: Chas McDevitt & Shirley Douglas. *'Beauty And The Beat'* was one of the little phrases they used to advertise us. About the same time there was Nina & Frederik, and we were always being compared to them.

I haven't really any special memories from my UK touring days. There was the usual thing with the girls and that sort of thing. I can't remember much about the Freddie Bell tour in 1957 except the concerted movements and the bass player, as that was the first time we'd seen the Fender bass. We did have fun with the Treniers in 1958, because they were super guys. They didn't seem to like Jerry Lee — obviously because of the Southern connection — and they said: 'Oh, all he does on the piano is play zip fasteners' — 'cause he went 'zip' with his right hand. I found a poster some time ago for a performance of Jerry Lee Lewis and the Treniers at Peterborough with my flyer stuck over his photograph. I thought Jerry Lee was great. I even recorded one of his numbers, or — I think — I recorded it before he did. It was my last record for Oriole in 1960, which was *Teenage Letter*.

LEW & LESLIE GRADE LTD. present:	IMPORTANT ANNOUNCEMENT	
TERRY WAYNE Columbia's NEW Singing Star	*Re* *Jerry Lee Lewis* The Rank Organisation feel they are carrying out the wishes of the majority in withdrawing this name from the bill, but appreciate that there may be some who will not now want to come to this show. For these, refund in cash will be made at the Booking Office in exchange for tickets already purchased.	**THE CHAS McDEVITT GROUP** featuring SHIRLEY DOUGLAS

We got properly paid for our tours; very few people welshed on us. Whether we got enough is another matter, and you never, ever, get enough. I remember when we first hit £1,000 a week, we thought it was a real hoot. We were on a ten-week Moss Empire tour in 1957 — after the Freddie Bell tour I think — and on a 60:40 percentage split between ourselves and the promoters. And they were record-breaking weeks. I remember, in 1957 again, we were offered a summer season in Blackpool. Our manager was on the phone and he said: 'What shall I ask for?' and we said: 'Ask for £1,000.' He asked for £1,000 and we were rolling around the floor laughing. We didn't get it of course for those weeks, because it was a whole season at £1,000 a week, but we hit £1,000 a couple of times on the Moss Empire tour. Apart from the Moss Empires, we were doing one-nighters where the money could vary. The band members were on a weekly wage of about £25, and whatever else was left we split three ways. Sometimes we didn't get anything. Our record royalty rate with Oriole was a penny a record for the group. Even the split of that was difficult. You see, with Nancy only ever appearing on one side, the boys said: 'Oh well, I'm on *both* sides, I should get twice as much.' That was how it was decided. I mean, we didn't know which was going to be the 'A' side.

I don't really know what we got out of the tours as artists apart from money and fun. At one stage we were almost a co-operative group: we were all getting the same. As the original members left, new members came in on a salary, employed by Nancy, Marc Sharratt and myself, with the manager getting his commission. When they left, it was just the manager and myself. No-one really looked after the money properly. The money went out as fast as it came in. We were buying our own van; paying for it and paying for the manager to drive us around.

I wasn't particularly into the business side. When I started producing records even, I wasn't really fully *au fait* with it all. I should have done more at that time when I was writing more songs. Even when the chart success died, we never really stopped making records and we'd go from one label to the next, and, although the records weren't chart successes, we still managed to sell them.

There were no particular friendships forged with other artists from those days; everything was fun up to that time. We got quite friendly with the Treniers and they'd come over here in later years. Their bass player would come over and play for the Harlem Globetrotters. In the UK, one of my best mates is Joe Brown and, through the Water Rats, a lot of other people from the business. Different people become stars over the years, like Brian May. He and I sang a song at the last *Water Rats' Ball* on a giant video screen. There was Lonnie Donegan in later years, but at the time we didn't have much to do with each other. I still see Dickie Bishop occasionally; Ray Bush as well, but he's in America most of the time. Although Russ Hamilton was a fellow Oriole artist, I never saw him and never worked with him. He doesn't surface at the Variety Club either.

As for girls, drink and drugs, there were hardly any drugs on the scene at all. One of the guys towards the end was smoking pot a lot, but it was mainly girls — and they were always around even before the success. No trouble with girls ever came to the surface, although I'm sure some of the lads got into trouble. We hardly drank either. Again, the guy that did the drugs was a drinker; and he used to get drunk and come off stage and say: 'I felt fabulous,' and was the cause of many a fight in the dressing room. I remember one of the guys said: 'You were shit,' and then a big fight started — because when he was like that he couldn't play at all. Again, there could have been reasons for that. He was a jazz musician; he played bass and he played jazz guitar, and playing with us was just a way of making money. It probably brought him down a bit and he turned to drink and that was it.

My own favourite artists who influenced me by their records in the early days were the New Orleans jazz players like Louis Armstrong and George Lewis, and then I transferred to Ken Colyer. Then the blues singers: early Muddy Waters and some of the first records of Little Walter & His Jukes, and today people like Snooks Eaglin. Anything to do with New Orleans music, whether it's blues, jazz or rock, I love. There's something inherent in that music which appeals to me. Whether it's the French in me, I don't know. Apart from my mum, dad was in France for twenty years, and that's quite a French background. I also like Fats Domino and the Everly Brothers.

Musically, I didn't choose any particular path. I just followed and played what I liked, and played what I had to do to make a living. I didn't really progress musically at any stage. Once Buddy Holly died, my guitar tinkering finished, because I used to try to play like him, and after that I either had to have lead guitar players, or I just didn't progress.

I don't place any particular value on my place in popular music. People always say that *we* started them off; they mean Lonnie, mainly, but a lot of them specifically mention my group. Then, of course, people like John Lodge of the Moody Blues; John Paul Jones; John Entwhistle, and a guy from Mud, all used our bass guitar tutor, *Shirley Douglas' Easy Guide To Rhythm & Blues'*, because there was no other tutor on the market. So, in a way you feel

Chapter 6 – Chas McDevitt

at least you started something. We were in a race with Jet Harris to get the first one out and, when we got ours out, he abandoned the idea.

The music industry has always been controlled, but it was controlled the way I liked it, and it came out the way I liked it — eventually. Now, you've got to pick and choose, and what you're getting bombarded with is not necessarily what you want to hear. That's why there are so many specialist groups and magazines around these days. But it's a shame that a lot of people don't get off the ground, like Cajun music. That was getting quite a following in this country, and eventually it just didn't catch on and all the magazines closed down. It's a shame.

I have no idea what I would like to have written or recorded: I've just never thought along those lines. I have favourite songs that I like to hear, but whether I could do them justice is another thing. At the moment I'm into fado music, which is Portugese. It's very soulful music — almost akin to the blues — and usually sung by eighty-year old women all dressed in black. There's a young woman around called Mariza — she's actually been on the Jools Holland show — who's absolutely stunning and she's a current favourite. Rick Hardy *[aka Rick Richards]*, a mate of mine, was in the first rock group to go to Hamburg — the Jets, with Tony Sheridan — and he has suddenly been discovered by the country's veteran rockers, so he goes over there for their convention. Also, he was the guy that introduced the Shadows to Cliff Richard, so he goes over to the continent for the *Shadows Convention*. He's into fado music, and he was over in Lisbon last week and he gave one of these eighty-year olds €100 just for her shawl! And a cult can become a form. That's just one aspect; I like all sorts of music.

If I could go back... oh, I don't know... I'd consolidate things more as I go along and try and get into the production side a bit more, but I'm too easygoing and happy-go-lucky, you know, to have always been a business man at it. I mean, when I had that coffee bar, the Freight Train, in Berwick Street for ten years from 1958 to 1968, I should have done things then. But I just sat back. I thought: 'Well, I'm earning enough for the coffee bar, why push things?' That's where Hank Marvin met his first wife; they used to wait there for their girlfriends, who used to work in the night clubs around there. And that's where Johnny Kidd wrote *Shakin' All Over* in the basement one night. I had Cliff Richard playing there, and the Drifters. I was away on tour with the Treniers *[in 1958]* and I had a letter from them saying: 'Thanks very much for letting us play in your coffee bar. We made quite a few new fans and we'd like to come again, but we found playing for four hours a little bit long. Could you arrange for your staff to arrive on time next time so we don't have to wait out on the pavement.'

Oh yeah, the Freight Train made money for me. I owned it and it was the best site in the West End for a jukebox. We were open all night, so consequently it had a long span of playing. In that sense, I was a businessman, but I just played at it really. I mean, I'd go away on tours and leave the place in the hands of managers and, although it made money, they were creaming off a bit. We didn't have any trouble from the gangster types who were around in London's Soho at that time, but the yobs used to cause a bit of trouble with fights in the area. Then there was the time of the

Cyprus-Turkish thing, and you'd get a few stabbings out in the street.

My marriage to Shirley is my only one; we split up in 1976. I have a daughter, Kerry, who is the Deputy Stage Manager of the National Theatre in London. She's been interested in the theatre since her schooldays. She started as an actress and toured with Dame Peggy Mount and people like that. But she likes singing and, whenever I get my group together, she plays washboard with me and sings if she's not working. She's just been to New Orleans for ten days and sat in with a Cajun band over there and saw Wayne Toups, a big favourite of mine, who's a zydeco player — it's like Cajun music with a beat. Also, she saw John Cleary who plays with Taj Mahal, Bonnie Raitt and Dr. John. He's English, but now has his own group, the Absolute Monster Gentlemen, and recently starred in the *New Orleans Jazz Festival.*

I can't really think of many low spots in my life or career. One low spot was Marc Sharratt died after we'd just done a gig in Holland in 1991. It was a head-on crash. His mother lived in Camberley still, and he had to do some plastering for her and he came here afterwards. We went to the airport and flew to Holland and did the show. He came back from Holland; back to his mum's; finished the plastering, and went off home on his 58th birthday. He lived in Rye — he was an antiques dealer, but still came out and played with me. A hundred yards from his home, he was in a head-on crash with another car which killed him. He was a lifelong friend, so that was a blow. He might have fallen asleep, but the other car was driven by an old couple, and I know the sun was low in the sky and they could have been dazzled — so we'll never know. But that was quite a shock. As I said, my daughter just came back from New Orleans and I was there in 1992 a year after he died. Marc always wanted to go to New Orleans, so I paid for a stone to be made to be put on Canal Walk — where you can place stones engraved with people's names — with his name and dates of birth and death. And Kerry's just come back with a photograph of the stone. In my music career, the high spot wasn't having a hit with *Freight Train;* the real high was in going over to America and playing it and doing the *Ed Sullivan Show* and things like that. I can't think of any low spots. The highest spot in my life has to be the birth of my daughter, Kerry.

Outside of music, I've been King Rat for the last two years and, in fact, tonight we've got a dinner with the Lady Ratlings. We don't do a lot with them, but tonight they're honouring Lady Sheila Butlin, who's very generous to both charities, and I've got to go there and make a presentation to her. We've got a show with Prince Philip in a couple of weeks time at Windsor; and we've got an in-house dinner where just the Water Rats come; and I've arranged for all the Water Rats who've received honours, like OBEs, to have dinner with Prince Michael. In between times, we put on shows to raise money for the Rats. I was in Weston-super-Mare all last week for the *Music Hall Week* and doing shows there. I'll be doing a show in Leeds with Vince Eager for a Billy Fury tribute. In fact, Vince has got an *Oh Boy!* show together with the okay of Jack Good to use the name. I'll be busy with the Water Rats until the end of my year in November, but I'm not chasing work any more. If it comes in, it comes in.

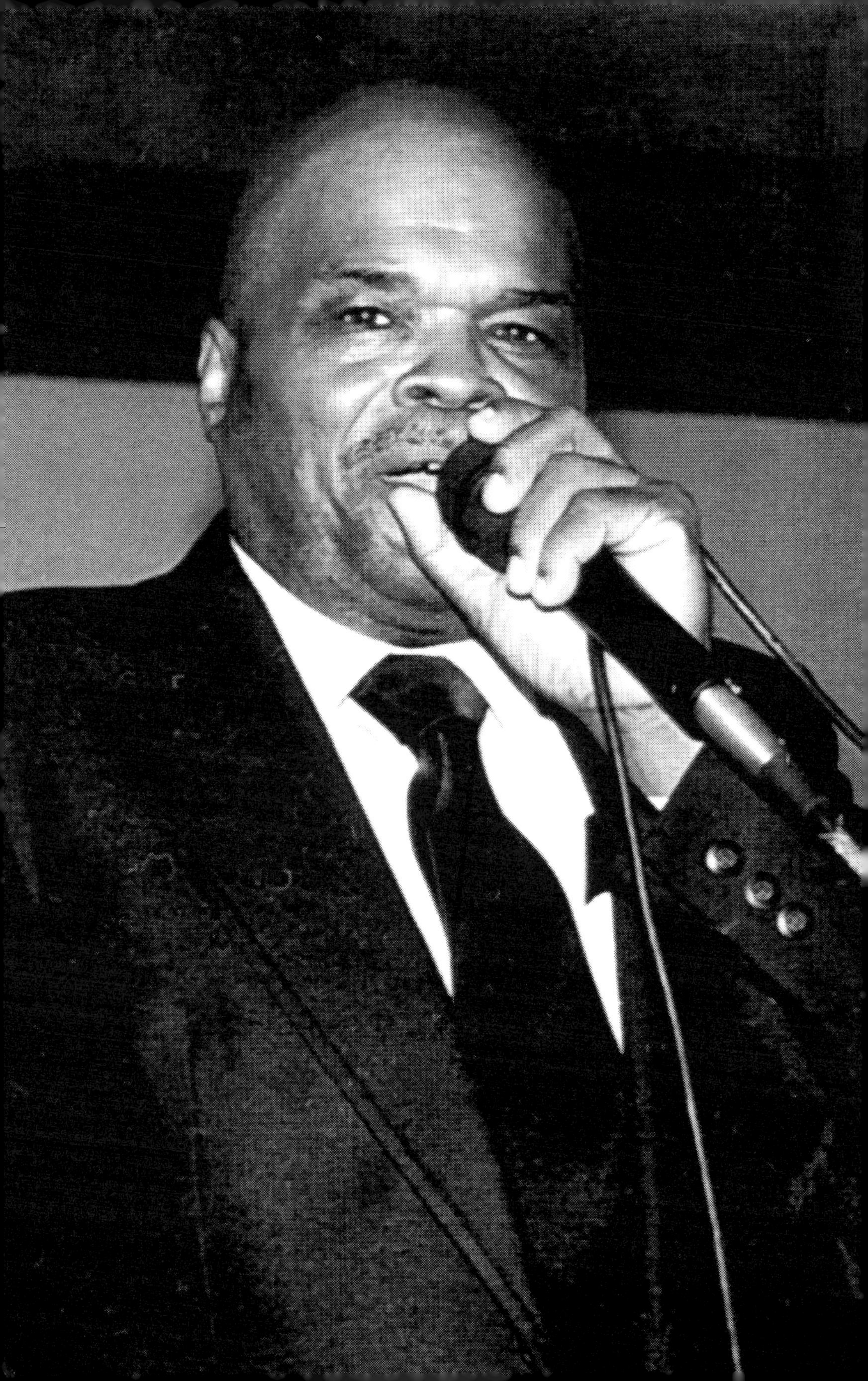

7

SEA OF LOVE
Phil Phillips

Phil Phillips attained legendary status in the summer of 1959 with his self-penned swamp pop classic, *Sea Of Love*, but almost immediately became a casualty of the record industry's oppressive financial practices. There was to be no follow-up to his million-selling smash hit, and the album he'd already recorded was never released. Totally disillusioned with his treatment, he curtailed his singing career and became a radio deejay in Louisiana, but has now returned to the recording studio after a break of several decades and is once again making appearances when health permits.

I was born Philip Baptiste and raised in a city called Lake Charles in the state of Louisiana. Even as a child I loved to sing and started at the age of eight. My mother often encouraged me. Both she and my father loved to sing, as well as my brothers, with whom I later formed a spiritual group called the Gateway Quartet. I was often called upon to do solos in church.

Although singing was my passion at a young age, my mother stressed for me to get an education. Coincidentally, it was at school that I gave my first amateur performance on stage in the auditorium. I sang a song called *Sweet Slumber.* I received a standing ovation and compliments from my fellow classmates, as well as my teachers. I was encouraged to pursue a career in music, which I had intended on doing. Throughout my youth, I sang in church and in clubs. I also played guitar. Music was in my blood and so I often surrounded myself with it. Some of my favorite artists were: Roy Hamilton, whom I thought had a beautiful unique voice; Mahalia Jackson, whom I thought was one of the greatest female gospel singers, if not the best; and the Jubalaires, who had such perfect harmony. But my all-time favorite was the Golden Gate Quartet, a spiritual group I deeply admired. They were a group that didn't need musical instruments. Their harmonic, powerful voices could fill out a song and their phrasing could make you visualize every lyric. They were true professionals, both on stage as a group and off stage as friends — a trait in any group that's very hard to find.

While seeking to start a musical career, I worked as a bellhop at a motel in Lake Charles called Chateau Charles. My girlfriend at the time was a young lady called Verdie Mae. Although I would express to her on numerous occasions how much I loved her, she would always tell me: 'No, you don't

Chapter 7 – Phil Phillips

really love me.' One night in 1957, while standing on her front porch, I started thinking: 'If only I could take her to the sea and tell her how much I loved her, it would prove my love for her.' I had my guitar. Suddenly, a melody came into my mind and I started to strum the melody on my guitar. Verdie Mae was sitting on the porch with me, watching me. I kept strumming the melody and the lyrics started to come to me and I sang it aloud as it came: 'Come with me, my love... To the sea, the sea of love... I want to tell you how much I love you.' Within twenty to thirty minutes, I'd written and composed *Sea Of Love*. Verdie Mae was shocked to see me write the song so quickly. She was, then, finally convinced that I loved her. She really loved the song and would ask me to sing it to her. It wasn't long before others started to hear it. I would receive many compliments on the song. I remember singing it one day and a friend of mine told me: 'Phil, you may not know it, but you are walking around with a million dollars in your hands.' More and more people started to tell me that, and word got around. I retained my original lyrics.

I was taking steps to gain interest by record labels, when one day a man who owned a record label, George Khoury, approached me about the song. I played it for him and he was immediately thrilled by it, and told me it was a hit and that he wanted to record it. He then, in turn, introduced me to a man he knew named Eddie Shuler, who owned a recording studio. Both were located in Lake Charles around the corner from each other. I then organized a group to sing backup and gave them the name 'The Twilights'. The Twilights and I, accompanied by musicians and a group called Cookie & The Cupcakes, recorded the song in about eight to ten takes in Mr. Shuler's studio for Khourys Records. The lyrics and melody remained the same. The very lyrics I first sang to Verdie Mae on her front porch are the very lyrics that were recorded and are on the record *Sea Of Love* — *exactly*. The lyrics were never changed. I arranged the background vocals, and Cookie & The Cupcakes arranged the music with my input with the pianist. Neither Eddie Shuler nor George Khoury had anything to do with the arrangements or the vocals to *Sea Of Love*. We also recorded a song as the flip side to *Sea Of Love* called *Juella*, which I wrote and composed as well. Juella was a former girlfriend of mine.

Sea Of Love was my first professional recording. I was very pleased with it: it had come out the way I'd envisioned it. I wanted to come out *strong*, therefore I decided to change my name from Philip Baptiste to what I thought was a more catchy stage name — Phil Phillips.

Chapter 7 – Phil Phillips

I made my professional debut when I sang in different nightclubs to promote *Sea Of Love*. Word started to spread and we started trying to get it played on local radio stations. I cannot recall the *[Baton Rouge]* radio station, but a disc jockey, who loved *Sea Of Love* so much that he played it over and over and over again, broke *Sea Of Love* to listeners. The disc jockey was even threatened to be fired for playing the song so often. He, in turn, locked himself in the sound booth and continued to play the song over and over and over again. His actions gained tremendous attention and interest, and *Sea Of Love* exploded onto the airwaves and was in great demand shortly after that. I can't recall where I was or how I felt when *Sea Of Love* charted. For the sole purpose of getting a wider distribution, Mr. Khoury leased the record to Mercury Records. The song became an instant hit. Needless to say, I quit my job at the Chateau Charles Motel.

I started performing on television shows such as the *Alan Freed Show* and Dick Clark's *American Bandstand*. I also toured with the *Dick Clark Caravan Of Stars* along with artists like Paul Anka, the Coasters, the Drifters, Annette Funicello, LaVern Baker, etc. I still have many good memories of us all having a lot of fun performing and traveling together, talking about the industry, etc. I was also fortunate enough not to have any problems with segregation. Although the song was a hit, I always managed to stay grounded. My success with *Sea Of Love* never changed my relationships with family, friends or Verdie Mae. Although we did not stay together, Verdie Mae was very happy about the song's success. She was very happy for me, as everyone else was, and we remained friends.

I did receive a gold disc from Mercury for one million sales of *Sea Of Love*. Unfortunately, because of injustice, my career was cut very short. When *Sea Of Love* was released, I noticed that Mr. Khoury's name appeared on the record as a writer when, in fact, *no-one* co-wrote *Sea Of Love* with me. It was because his name was added as a writer, he was not being forthcoming about my royalties, nor paying me, that I decided to take legal action against Mr. Khoury. It was because of my decision to fight for what

Chapter 7 – Phil Phillips

was rightfully and legally mine that a full album I'd recorded was never released. I'm not sure what Mercury were planning to call the album, perhaps *'Phil Phillips'*. Mercury Records may have that information, as well as information regarding specific tracks. As it's been so many years, I can't remember all of them, but some of them were: *Weeping Willow, Skylark, Stormy Weather* and *The Ghost Of St. Maria*. I wrote *Weeping Willow*, and there were others on the album written by me as well, but I am unable to recall which ones specifically, as I've written many songs. I do not have the masters to any of the songs; Mercury Records does. Therefore, I am not able to press any of them.

My career was intentionally killed. Khoury, who was also my manager, made no efforts to rectify the situation and abruptly ended any efforts to promote and further my career. I never received justice then, and forty-five years later I have yet to receive justice. I have yet to receive retribution despite all my sincere efforts to receive it. After the falling-out, I no longer performed in clubs and became a disc jockey, and was one for many years before retiring in 1986. Although my career was no longer, I was fortunate to have a beautiful blessing enter into my life unexpectedly: I met and married my beautiful, loving wife, Winnie. We had seven children.

Sea of Sales!
SEA OF LOVE
PHIL PHILLIPS
71465
Mercury RECORDS

I continued and still continue to write songs for my own pleasure with hopes of one day getting them released by a major recording studio, and I sing my original songs and spirituals I've written as well. I still perform at rock'n'roll shows. I performed at the *Swamp Pop Ponderosa Stomp* music festival in New Orleans, Louisiana *[May 2003]*. People constantly tell me I have the same voice and that's it's a unique sound. I like to perform *Sea Of Love* the same as the original because the fans like to hear it that way. They often tell me that it's like hearing the original all over again. So, in that way, *Sea Of Love* is always fresh to them.

I classify *Sea Of Love* as rock'n'roll-pop and, when I wrote it, I'd always had the intention of recording it myself, which I did. But it makes me happy and amazes me how, over the years, so many artists from different musical genres have done great versions of the song — including Del Shannon and the Honeydrippers. I especially like the Honeydrippers' version. I thought they did a *fantastic* job! When they used the title and the song for the Al Pacino movie, *Sea Of Love*, I thought it was fantastic. Until you asked me about Marty Wilde's 1959 UK hit with *Sea Of Love*, I didn't know about

Chapter 7 – Phil Phillips

Mr. Wilde at all. You telling me about it is the first I've heard of it. No-one even told me about it and I never profited from it. I've been asked on more than one occasion if I myself could've recorded another artist's song, what would it be. Being a spiritual person, I'd always hoped to record *You'll Never Walk Alone*.

Looking back, *Sea Of Love* has been like a double-edged sword for me in that, for a short period, I was doing what I love to do — recording records. But, unfortunately, I have never received justice for all the time, hard work and dedication I put into it all. I was cheated in an enormous way and have spent most of my life fighting for justice. *Sea Of Love* brought about one of the highest points in my life — I became successful almost overnight. And it brought about one of the lowest points in my life — they put the kill on my career, an inconceivable injustice that has never been rectified.

If I could go back in time and change anything, I would obviously work with different people. I would work with trustworthy people that I could depend on. I would go back and change that aspect, not only for the benefit of my own career, but for the benefit of my wife's and children's lives. It has not been easy for my family and me to go through such injustice for all these years. We have all truly suffered emotional, physical and mental turmoil. It never ceases to amaze me how an injustice that was initially done so many years ago could have such a tremendous effect, still, this very day. It's an injustice that affected not only my career, but it affected chances for my children's careers. My children have not been able to get into showbusiness, largely because the injustice that was done to me effectively locked doors that could've easily been opened for them.

It is unbelievable and sad that the same lies — such as me giving up my rights as an artist and writer — that have plagued my fight for justice over the years, are still being sold as the truth to this very day. It is also very sad that what could've possibly become an enormously successful, just and honorable business relationship between me, Mr. Khoury and Mr. Shuler had to end because they chose not to show the same honor and sincerity I went into it with. I'm not even being paid — nor have I ever been paid — as an artist for *Sea Of Love*. There have been songs released on me overseas that I never even knew about until I was told about them from friends and loyal fans in the UK. What was and is rightfully mine — what I honestly earned — was and has continued to be stolen from me.

I am truly grateful for my fans. The love I receive from fans all over the world is quite heartwarming. I have been inducted into rock'n'roll halls of fame, and it brings me such joy to know that the lyrics and music I wrote so long ago still bring so much joy and memories to people today. I recently re-recorded *Sea Of Love*, as well as a spiritual, *Be Mindful What You Do*, on a CD single in a local home studio. As the saying goes: 'The future none can see'. I can only hope that I receive due justice one day, that the single is picked up by a recording studio, and that my children are able to break into the business and have truly successful, enduring careers.

Photo: Paul Harris

8

WHOLE LOTTA MAN
Marvin Rainwater

A larger-than-life character steeped in traditional country music, Marvin Rainwater started his hitmaking career with *Gonna Find Me A Bluebird* and *The Majesty Of Love* (a duet with Connie Francis), and went on to top the UK charts in 1958 with *Whole Lotta Woman*, but after a couple of smaller hits his popularity faded. Somewhere along the line, a real talent — still underrated to this day — missed its way. After battling throat cancer, Rainwater re-emerged during the rockabilly revival of the 1970s and nowadays continues to successfully combine his outside business interests with recording and performing.

I was born Marvin Karlton Rainwater on July 2, 1925 in Wichita, Kansas. Mother's maiden name was Stella Arbell Miller and my father was Cicero Percy Rainwater. I had one older brother, Don (George Donald) who died last year and have two younger brothers, Ray (Percy Raymond) and Bob (Robert Eugene), and a sister, Patty (Patricia Lucille). Some say that our surname originated from English, some say French and some say Indian, but I don't know for sure. I am no relation whatsoever to Cedric Rainwater the bluegrass guitarist, as Rainwater was not his real name — he used it as a stage name. Father was an auto and truck mechanic and mother was a housewife. We lived in Wichita and Esben, Kansas; Muskogee and Tulsa, Oklahoma; Georgia, Alabama and Tennessee.

I studied classical piano when I was a little boy. My mama took in washings — which was a lot of work for her — and got us a piano. I practised on it for eight hours a day until my dad would come home and he'd run me off. Dad didn't encourage me too much with the music, but I loved him and he taught me everything I know. I practised on that classical music until I cut off part of my right thumb in an air grease-gun accident at a Greyhound Bus garage when I was still at high school, and that was the end of my classical career. It was at this time that I took up the guitar and I also played a little tenor banjo and harp. I took some guitar lessons, but I am mainly self-taught. My brother Bob sings and writes songs, and my sister Patty and I have recorded a lot of songs together. She is a great singer and a great songwriter. Mama couldn't play music or sing, so she was so happy when one of her children did.

The first music I remember is mama singing to me. After that, it would

Chapter 8 – Marvin Rainwater

Marvin Rainwater in 1987. *(Photo: Paul Harris)*

be *Grand Ole Opry* on the radio and artists like Gene Autry, Jimmie Rodgers and Roy Rogers. I loved all of old Hank Williams Sr's stuff — it really turned me on. And I love Webb Pierce's music. Roy Acuff is the one that got me started in country when I was in the navy. We'd listen to his old songs like *The Precious Jewel*: 'A jewel on earth, a jewel in heaven / More precious than diamonds, more precious than gold...'. Ohh, those songs hit us right to the roots of our being, so I gotta give those people a lot of credit for influencing me and a lot of other people. So, I waited till I got in the navy to get interested in country music, and I've been in it ever since.

My first amateur performance took place locally. There was a little grange hall up the road in Sunnydale, about thirty miles west of Wichita, and I took my little tow-haired brother, Ray, up there with me. I think I was about nine and he was about seven. We did a show for the people there at the grange: I played piano and Ray sang *My Buddy*. He stole the show, and I made him quit singing. *[laughs]* I made my very first radio broadcast around 1940, when I'd be about fifteen years old. It was in Wichita, Kansas on KFBI Radio and I sang *Bury Me Beneath The Willow*.

I went to high school in Wichita and also Walla Walla College in Washington state, where I started a course which I hoped would lead me to study medicine. I guess I was not a good student because I was too interested in telling jokes and making people laugh. My favorite subject was Mathematics, which I got an 'A' in on my report card, but I got a 'D', I think, or maybe a 'F' in Biology & Anatomy, which appertained to what I was hoping to study! So, I guess I went to college for the wrong purpose. After a short spell at Walla Walla College I had to go into the navy. I intended to be a doctor, but it's just as well it didn't work out because that's not what I'm cut out to be.

During my two years in the navy, I never served aboard a ship, but was employed as a Medical Corps man and storekeeper in Philadelphia, Washington, DC and Bremerton, Washington. I was discharged sometime in 1944 and went out to Oregon to work for my uncle, Joe Rainwater — daddy's brother — in his logging and sawmill business. I also worked for Anton Biro, my daddy's sister's husband, who was a Hungarian. I learned a lot from him — except for how to speak English! He was a genius with machinery and equipment and built a lot of original parts for his sawmill. He got run over by a carload of old ladies and died a long time ago. I sure liked him. In 1944, I met and married my first wife, Charlene Ruepke, in Oregon.

Was I *really* a lumberjack in Oregon? *[in a mock-aggressive, storytelling voice]* Yes, I *was* really a lumberjack, and I climbed trees, and I went up the side of a mountain with a gas can in one hand and a big, heavy chainsaw in the other and cut timber all day until noon!

Yes, I logged in Oregon after the navy, and then in Virginia (Washington, DC) and Minnesota. I used to climb trees and cut the top out, and the tree would swing back and forth about fifteen feet — quite exhilarating — but I would be writing a song and several times put my life in jeopardy by inattention.

While working at these jobs, I was performing as an amateur. I've never been part of a group, I've always been solo. Of course, I need a band to sing, but I just go out as a single act.

Chapter 8 – Marvin Rainwater

I turned professional in 1951, when I worked a little club in Georgetown, up there in Washington, DC. I can't remember the name of the club, but I paid my band $200 a week and I got paid $100 a week for me *and* the band, and so it cost me $100 a week to be a professional! This went on for quite a long while. Friends called me 'Starvin' Marvin' when I started out singing — that was a pet name for me, 'cause that's all I ever did... starve.

So, I finally decided to try my luck at songwriting and moved back to Virginia, Washington, DC. There, I worked for my brother, Ray, who had a tree expert business, and got close to the Library of Congress, where you copyright songs. Also, that is where I met Ben Adelman, who was in partnership with Bill McCall of Four Star Records out in California. Bill heard my stuff and put out a record on Rainwater Records — a label he started just to put out my stuff.

It was in 1955 that Bill McCall put out *I Gotta Go Get My Baby* b/w *Daddy's Glad You Came Home* on Rainwater — also on Four Star and Coral. Subsequently, Teresa Brewer cut *I Gotta Go Get My Baby*. Justin Tubb went to No.1 with that song, which was also cut by several other artists including Rose Maddox. So, this song is responsible for any success I ever had. It got me started as a writer and then a singer. My style then was pure down-to-earth country music, but I just loved music no matter what it was — classical, country, rockabilly, rock, pop... anything. I just loved music and still do.

In May 1955, my brother Ray got me on the Arthur Godfrey show. He contacted them and sweet-talked them into having me, and I appeared off and on for a year on the morning show. When I sang *Baby* on his show, I got response from labels, which caused me to eventually sign with MGM. Arthur Godfrey was real good to me and was a wonderful man. On account of his show I got on Red Foley's show, the *Ozark Jubilee*, down in Missouri and was there for four or five years, from 1955 through 1960.

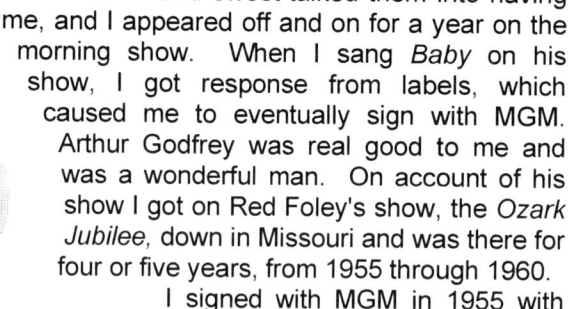

I signed with MGM in 1955 with Mr. Frank Walker, the president of MGM Records, on account of I thought so much of Hank Williams Sr, and he did too. That's why he put me on this label. The first record I cut for them was *Albino Stallion* in 1955. Eventually, in 1956, I wrote and recorded my first hit, *Gonna Find Me A Bluebird*, and my career took off — if you think three hundred one-nighters a year, at low money, a career.

Chapter 8 – Marvin Rainwater

I appeared on the *Ed Sullivan Show* to plug *Bluebird*. I don't really remember hearing it for the first time on the radio, but it made me feel good to see it go up in the country charts and it crossed over into the general popular charts. MGM was where I released most of my records. Rockabilly songs like *Hot And Cold, Boo Hoo*, etc. went unnoticed in the MGM catalogue for years, but did quite well in Europe.

I think it was in 1956, when I was doing a show in Memphis with Johnny Cash and others, I was onstage singing when all at once a couple of dozen teenagers rushed the stage. I backed off and thought: 'Man, I'm being *mobbed* — I've got it made!' But I never felt the impact of the rushing bodies. They climbed up on the stage and ran through the curtains at the side, screaming and shouting. It seems that Elvis Presley had come to see Johnny, and he decided to just walk out of the curtains a little ways and shake his hips at the crowd. That was unbeknownst to me. Well, the young 'uns swarmed him, but it was quite a blow to my ego!

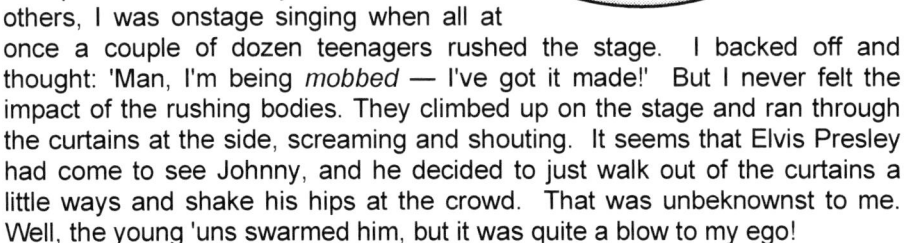

In 1957, they came to me with a girl named Connie Francis and asked me if I'd cut a record with her. When I heard her voice I said: 'I certainly will!' We cut *The Majesty of Love* and one of my songs, *You, My Darlin', You*, on September 5, 1957 in New York City, and I thought they were two good recordings. I'm still very proud of those. They weren't separately mixed: we cut them together right at the same time. I don't think that I lost out because MGM were pushing Connie Francis. She did well and went on to get an award for being the best singer in the world, and I thought that was great.

My brother, Ray, and our manager, Norm Riley, thought up the publicity of me being a full-blooded Cherokee Indian. They thought it would work — and I loved the costumes. My mother and father were rather indifferent to the Cherokee publicity, as they weren't sure about our family tree anyway. Real Cherokees trying to converse with me happened many times, but no-one ever rescued me — and what a tongue-lashing I got, such as: 'You blue-eyed punk, you no Indian!'

I felt like writing a rockabilly song, so I wrote *Whole Lotta Woman* in about 1958. I mean that *beep* that I had on there was rockabilly: I didn't know it at the time, but that's what it turned out to be. It was just something that was done inside of me and I thought it was gonna be a big hit. The song, inspired by several lovely ladies, was recorded in Nashville and Jim Vienneau produced it. I don't know how many takes, because I went flat on the *'I know I bin **had**'* line. In those days, we couldn't overdub the voice as it was all mixed up with the other music, and I was very unhappy with that flat note and nobody could change it. So, I said: 'Let's go back and do it unison, and when I get to that part you bring it down a little and I'll hit it hard.' And we did, and it turned out that it gave that song a sort-of 'radio frequency' sound — some kind of a strange, haunting sound that he gave it by using that unison, and that really helped the record.

I didn't play on the session. Grady Martin is the one that did that great six-string bass guitar walking around, Floyd Cramer played that lovely piano, and I think it was Harold Bradley who played the wild lead guitar — it was really great what he did. There was a radio station in Buffalo, New York, started playing the record really heavy, and then all of a sudden they got the word that the record was banned because it was 'dirty'. They said *'I'd been had'* was a dirty line and they couldn't use it, so all the networks quit playing the song and we thought the record had had it, it was done. I felt very bad about that, because I *really* felt that song had a chance to go. My brother, Ray, thought that was funny. He said it was no good, and everybody else said it was no good. Yet, all of a sudden, it started showing up in England and climbed the charts over there and went to No.1. When I found it had gone to No.1 in England, I jumped ten feet in the air! So, I had my revenge, as it turned out they were a little wrong and had to eat some real crow on that one!

At the outset, *Whole Lotta Woman* was promoted by me in the States. I went on shows like Dick Clark's *American Bandstand.* This was a great show — we just didn't get paid for it — but it did great for helping our records out. It didn't do me any good anyhow, as they banned my record and it wasn't allowed to be played in the United States. However, it was because of songs like *Whole Lotta Woman* I got to go to England and then around the world and back to my rockabilly roots. I toured in 1958 all over England, Scotland, Wales and Ireland with the No.1 record in the country.

I enjoyed every show we did on my UK variety tour in 1958 with all the different acts on the bill, like ventriloquists, comedians and stuff. I thought it was great, and I loved the reception I got from the wonderful, wonderful British people. You'll have ask my brother what we got paid for that tour. I really don't know what we got paid, but we made quite a lot of money.

One of the highlights of the 1958 UK tour was

Chapter 8 – Marvin Rainwater

> **Congratulations**
>
> # MARVIN
>
> OUR SINCERE THANKS TO ALL WHO HELPED MAKE
>
> **MARVIN RAINWATER'S**
>
> **"WHOLE LOTTA WOMAN"**
>
> **M-G-M** No. 1
>
> E.M.I. RECORDS LTD, 8-11 Great Castle Street, W.1.

appearing on the *Sunday Night At The London Palladium* television show. Johnny Duncan & The Blue Grass Boys did a superb job of backing me. What a thrill! On that tour I used Dreadnaught acoustic Martins.

I did try and put over a country show in my first visit: I didn't have the material to do otherwise. If I had known that *Hot And Cold* and *Boo Hoo,* etc. were popular, I would have had a lot better show for the times, but my judgment has always been flawed for some reason. The audiences and critics *still* don't know what to make of me. Neither do I! My cross between a genius and an idiot puts me into a unique category. Maybe it was because I fell off a porch headfirst onto a big rock when I was a kid that caused it, or maybe it was because my older brother, George Donald Rainwater, swung a baseball bat and hit me squarely in the forehead (not his fault). These, or some other factors have — at times — put me into a state of mental distortion, but I do have my moments of satisfaction. Hey, that's a good title! Think I'll write *Mental Distortion* — ha! Would you like a copy of my recording, *Bungee Jumpin' With The Livin' Dead*???

I have some funny memories from that UK tour. We went clear up to the Shetland Islands — it was in April. Everything was going on fine, except it was very damp and cold up there. My room got very cold all of a sudden and I felt like I was freezing to death. I piled more covers on and I *still* couldn't get warm, so I went down to the desk and I asked the woman: 'What happened to the heat?'

She said: 'It's April, darling.'
I said: 'I know, but where's the heat?'
She said: 'We turn the heat off in April, darling.'
I said: 'Oh, mercy!'

We had to find a follow-up to *Whole Lotta Woman* and I hadn't written one yet — I was too busy singing that one. I wish I had a chance to do it over, 'cause I could come up with some *real* dandies, but anyhow we found a song I love very much called *I Dig You Baby*. Although I can't remember the precise details, a guy called Stevenson — I forget his first name[*] — and I were co-writers on this record. I remember working on the lyrics with him, but I think he was responsible for the hip phrases of *'I dig you baby'* and *'You're too much, the most'* — I just sang 'em! It was published by Geronimo Music and we had part of that company. There was no problem to keeping composers' credits separate back in those days: they didn't ask for half the writing like they do now. If you wrote it, you wrote it; and if you didn't, you didn't. And you didn't have to share your writing with anybody. With some of my songs, I had a share of the publishing. On others, I just got the writing on it.

After *I Dig You Baby*, my career just kept on a-going and I just kept singing around the world, on and on and on. With such a gruelling agenda — two shows a night for three years — my voice soon gave way and collapsed, and after that I had an awful time recording for a long time. I recorded a whole lotta records for MGM after *I Dig You Baby*, but I don't remember all the names of the songs. It was dozens and dozens, maybe hundreds. I had considerable success with *Half Breed* in 1960. I did songs with my sister — *Because I'm A Dreamer* and *Two Fools In Love* — and I did *Wayward Angel*, and all kinds. Then I did some rockabilly stuff: *Boo Hoo* and *Hot And Cold*, which was in the bootleg charts about 25-30 years, and *Gamblin' Man* and *Love Me Baby* and all those rockabilly things I love so much. Now they're all coming back: those people over in Europe love rockabilly, so I've been traveling over there doing a lotta shows for them and having a wonderful time.

I was treated very well at MGM. Mr. Walker used to take me into his office and we'd talk about Hank Williams. I crossed paths with fellow recording artists Tommy Edwards and Conway Twitty — who also had big hits with MGM — and was great friends with Conway Twitty especially. Boy, it'd take me a long

---

[*] Augustus.

time to list the friends I made in this business: Johnny Cash, Charlie Louvin, Freddie Hart, Jimmy Dickens, Webb Pierce, Kitty Wells, Johnny Wright, Bobby Bare... just on and on and on — I've worked with just about every one of them... Hawkshaw Hawkins, Jeannie Shepherd... I've just worked the road with so many of these people over the years and I love every one of them.

Did I get all my royalties? Well, I suppose so. I never did audit them or anything — my brother Ray managed me and looked after my interests — but I got quite a lot of money from them.

I had to leave that wonderful label, MGM, in the mid-Sixties because my voice was so shattered. I couldn't record good enough to release. I had no control of my voice, went flat and got very hoarse. I don't remember when my voice gave out completely, but after MGM and I parted, I just recorded on my own label and some other little labels. In 1967, I moved from Falls Church, Virginia to Chicago and joined my friend, Bill Guess, in recordings which we made in Nashville. We started the Brave label and built our Brave Studios in Harvey, Illinois. When Bill died, I moved to Aitkin, Minnesota and started another label, Okie Records. I recorded several records on Okie.

At that time I actually did think about leaving showbusiness, but I didn't. Had I not remained in the business, then I had the chance to be a booking agent down in Nashville. I've been in business for myself all my life, having log trucks, trimming trees and doing all kinds of things, so I don't think it would be real hard to find something to do. I never really counted on anybody to give me a pay check, 'cause I always went out and scrounged for myself and managed to come up with something. When you get used to that, it's no problem.

I kept hanging in there and in 1975 I found out that I had cancer in my throat. I had been a heavy smoker — five packs a day — for years. In the same year, I had an operation at the Mayo Clinic in Rochester, Minnesota. They went down there and cut out the glands — the thyroid glands and the other glands — and got rid of it. I had nodules on my vocal chords and they cut those off, and my voice came back after I conquered the cancer, but it came back high. It wasn't as low as it used to be. It was real deep baritone before and I couldn't hit high notes. Now, I can hit high notes but have trouble with the low ones. It's weird, but that's what life gives you. You gotta live with it.

How did I deal with the temptations of ladies, drink and drugs? *[laughs]* I loved 'em all! Yes, there was pressure with the success and it cost me my marriage, being gone all the time and not ever being home. That's hard on a family, and they don't stick around too long, but music is in my blood and I had to stick with it. I have had three wives. One of them was Charlene, who I mentioned earlier, and her children, Jimmy (Marvin James) and Judy. Then I got married again, to Barbara, and she had a boy and two girls: Wade Tracy, Barbara Allen and Loralee. Barbie (Barbara Allen) and Loralee sing, but are busy with families. Emily (Barbie's teenager) has a lovely voice and I might promote her one of these days. Now I'm married to Sheree and she's a cute little thing. She sings once in a while and she plays sax, and I love to hear her play sax on *Whole Lotta Woman.*

Given the choice of any, which song would I like to have written? Well, that would have to be the song I recorded, written by Jimmy Walker, called *Daddy's Footprints*. Ohh, what a story about him: the man stumbling back and forth half-drunk and his little boy tagging along, just worshipping every step he took. That song really knocks me out and it does disc jockeys, too. And the record I would've liked to have recorded? Well, I guess it would be a toss-up between Bob Seger's *Old Time Rock'n'Roll* or Creedence Clearwater Revival's *Proud Mary*. I love those two songs; I do 'em all the time. Today I play a '58 Jazzmaster — lots of finger and a real workhorse.

I'm very proud of my place in musical history. Even though it had a lot of ups and downs, I enjoyed it. I enjoyed making people laugh, and I enjoyed singing for people if they liked the songs I was doing. 'Specially, I like rockabilly, 'cause the young kids just jump up and down and sing the songs with ya and they love every word you sing. And that makes me go into a trance — I really do my best for them.

I own a lot of my own masters. Since the break-up with MGM nobody wanted them, but now that I've got things organized again I've got a great catalog of my own material that I own everything to. I've got a brand new CD right now full of wild rockabilly music that'll be on the market real soon. It's called *'Rockabilly Wildman'*, and I believe it will be on the Rollercoaster label. On this CD I've tried to capture the way I feel about rockabillies and I just hope they understand and enjoy what I am doing.

You really can't get the enthusiasm going like we do at rockabilly shows. I don't have to try to keep *Hot And Cold* fresh, because every time I sing it, they make me sing it about three times — and I don't know why! *[laughs]* Roy Clark played the lead guitar on that, and I think that might be the reason why. Every time I do it, the musicians work real hard on it and learn it *exactly* right, and it brings the house down. It's just a song that's *weird*. In the last few years I have been contacted by promoters around the world and they have booked me on rockabilly shows in England, France, Finland, Germany, Sweden, and Las Vegas and Wisconsin in the States.

I guess the lowest spot in my career, and maybe in my life, was when I found out that I had cancer in my throat. It explained all the problems I'd had for five, six or ten years before that, because my voice just kept getting hoarse and hoarse. It got where I couldn't speak, couldn't sing at all, and I still wanted to sing and I couldn't. When I found out what the problem was, that was the lowest point in my career, I think. So, I took the chance to go in and have it removed and cut out of my throat. I guess the high spot was when they got rid of it and told me I was clean, and I hope that it *stays* clean. The Good Lord willing, we'll keep on a-pickin' and a-grinnin'.

Am I a religious man? Well, I had somewhat of a religious upbringing by my grandmother on my daddy's side and didn't get to be a 'wildman' till much later in life. Caroline Rainwater had nine children, one of which was my dad, and at least two of her children are still living. A lot of my family lived to be 100.

Photo: Paul Harris

My daddy's brother, George, is still alive and kicking in Tennessee and going on 100, and daddy's sister, Lucy, is still somewhere in California and I think she reached 100 some time ago. Granny lived to be 102 and cooked dad's breakfast every morning. She was a vegetarian and followed the Seventh Day Adventist religion, in which she indoctrinated me. I have a new CD about faith and love, and the lead song is *Someone's Watching Over Me*. In that song I summed up how I feel: I could never be ashamed of my Jesus, and I just hope he's not ashamed of me.

It pleases me greatly to know that *Whole Lotta Woman* has not been forgotten because I, at the time, thought that I had written a wonderful song telling a woman how great she was. All the people put it down and tried to stop it, and the fact that it was banned in the United States — all that worked against it. But the English people went ahead and said: 'Hey! He's written a great song about a woman, and I like it.' I'm sure happy that they did that, 'cause I would've been real sad if that hadn't happened.

If I could go back, would I do anything differently? Well, I probably *should.* When I think back on it, I probably should've paid more attention to what I was doing, but I was having so much *fun* that I couldn't pay attention! I just had to enjoy it — and I did — from one end to the other.

Herb Reed

9

GROUP IN A MILLION
Herb Reed / The Platters

Loved around the world for their sophisticated sound, the Platters were the most popular vocal group during the first five years of the rock'n'roll era with such classics as *Only You, The Great Pretender, My Prayer, Twilight Time* and *Smoke Gets In Your Eyes.* Herb Reed, founder member, leader and original lead singer, has been a Platter for over fifty years and is still performing, bringing the group's unique magic to yet another generation.

Forget about personal questions; I am not interested in baring my soul to the general public. Forget all about that please. If you want to know something about music or the Platters I'll be happy to answer that, but going into my personal life and stuff like that, I'm not gonna do that.

I was quite young at the time I settled in Los Angeles, California. My earliest musical influences would be gospel groups such as the Golden Gate Quartet and the Mighty Clouds Of Joy. So far as a popular group was concerned, it would be the Ink Spots. Those were my earliest influences. I never found out that I could sing yet, to be honest with you. *[laughs]* I had no singing lessons as a child and my family encouraged me *not at all*. There was no musical talent in the family whatsoever. It was a *fluke! [laughs]* I've always thought I was fairly decent in the background — but leads, no. I've had a deep voice for quite a number of years now and was unable to control it vocally, so I always just wanted to stay in the background with the 'oohs' and 'aahs'. I don't play any musical instruments: two fingers on a piano and two, three or four chords on the guitar.

My first amateur performance took place in Los Angeles. In those particular days, there were what was called 'amateur shows' in nightclubs, and we entered an amateur show and sang a song by a popular group of the day called the Ravens. I did the lead singing and we won First Prize, which was about four dollars for the whole group, and I was as pleased as hell with the four dollars. The song we did was *Write Me A Letter.* That group was called 'The Platters' and was the very first group. There were no other groups before that — I was just singing in the school choir at Lincoln High in L.A.

The Platters came about because I had the idea of a starting a group of my own, and I spoke to Alex Hodge and asked him did he know anyone who could sing. He said yes. So, he introduced me to Cornell Gunter and then later on to Joe Jefferson. So, we just kept hanging around singing and enjoying each other; not thinking about a career, not thinking about recording, not thinking about being famous — nothing. Just kids enjoying each other's camaraderie. Then, we started to harmonizing, just for the fun of it. Again, we were not thinking about a career; we were not thinking about going out and doing anything. Just harmonizing and having fun. Then we heard about the amateur show at a nightclub and it wasn't far from where we lived. We had learned this one particular song that I've mentioned and we decided we would do it, and we did it. In those days, you had to pay in order to go into the club, and we could not afford to pay to get in. So, what we did, we would go in and we would do a rehearsal with the band that they had, because we were all acappella. The musicians knew all the songs. So, we'd do that and then go outside and we'd wait. And then they'd call us in and we would do our song, and then we would go outside, around the ticket booth, and wait until they'd call for judging.

When I founded and formed the Platters in 1953, the group was made up of Joe Jefferson, Cornell Gunter — who later joined the Coasters — Alex Hodge and myself. I never really considered Joe Jefferson to be one of the Platters, 'cause he never recorded anything with us. He was just a guy in the neighborhood that we asked because he could carry a particular note, and then he did one — I repeat *one* — amateur show and that was it. No recordings, no other amateur shows, nothing. He couldn't sing: his throat just gave out at the very first amateur show. So, it's easy to give him credit for nothing, actually. We started out singing songs of that era, and we were into whatever was popular. Whatever we knew that the people knew, that's what we did. Slow, soft, uptempo — things like that, danceable.

I got the group name from listening to disc jockeys refer to records as being 'platters'. They used to say: 'And now we're gonna spin another platter by so-and-so' or 'Here's a platter by so-and-so.' That's where I got the idea. I must tell you that nobody liked that name. I mean, the group said it was okay, but they weren't over the moon about it. The record company didn't like it. Our manager didn't like it. They wanted to change it, and I was adamant about not changing it — and I'm glad I didn't! They had a series of names they wanted to do, but I liked 'The Platters'. I explained to the gang what it meant, and why, and we kept it. I was very adamant about not changing.

No records were made with the original line-up. After I had found David Lynch and Tony Williams, we were doing local TV and background singing for other singers that were recording and needed background singers. I can't remember the names of those singers. I didn't count them — we were doing two or three of 'em a day. We used to have fun doing that and, like I said, nobody thought about it being a living, or success, or anything. We got paid for doing the backing work. One of those so-called 'legitimate' recording jobs was back-up behind a musician. We got there at nine o'clock at night and left at two o'clock in the morning, and this cheap bastard paid us six dollars for five people! I don't want to name him, but that's all we got. Can you *imagine* that? Nine in the evening to two in the morning, and he paid us six dollars for five people!

Cornell Gunter was one of the group, just having fun and doing one or

Chapter 9 – Herb Reed / The Platters

two little things together. He was also rehearsing with a group that went on to become the Coasters.

What happened was that... I remember one night he said: 'Come on, go with me to the record company. They've released our record and I'm going down to the record store to sign autographs.' I didn't know what he was talking about. So, I went with him and he's signing autographs and I said: 'What the hell's going on?' And he had all along been singing and rehearsing with this other group. They were the Robins, before they evolved into the Coasters. So, he left before we started anything record-wise.

Yes, I was humorous onstage with the Platters, but no, no, no, there was never a chance of me becoming a Coaster, although I was friends with Cornell. What happens is that you meet people you like, and then they get along. They suggest a date, and people give a good argument as to what to do, etc. You do that without question. It's just that you respect other people's opinions and you pull it back. Therefore, there was not any frustration, or anything like that I felt like I should be maybe be funny and they thought I should be serious.

David Lynch and Tony Williams I found in Los Angeles. In fact, I'd heard that Tony Williams had auditioned for something in a theater somewhere and that he was very, very, good. So, I found out where he was living and I went by to see him and told him what I was doing, that we had a group and would he like to join it, etc. He said: 'Okay, fine.' At the time, I was considered to be the lead singer and Tony Williams was just background. Tony had no desires whatsoever to be a star or anything like that. All he cared about was being in the background doing his 'oohs' and his 'aahs', and he had no interest in being lead singer. In fact, I had to constantly, constantly tell him about different songs that I thought he would be good at singing. He smiled, said: 'Okay, thank you, ba-ba-ba-ba...' It took a long time before I got him to even come forward to do a lead number. He wasn't shy: he was not interested. In fact, with all the hit records we had with him singing lead on 'em, he never thought that he was great. He never thought that he was good. I never heard him brag. He never wanted to be the first one to a photo session, or to be in the spotlight with pictures and this, that and the other. Never. He was just a very quiet, laid-back guy who enjoyed being in the studio, but after he left the studio or left the stage, that was it — he was non-existent.

I wanted Tony Williams to come forward to be the lead singer because he had a fantastic voice. He had an *unbelievable* voice. You know, he believed he could sing two songs: one was *Ebb Tide* and the other song was *Trees*. And he believed they were the only two songs he could sing! As fate would have it, one night we heard him sing *Trees,* which was *unbelievable*. So, at the amateur show, we decided to put in *Trees* instead of my tune. And that was the only night we won *Second* Prize! Isn't that amazing! So we said: 'Okay, that's it,' and he didn't do lead at any more amateur shows. I did all of them from then on out. I was the boss of the group and the members were all friends. With salaries we had everything equal.

Believe it or not, I found David Lynch when I was at a hot dog stand.

Chapter 9 – Herb Reed / The Platters

The Platters *(left to right)*: David Lynch, Herb Reed, Tony Williams, Zola Taylor and Paul Robi.

This guy walked up when I was stood there talking to the guy behind the counter. We were talking about music and this guy joined in. I asked him if he could sing and he said yeah, so I told him what we were doing and that we were rehearsing. So, he came over and we liked him as a person, and he knew his parts. He was a second tenor and very good, so he joined the group.

We started doing a number of amateur shows because of the money, and a talent scout from Chicago by the name of Ralph Bass spotted us. He was very famous as a talent scout, but at the time we didn't know anything about talent scouts or anyone. He liked us and asked if we would like to do some recording and we said yeah. That was with Federal Records. So, we went into the studio and he said: 'Okay, here's some radio tunes.' He liked how we sounded, but he understood that we didn't, so he said: 'Okay here's what you do: you go in the studio and you keep going in the studio until such time as you think you've got a sound that you can live with.' So he gave us unlimited studio time to try and find a sound. Finally, we thought we had something going for us and just kept on trying until we got lucky.

My singing of *Write Me A Letter* was the song Ralph Bass noticed when he found us. In fact, the very, very first recordings of the Platters — the first time we were recorded as a group called 'The Platters' — was my singing the 'A' side and the 'B' side. They were two of my original songs; one was

Chapter 9 – Herb Reed / The Platters

called *Hey! Now,* and I can't remember the other name[*]. They were so bad, they were *embarrassing!* I wish that I could buy up those copies and destroy them. No records were made before those Federal recordings.

I didn't meet Buck Ram until around 1954. Alex Hodge had heard that there was a songwriter from Chicago who was in town looking to manage a group of nice people, so we went out to his office and just casually talked. He didn't make any commitments about managing us or anything like that. It took a while for him to make up his mind. We didn't bug him because we were not striving for a career, we were not hungry for success or anything. At that point, he had just heard one or two songs from us that we did in his office, acappella. The latter part of 1954 was when he became the manager.

I joined Zola Taylor to the group. When we were rehearsing at Alex Hodge's house, she was there rehearsing with some girls. It could have been with Shirley Gunter *[Cornell's sister]* & The Queens or something like that, but they never got off the ground. I heard Zola singing one particular part that I liked, and she was very, very cute as a girl, so I suggested her, and after talking to her she thought it was great, so that's what we did. No, there was never any romance between Zola and any of the group: she was too young, she was fifteen years old.

I don't know anything at all about Alex Hodge being in trouble with the law. I heard a rumor, but he never said anything to me, and nobody ever called me and said he was in trouble. I was there when he left. But, you know, truthfully, he wasn't that interested in any kind of discipline so far as rehearsals and learning tunes were concerned. He was just too busy enjoying himself doing whatever he was doing. When I realized that I could make a decent living with this, and I liked doing the things we were doing in these early recordings, I thought maybe we did have a choice of making some bucks. But I didn't put my heart and soul into it, you know. I just thought that we should be prepared for whatever we had to do in the future.

Paul Robi came from the gutter. Well... *[laughs]* No, Paul was a local guy going to school in Los Angeles, although originally he was from Oklahoma. We knew him, and in those days people were friendly towards one another. We said we needed another guy to replace Alex, so we said to him: 'Do you wanna check out and join the group?' He said: 'No, I don't like groups 'cause they like too many girls.' We didn't know what he was talking about, because we were kids ourselves and we were shy. And girls never entered into our lives *at all* — not in conversation with the guys, not in looking at girls. We didn't pay no attention to girls, 'cause you had to have *money* to go with a girl: you had to have money to take her to the movies, or buy her a meal or somethin'. They never entered our lives, so we didn't know what the hell he was talking about, this guy. To make a long story short, one day, when we went over to see Buck Ram, Paul was at the office and Buck Ram said: 'You know Paul, don't you?' And then he started talking about Paul — he could sing very well and he knew harmony — and he strongly suggested that we give him a shot. We said okay. So, we did a few things, and he could do it, and that's what happened — we gave him a shot. At the time, Paul was

---
[*] *Give Thanks* [Federal 12153] 1953.

Chapter 9 – Herb Reed / The Platters

just on the scene singing background, I would suggest, not lead. You've got to understand that, in them particular days, in the very beginning, I was the lead singer — because I had the bass voice and a group called the Ravens was so popular. I could imitate the guy* to a 'T' and, as a result of that, I was considered to be the most popular, and these were the songs that we were going with, because of the Ravens and my ability to hit their singer's notes.

Buck Ram became *the* man so far as recordings were concerned. There were two that he suggested with me which I turned down, and then he became, to be honest with you, power-mad, and we started getting all kinds of *crap*: just testing things, you know. And then we got to a point where we were just doing a lot of 'fishing', as we called it. You know: 'Well, here's a tune. Do you know the song?'

'No.'

'Aah-da-da de-de la-da-da...'

'Oh yeah, it goes like that, yeah: ba-ba-ba-ba...'

And all along they were recording these rehearsals and, you know, those sons-of-bitches put those rehearsals out, later on, as so-called 'unreleased recordings' of the Platters! Songs that we didn't even know the words to, didn't know the melody — we were singing out of tune, just kabitzing around trying to find a high wind. And they released those songs later on as 'unreleased recordings'! That was Buck Ram and Mercury. I tell you, that is the most embarrassing thing that you could possibly hear as a professional artist: to hear a host of tapes when you were out of tune, didn't know the melody and didn't know the words. And they released these songs as recordings! *Nobody* releases rehearsal tapes! Buck Ram was a witness to all that shit. There's no question he was in on all of that. He became power-mad and money-hungry.

Buck Ram was a hit-and-miss kind of guy. If he was having a good day, he was okay. If he wasn't having a good day, he wasn't okay. He was just like a manager someplace out in Hollywood, and we were in inner city Los Angeles. There was no social contact except during a meeting of some kind, when we would go out to his house and have a sandwich or something, but there was no inviting out for dinners, nothing like that at all. I try to remember Jean Bennett being

---

* Jimmy Ricks.

Chapter 9 – Herb Reed / The Platters

in his office the first day we went out there. She was in a corner, where I just got a glimpse of her. I never saw her full face or full figure. She was just a face who was in a corner someplace and I had a look around and there she was, and that was about the extent I saw Jean Bennett. But I didn't know anything about her after that. I heard she was his secretary, but that was all.

As a black group, having a white manager helped us in a lot of ways, and in some ways it hindered, because he was Jewish. A lot of people were just as prejudiced against Jewish as they were anybody else. But it did help in a number of ways, because in those days a black manager couldn't do anything — he had no shot. No, Buck Ram never conducted an orchestra when we were performing, never. He didn't do *nothin'*. We had a piano player, name of Rupert Branker, who conducted the orchestra. He was our musical director. Buck Ram never directed a goddamn thing. He was just our manager. Paul Robi did the vocal arrangements and I did all the dancing and routines.

The Platters were more popular with white audiences than black audiences. However, we did the Apollo, New York, twice. They wanted us to come back the third time, but we said: 'No way are we gonna do any work for you bastards' — because they would have you doing four, five shows a night. And we said: 'Screw this!' So, we turned down the Apollo. In fact, I did the Apollo again — for a special show up there — some three years ago, after twenty-odd years.

How did I feel when *My Prayer* went to No.1? I don't even remember recording the song. We did not know anything about recording *My Prayer,* or when it was, or where it was, or anything. I have no knowledge whatsoever. We were recording things, and then the next thing you know these things were put in an album and then they were put out. But knowing when they were released, nobody told you. You gotta understand something, mister: in those days, you couldn't even get one of your recordings. In fact, if you wanted a record of the Platters, you had to go out and *buy* it! The record companies would not give you five free records! So, nobody called you up and told you they were gonna release this recording next week, or next month, or anything. You got no information at all. They released what they wanted to release, when they wanted to release it. They told you nothing.

Nobody even called you up and told you you had a hit record. Nobody would call you and say: 'Oh, by the way, your song is moving up the charts.' *Shit!* No sir. It was worse than that, because you gotta understand something. Nobody gave us a party to celebrate another hit recording. Nobody gave us a party to celebrate a gold recording. Nobody gave us a big dinner to celebrate another million seller. Nobody called me on the 'phone to say: 'Hey! you got a hit recording.' Shit, *you got absolutely nothing!* Yes, of course it was because we were black.

Gold discs? Let me tell you something about that — now, listen carefully. The first gold disc we got from Mercury Records, they took a 78 rpm recording, sprayed it with gold paint, and sent it to us as a gold record. When it got there, some of the gold paint had rubbed off and you could see the black underneath it — and only the one copy between five. That's how cheap those sons-of-bitches were: they took a vinyl record, sprayed it with gold paint and sent it to us! In those days, mister, nobody gave you any respect except your audiences. Your audiences were extremely nice to you. They wanted to know you, they wanted to meet you, they wanted autographs, they wanted pictures with you, etc. They were very, very nice to you — that's what kept you in the business. But the business end of it, you didn't give a damn about the business end of it at all. In fact, I'll be honest with you, I never cared *anything* about all that success. I never cared anything about having a No.1 recording or having a million-seller. I never cared, and Tony Williams didn't give a shit about it. Nobody cared about it. Nobody said: 'Hey! man, guess what? We got a hit record!' Nobody celebrated in the dressing rooms, nobody commented on anything, because the way people treated us it didn't mean anything. You understand that? You got a No.1 record in the country and the record company is selling millions, and they won't give you *five free records!* What do you think of *that*?

We did have some choice over recording material. We recorded whenever we were in voice and we had time to relax. The reason we couldn't remember records like *My Prayer* was because we were recorded so often and in different places that you just didn't pay no attention to that. What you did is that, when a song was proposed, you got together, you worked it out, etc. They'd call a session, you'd go, you'd do it and you'd forget about it. I didn't like *Twilight Time* and I never paid any attention to *My Prayer* at all, but I thought we did a good job on *Smoke Gets In Your Eyes*, 'cause we learnt that song in fifteen minutes and recorded it in Paris, France. So, I thought we did a good job on that one. But the other stuff didn't mean nothing to us.

My own favorite Platters' records were things that never made a hit — some of our early things on Federal. I do know that we had struggled so much in the studio trying to find a sound, and we finally started getting things right. And we were really pleased with the things that we did on Federal. My fondest memories are of those songs that never made it. Although I just can't think of them right now, I can still remember the feeling, you know. Buck Ram wasn't involved with those recordings at all.

Did Buck Ram treat us fairly as a manager? Ah, well, the thing was that... you see, you gotta understand something: in those days, you were extremely ignorant of the business and you didn't know the game. You dig it? And so, you'd do a local TV show and you didn't know that they paid you to be on that show, and Buck Ram would pocket that money for all those shows. We never even seen the money, and we didn't even know we were *getting* money. Things like that, you know. When we toured England in 1957, we had an accountant by then. *[laughs]*

Mercury didn't treat us fairly for royalties either. Mercury were thieves and they *still* are thieves, although they no longer exist. We pursued them one time for audit and we had a nice piece of money from the audit because they were robbing us, you know.

I remember our touring days very well. I remember arriving in England for the first time *[1957]* and the *Melody Maker* said in their big block headline: 'WELCOME TO THE PLATTERS'. I recall playing some places first, then the Palladium, and all the niceness, and everything about the people and the audience. Oh, just a pleasure! England has always been our favorite place to tour in. England was an absolutely *unbelievable* place to us. We had never been around as many nice white people in our whole lives! It was a blessing to us, it really was.

Back home, we did three of the biggest tours of America, all for Irvin Feld. They were called *The Biggest Show Of Stars* for that year. We would tour with everyone from Bill Haley to Frankie Lymon & The Teenagers. I did a lot of Dick Clark's shows, but I never did any tour, 'cause Dick Clark wouldn't pay no money then.

The court case *[against the group's male members]* in 1959 was such a bullshit thing. It was a prejudiced night clerk that saw one of the guys with a white chick. He said that only a whore would go with a black guy, and then he called a cop who said we had whores there, and the judge shot it out. Buck Ram, he just stayed in the background, he didn't come on the scene at all. The minute that it was over with, he brought us to England.

We didn't keep in touch or remain friends when we split up. What happened was that we didn't break up all at once. Zola left first, then Tony, and then Paul Robi and David Lynch. I moved from Los Angeles to New England, where I am now. I'm 250 miles north of New York near the Canadian border. They stayed in California, so therefore there were no friendships involved there.

In my career I haven't had any what you could call really low, low points, because you always believe that you can solve any problems that may crop up. But, when David Lynch passed away, that was a low point, and of course when Paul Robi passed away, and then Tony. I had met Tony for the first time in twenty years, in 1990, when we were inducted into the Rock & Roll Hall of Fame in New York and sat at the same table. After receipt of the awards, he disappeared and I never saw him any more. I heard two years later that he passed away.

You would not believe the highest point in my career! I was something like seventeen years old and learning to drive in Los Angeles. Every time they saw me, the police never gave me break, they *always* gave me a ticket. That's right, because I was black — exactly. I persisted driving without a license as I was trying to learn. *[laughs]* So, what happened was that I was always up to my ears in tickets, and the gentleman at a service station that became my dear, dear friend, was always bailing me out. Finally, I got my driver's license and, when I went by the station to show it to him and I took off and headed to a particular junction, just to be driving, I felt so great, so good, that I have never had that feeling again, never. The police didn't bother me after that, because when I got my license I didn't drive that much as I couldn't afford the gas! *[laughs]*

My favorite artist was Brook Benton. I like the Four Tops, the Temptations and Al Martino, who is my favorite singer now. If I could go back, I would not try to record — I mean solo, that is. I would not try to sing solo. I think the things that I did on those early recordings — please understand one thing — here's an example, a perfect example: you go into a studio and you've got X amount of songs to sing that day, okay? So, the norm is that you've got the lyrics with you and the musicians are there. They have been rehearsed by the music director while you are waiting around while it's all getting ready. You go into a booth and start recording and singing with the band for the first time. Now, you are not sure of the lyrics 'cause you're reading them, you're not sure of the arrangement because you never heard it before, so you are really stumbling in a way through the lyrics and through the melody. And then they say: 'Okay, that's it!' And you say: 'What you talking about? I'm not even sure about this...' and they tell you: 'No, that's it, that's it — no, no, no.' They won't give you a second chance. So, all the mistakes you made — singing out of tune, or being flat or sharp, or being behind the beat or before the beat — didn't matter to those goddamn bastards. They would not let you record any more, 'cause they saved all their time for the *lead singer*. Do you understand that? The record company did not care about me, Zola, David or Robi. All they cared about was Tony Williams, because he had gotten the hits and they wanted all the studio time devoted to him. Although we all recorded together live with the musicians, they would only concentrate on his errors. They wouldn't identify my being out of tune, or too sharp, or too flat or not.

Today, I'm feeling and doing good, to be honest with you. I believe in God, but I don't have a particular denomination that I'm with. I believe in God Almighty. I was never an abuser — meaning I never did drink, never did dope, and I've always tried to eat right. I was not a health nut, but just a positive thinker and a person who likes people and enjoys the challenge of my work, and enjoyed the creativeness of the work. With touring, each place is a new experience no matter how many times you've been there, because each audience is new and it's a new challenge. I think you have to like challenges and be somewhat creative in order to be in this business. As of now, I am having the time of my life. I'm picking and choosing, and doing a lot of cruise ships and I go all over the world with them. I pick and choose a lot of places I want to work in America, and I live in the state of Massachusetts, which is in that beautiful part of America called New England. I have a great girl and a lot of great, great friends, so I'm a happy, happy man. I don't care anything about being a success again so far as recordings or anything else is concerned. I'm satisfied with what I got.

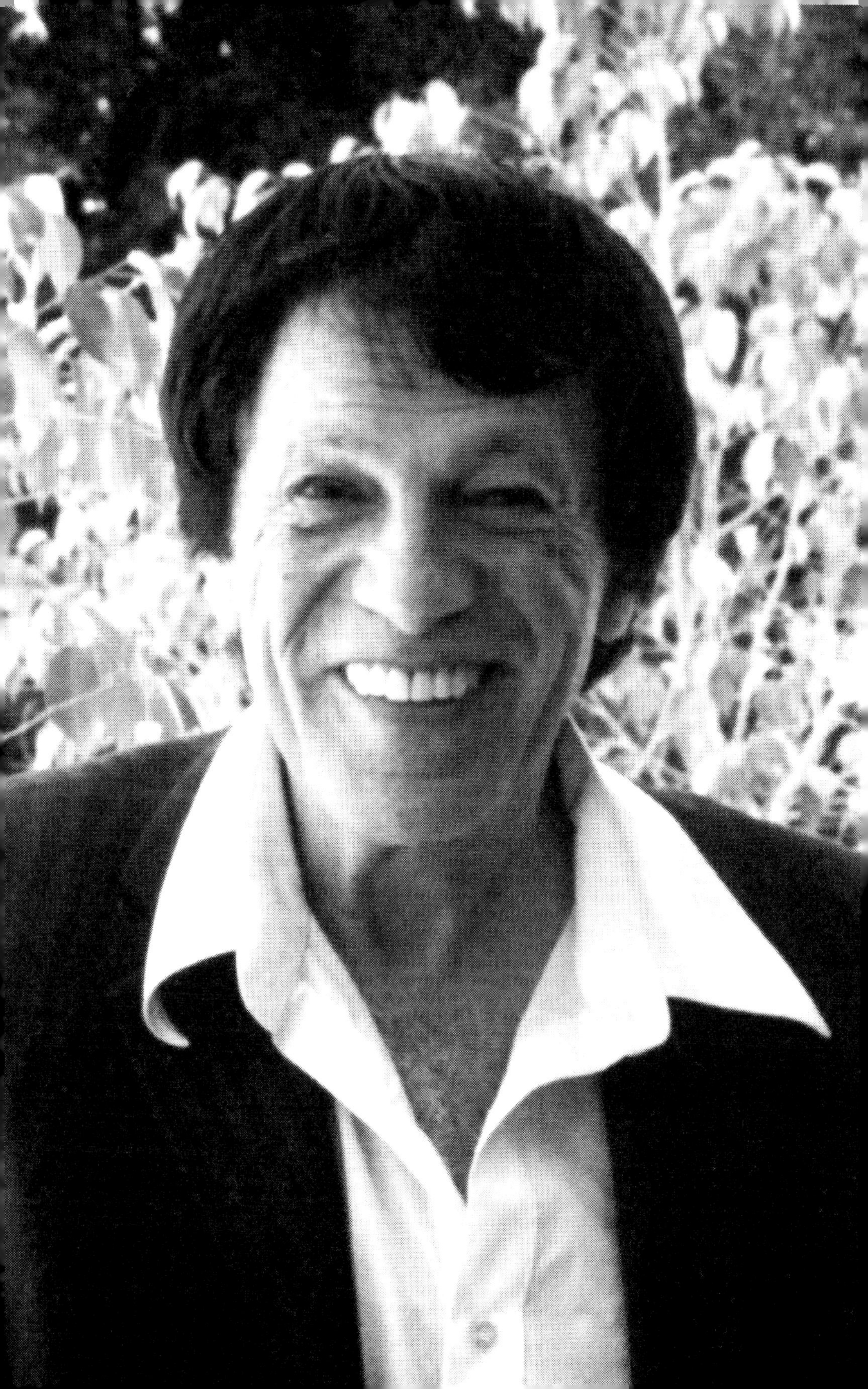

10

THE SINGIN' IDOL
Tommy Sands

Country-singing child prodigy, rock'n'roller and gifted actor, Tommy Sands was a talent to watch. He got his big break in 1957 when his former manager, Colonel Tom Parker, recommended him for the lead role in *The Singin' Idol*, a TV drama loosely based on the meteoric rise of Elvis Presley. Public response to the play was so great that Sands was immediately signed by Capitol and 20th Century Fox. His first release, *Teen-Age Crush*, sold a million, though subsequent, equally excellent efforts fared less well. A combined movie and recording career followed, as well as a highly-publicised marriage to (and subsequent divorce from) Nancy Sinatra. Today, Tommy is still in demand and is finally receiving recognition for his considerable talent.

I was born Thomas Adrian Sands on August 27, 1937 in Chicago, Illinois. Father was Ben Sands, a professional orchestra pianist and conductor, who had been a pianist with Art Kassel's band and also with another great bandleader in the early Twenties. Mother was Grace Lou (*née* Dickson), a housewife and nurse. Mom had no musical inclination or talent and was certainly never a vocalist with Art Kassel's band, Kassles In The Air, or anything like that. My father was where I got my musical talent from. I had one half-brother, Edward Dearn, who was eleven years older and is now deceased. Edward had no musical talent.

Dad played hotel lounges in Chicago, but when he would be on tour with the band — usually during the winter — mom would take Edward and I down to Greenwood, near Shreveport in Louisiana, to stay with my mom's uncle and my great uncle, Charles Dickson, at his farm. I was about three or four years old when we first started going to Greenwood and I joined Greenwood Methodist Church when I was five. Over the years I attended four schools in Chicago: I went to Lincoln Elementary, LaSalle Elementary, Oglesby Grammar, and then to Calumet High School for a year. In Shreveport, I went to Greenwood Elementary School. In Houston, Texas, I went to Sidney Lanier Elementary and later to Lamar High School in the ninth grade. In the States you start Grade 1 when you're six, so I would be around fourteen. I was a straight-A student, but left high school before graduation. We were back and forth between Chicago and Shreveport from the time I was three until I was seventeen years old.

Chapter 10 – Tommy Sands

My earliest musical influences would be from the radio. There was Hank Williams, Hank Thompson, and there was a local guy that was on the radio early in the mornings that I used to listen to named Harmie Smith. There was Kitty Wells, Johnnie & Jack and the Tennessee Mountain Boys. As a boy I bought all the records that I wanted to learn the songs to. I didn't listen to records at Hard Cash Wilkerson's J&S Music Store — I just got my guitar there. We had a Victrola at the farm, which was out in the country between Greenwood and Shreveport, and I used learn the songs on the Victrola. And Little Jimmy Dickens — he was a *big* influence on me when I was a little boy. I used to imitate him and sing *Sleeping At the Foot Of The Bed* and a lot of his songs. I was into country & western music — until I met Elvis later on.

My mother was not the driving force for my showbusiness career. It was really on my own. I wanted to sing and play the guitar from the time I can remember, and she bought me a new Martin guitar when I was five. So, at that age I began singing and playing. There was no formal education in music, but the family encouraged me and my father helped me understand music. My first performance was really the day I paid off my guitar, when I was about six or seven years old. I went into town on the bus, paid off my guitar and went down to KWKH Radio Station and auditioned for a man, Otis 'Pop' Echols, who had a noon radio broadcast called *The Melody Ranch*. He put me on the air that same day. The first song I sang was *Oklahoma Hills*. Mom and Uncle Charles heard me on the radio. After that, I was on the radio twice a week for $2.50 per performance.

I first worked on KWKH's *Louisiana Hayride* when I was eight and was there in 1947 and 1948. I'm sure it wasn't 1949-50, because when I was twelve I moved to Houston. I don't know if it was as a result of me being on the station's *Melody Ranch* or not, but I just auditioned for the show's producer, Horace Logan, and he put me on. The *Louisiana Hayride* was a radio show and also a live broadcast in a large auditorium which seated about five thousand people. They had a lot of big stars on there: Slim Whitman, Jim Reeves, Johnny Cash... later on Elvis Presley, Johnnie & Jack, the Tennessee Mountain Boys, Kitty Wells, Johnny Horton and many more.

Later, Horace Logan fired me. He said that I couldn't sing, that I should be an actor; I didn't have a voice. Around that time, when I was seven or eight I guess, and going between Shreveport and Chicago, I appeared on Chicago's WBKB-TV's *Lady Of the Mountain*, which featured the singer and guitar player Barbara Ellen Rogers. She used to tell me folk tales and show me how to make things, as you would in the mountains, and we would play songs together.

I don't remember singing *My Mommy Bought Me An Ice Cream Cone* on KWKH when I was eleven or so; I don't remember that song. I never really sang with Harmie Smith. As I've mentioned, I used to listen to him every morning at about five o'clock. He was on very early, and I used to get up early because my mother would take the bus to go to work: she was a nurse. When she got up I would turn on the radio and start listening to all the morning radio broadcasts.

Tillman Franks was a bass player in a Shreveport band that played on

KWKH and who, in the past, had worked in a country & western band with Pop Echols. It was Tillman who took me to Houston in 1950 when I was twelve. Mom had already moved down there and she was waiting for me. Tillman introduced me to Biff Collie, who was the one that booked me all during my years down there. Biff, who played trumpet, became my closest friend. He was a disc jockey who hosted KPRC Radio's *Hoedown Corner* show, which was sponsored by Sun Up Ice Cream. I got a spot on the show, but I can't remember the first song I sang. I made my first record in Houston; it was released in 1950 on the Freedom label, and I wrote both sides: *Love Pains* b/w *Syrup Soppin' Blues*. I was billed on the record as 'Little Tommy Sands (The West's Wonder Boy)'. I have no idea who owned Freedom Records.

I don't remember when my mom and dad divorced, or how old I was. I really don't remember. They were separated so much that I don't remember when the actual divorce happened. When they finally split, I went with my mom and lived with her, but then she got sick and I lived with foster parents, Treva and Jack Perno in Chicago. I lived with them twice during the years — let's say... 1950 to 1952. When mom got better, I returned to live with her in Houston.

The first time I got into acting was in Houston. I was twelve years old and I got the lead role in a play called *The Magic Fallacy* at the Alley Theatre, which is still there. It's a big theater now. My director was Nina Vance, and I won the Sidney Holmes Memorial Award as the best professional actor for the year, 1950, in the state of Texas. That was my first real acting experience. I hadn't studied acting; I'd had no acting lessons, and no previous acting experience apart from playing in a couple of school plays at Oglesby Grammar in south Chicago, when I lived with the Pernos, but they were minor. I hadn't taken to acting with the idea of breaking into films, but I wanted to be like my idol, James Dean.

Colonel Tom Parker picked me up in 1952, when I was appearing at Cook's Hoedown Club. I had been singing there week nights since I went to Houston in 1950. He was a friend of Gabe Tucker's, the bandleader I was singing for, and he called me over to his table after my first set and said that he wanted to manage me. He talked to my mom and signed contracts and took me out on the road that summer when I was out of school. And every summer for the next two or three years he took me around the country and taught me the business. I was signed to Colonel Parker's Jamboree Attractions, because he already managed Eddy Arnold and could only handle one person at a time under his own name. While in Houston, I sang with Hank Williams a lot — in south Texas and southern Louisiana. This was around 1952-53, and the shows would be shows in school auditoriums, bars and things like that. There was also a Tex Williams, but I never worked with him. The first time I met Elvis was in 1954 at the Eagles Hall in Houston, and I was on shows with him in southern Louisiana and south Texas which Biff Collie promoted in 1955.

Mom and Colonel Parker did not get on and she had me break the contract about two years later. I wasn't happy with that as I liked the Colonel very much and he liked me. I liked everything about him. He was like a

Chapter 10 – Tommy Sands

father to me; I loved him. Mom and I fell out, and we had real arguments over that. I don't know what she didn't like about him — maybe he was too possessive. Colonel Parker was responsible for getting me signed to RCA records in 1952. I can't recall my first release for RCA, but I think it was *Love Pains*, which they re-recorded with Chet Atkins and his band. I did seven records for RCA, but none of them sold and they dropped me in 1954. One of those records was *Don't Drop It*, a duet with Sunshine Ruby.

In 1954, I was working as a deejay on Houston's KNUZ Radio in the daytime, and at night I was singing at Cook's Hoedown Club. Ken Nelson from Capitol Records came to see me there. He came out and sat in my car that night and told me that, when my voice changed, he was gonna sign me to a contract — and he wound up doing that three years later. I didn't record for any other label between leaving RCA and signing for Capitol.

When I was in Houston, I sold door-to-door. Vacuum cleaners and dishwashing disposals — those are the two things I can remember — and *Encyclopædia Britannicas*. I was also a fry-cook in Chicago when I was living with the Pernos one year, when mom was sick down in Houston. It was only for a very short time, maybe a week. I didn't like the job and I quit.

I didn't graduate, and left high school in 1955 in the spring term and moved to Shreveport to get a very lucrative job as a deejay there on KCIJ Radio. I was there seven or eight months and saved the money for my mom and I to move out to California, because I wanted to get in the movies. By this time my brother, Edward, was in Anaheim, California.

In 1956, I interviewed for Cliffie Stone's *Hometown Jamboree* on KTLA-TV. I got the job that night and he put me on the air. I was living in Hollywood with my mom, and one night I got a call from Colonel Parker. He told me that Elvis had been offered a show on NBC-TV's *Kraft Theater*, which was loosely based on his life story. However, from the time they signed for the project until they finished it, Elvis had become the No.1 star in the world and they could no longer afford him. So, Colonel Parker suggested me and he flew me into New York to audition for it. I auditioned for Marion Dougherty the casting director. She signed me on the spot and I flew back to California.

Three weeks later, my dad and I flew back to New York and I did *The Singin' Idol,* a play by Paul Monash, playing the lead role of rock'n'roll singer Virgil Walker. There was one and a half songs in the play: *Teen-Age Crush* and half of *Ring-A-Ding-A-Ding*. It was a one-hour play broadcast on Wednesday, January 30, 1957 by NBC-TV and networked nationwide, and in one night

I became a star! When I was back in Hollywood, after I had gotten *The Singin' Idol,* Cliffie Stone signed me to be my manager for a few months. After that Ted Wick managed me. My success didn't affect my personal relationships. My parents were thrilled, and my brother Ed looked after my finances properly and safeguarded my interests.

After I signed to do *The Singin' Idol,* Ken Nelson of Capitol Records signed me to a five-year contract. There was no audition. My first release on Capitol was *Teen-Age Crush* b/w *Hep Dee Hootie (Cutie Wootie).* The recording was made in Studio A at Capitol in Hollywood. I don't remember how many takes were needed. Bob Bain played lead guitar; Buck Owens played rhythm guitar; Merrill Moore played piano and the Jordanaires sang back-ups. Ken Nelson produced it. I don't know anything about Joe and Audrey Allison, the writers of *Teen-Age Crush.* I didn't think the record would be a hit; I was disappointed. I liked the flip side *Hep Dee Hootie (Cutie Wootie). Teen-Age Crush* sold a million records in one week!

I can't remember where I was when I heard *Teen-Age Crush* on the radio for the first time. I think I heard it on KFWB's B. Mitchell Reed show and I was proud. When it got into the US Top Five I was thrilled. I didn't do any of the big shows to promote *Teen-Age Crush,* I just came back home. When I became a star, I did a slew of the big US TV shows during 1957. They had me on *This Is Your Life*, Ed Sullivan, Steve Allen, Perry Como, Dinah Shore, Patti Page, Jack Benny, Tennessee Ernie Ford and all the rest.

For the film version of *The Singin' Idol,* made by 20th Century Fox as *Sing Boy Sing [1958]* — which retained the lead role of Virgil Walker — I had to audition and did a screen test. Buddy Adler, the president of 20th Century Fox saw it and picked me up. I *hated* the film *Sing Boy Sing,* because they got a choreographer in there who messed up everything; made me look like a jumping jack — jumping all over the place. It was nowhere near as good as *The Singin' Idol,* which was mostly a drama with one song, whereas *Sing Boy Sing* was, like, fifteen songs and me jumping all over the place like a maniac. I didn't like it at all. The film's title song was written by me and Rod McKuen.

After *Teen-Age Crush* and the movie *Sing Boy Sing,* my record and film career developed badly. It followed in the direction of nightclubs, and I played the Waldorf, the Cocoanut Grove, the Sands and many more. As well

Chapter 10 – Tommy Sands

as touring the US, I toured twice for Lee Gordon in both Australia and New Zealand. The Platters and Frankie Avalon were on the first tour, and Jerry Lee Lewis was on the second tour. In Tasmania, the stage was warped down to the audience, and, as I ran on, I fell into the audience.

In 1960, I joined the US Air Force Reserve, which consisted of six months active service and five and a half years reserve. I did my active service at Lackland Air Force Base in San Antonio, Texas.

My marriage to Nancy Sinatra from 1960 to 1965 was my first marriage and, although I was being promoted as a teen idol, I don't think that the marriage affected my career in any way. As for my father-in-law, I loved Frank. He treated me well and used me in the film *None But The Brave [1965]*. Although he was also on Capitol, the idea of a duet with him was never floated. Frank was always very kind, and as for him trying to damage my recording and movie prospects after the divorce from Nancy, I don't believe any of it.

Ken Nelson was my A&R man at Capitol, and we chose together from the material submitted. The pressure I was put under for a successful follow-up to *Teen-Age Crush* was my own. *Ring-A-Ding-A-Ding* b/w *My Love Song* was the follow-up, but it did not fare well; it didn't make the charts. I wanted to be a rock singer like Elvis. Capitol's handling of my record career left a lot to be desired, but they tried their best. I saw my five-year contract out and they let me go when it was up. Capitol treated me fairly for royalty payments and I received a gold disc for one million sales of *Teen-Age Crush*. I still have it.

Following Capitol there were several other labels, including Vista, ABC-Paramount, Liberty, Imperial, Superscope and Brunswick, but I wasn't happy with my work on any of them. With a singing and acting career running parallel for some years, acting held the most appeal, but, as with my singing career, I only had a say as to what was offered to me. I did not go into theater musicals.

After the hits and movie scripts dried up, and I had been through a well-publicized divorce, I moved to Hawaii in 1967. I'd been there many times and I'd always loved it. There was no liver disease or mental breakdown, but I was so tired of working — I'd worked since I was five years old and hadn't had any time off — I needed a rest. I wanted to get away and just comb the beaches and climb the mountains, and just do everyday normal things that I wanted to do. I went there, fell in love with it, and stayed twenty years without going back to mainland USA. I lived in Hawaii Kai on Oahu in Honolulu. In 1968, I started my own show room at the Outrigger Hotel and sang there in '68 and '69. I also did *Hawaii Five-O* in 1968.

While there, I had a line of clothes that I represented in Hawaii called 'Off Shore'. I also had the *Tommy Sands Nightclub Tour* that I took around to my show and different other shows like Don Ho's show. Before I settled in Hawaii, I got into drugs and got hooked, but I finally quit in 1969 when I went to a drug rehab center. In 1972-73 I attended the University of Hawaii and took all the basic courses including Biology, Math, Sociology, History, French and Advanced English. I didn't qualify in anything, as I quit before I got a degree.

In the mid-Eighties I left Hawaii and returned to live in California — apart from 1988 when I moved to Florida for one year. Since then, I have continued to tour and I still work Europe, Australia (over twenty times) and two weeks ago I played The Hop here in Los Angeles — it is the Righteous Brothers' club. I enjoy touring, the nostalgia and festival shows, and keeping *Teen-Age Crush* fresh. I have never thought of leaving the business completely, and if I hadn't remained in it I don't know what I would have done. Music is my life.

I have been married two times: to Nancy Sinatra, and then to Sheila Lou Wallace from 1974 until 1988. I have one daughter, Jessica, who is 26 years old. She's a wonderful singer and is in Japan right now for six months, singing at Universal Theme Park. Outside of showbusiness I like movies. The birth of my daughter is the high spot in my life. The lowest spot in my career and life was when I was about 29 and had to move to Hawaii for a rest.

I value my success and place in musical history. Very much. I have no preference for writing or recording anyone else's material. My own favorite singers are Elvis Presley, Nat 'King' Cole and Frank Sinatra. I do miss the old ways of recording and don't listen to today's music very much. If I could go back in time, I would stay with Colonel Tom Parker. For the future, I plan a tour of England, Germany and Australia for later this year. *The Singin' Idol* television play is my favorite over everything and the high spot of my career.

Danny and the Juniors featuring *Joe Terry*
The Class Act of Original American Rock & Roll

11

ROCK'N'ROLL IS HERE TO STAY
Joe Terranova / Danny & The Juniors

At The Hop by Danny & The Juniors is one of the great anthems of rock'n'roll. An international smash hit and million-seller in 1958, it topped the US pop charts for several weeks and reached No.3 in the UK. *Rock And Roll Is Here to Stay* and several lesser hits followed, but nothing could equal the majesty of their debut single, and by the time the Beatles appeared Danny & The Juniors were no longer chart contenders. Now led by original founder member Joe Terranova, the group still appears at nostalgia events all over the world.

I was born Joseph Terranova in Philadelphia on January 30, 1941. My father Joseph was a stainless-steel worker for the Budd Company, who built railcars and chassis for motors. Mother, Victoria, was a housewife. I have one sister, Joan. The family stayed in Philadelphia and I went to the John Bartram High School there, but left in January 1958, five months before the June graduation time. I was an average student, and History was my favorite subject. Had I not left high school early because of our hit, I probably would have gone on to Drexel University in Philadelphia to be an architect or a draughtsman.

I was six when I found out I could sing. My Uncle John would stand me on the bar at the neighborhood tap-room and let me sing so that he could get free drinks. I loved the applause.

From the age of eight, I played trumpet and was in the All Philadelphia orchestra for students. There wasn't really any other musical talent in our family, although Uncle Ricki could sing — but not professionally. As a kid, I used to like Louis Prima and those small combos with their little jazz influences, which were the forerunners of rock'n'roll. My family saw my interest in music as a passing whim and didn't want me to get too serious, as they wanted me to go to college and get an education.

When I was fourteen years old, I sang in a church choir and put my own group together — Joe Terry & The Terriers — in Wildwood, New Jersey, where our family summered when the weather became too hot in the city. Wildwood was the Las Vegas of the East, and all the best musicians came to Wildwood — people like Steve Gibson & The Redcaps and the Treniers. We performed at Wildwood Civic Center, people clapped us and we liked it. In the wintertime, we went back to the city, and there I met Frank Maffei who was with the Juvenairs. He persuaded me to join when one of the original members, Artie Scottise, left, so then it was Danny Rapp, Dave White, Frank Maffei and me.

As the Juvenairs we used to go to different dances and sing three or four songs, and Dave White's stepfather used to take us to clubs — people thought that we were cute. We followed this up by entering talent contests till we got discovered. Our rehearsals were carried out on street corners, in Dave's car and in men's rooms at school. Men's rooms were our favorite as the echo sounded real good. Danny Rapp, a baritone, was the lead vocalist; Dave White was first tenor and backing vocals; Frank Maffei was second tenor and baritone and backing vocals; and I was baritone and backing vocals.

Our musical tastes were pretty varied, but in rock'n'roll we liked the Four Preps and Frankie Lymon & The Teenagers: we modeled ourselves on Frankie Lymon & The Teenagers. We got noticed when we were rehearsing on a different street corner to our normal ones. A guy, Johnny Medora, was putting his baby to bed and told us to be quiet. Then he changed his mind and said: 'Wait a second, sing one more.' On the strength of that, Johnny Medora, who was a recording artist[*], was impressed and took us to see Artie Singer, a Philadelphia record producer and owner of Singular Records.

Dave White wrote a song called *Do The Bop* on his own, and Artie Singer and Johnny Medora added their names to the writer's credit. The rest of us liked the song, thought it was a real cool sound and felt it could be very popular. We recorded an acetate demo — probably as the Juvenairs — and it was played a couple of weeks later for Dick Clark, who suggested that the bop dance was on the way out and, as the kids went to record hops to dance, *At The Hop* would be a better title. About the same time, Artie pointed out that we should have a unique name and that it was usually the lead singer who got mentioned first. Everyone agreed, because we thought that Danny may not always be the lead singer and that Danny & The Juniors was simply the group name. Dave White was really the leader, and he was upset that it wasn't Dave & The Juniors, but concessions were made to reflect what was going on in the group at that time. It was still a four-way even split of income, so everything remained the same except Danny's name was up front.

So, a few weeks later, as Danny & The Juniors, we recorded *At The Hop* for Singular Records at Reco Art Studios, Market Street, Philadelphia. It was recorded on a single-track Ampex and we used Sure mikes. I recall that it was the lucky thirteenth take that we used, and the flip-side, *Sometimes*, written by Dave White, was done in one take. Artie Singer produced the records and Amel Corsin was the engineer. It was released in August '57 and, after our record was played by Dick Clark on his *American Bandstand* TV program, we got a decidedly favorable reaction.

The first time I heard our record played on the radio was pretty exciting. Dad and I were in a car going to the drugstore when we heard it on the radio. As I recall, this was a request show and you were invited to phone in if you liked the record. My dad went home and called in as six or seven different people — he was very funny.

---

[*] Medora recorded under the name Johnny Madara/Madera.

At The Hop was released in August '57, and in October ABC-Paramount picked up the master from Singular Records. They paid $5,000 upfront for it, which at that time was the most ever paid for a master — unprecedented. Danny & The Juniors remained signed to Artie Singer and Singular and he did his deal with ABC. Our parents had to sign legal documents for us, as we were under-age, and we got a lawyer in to safeguard our interests. As it turned out, he was also a trademark lawyer and he told us to trademark the group name. So, the four of us went ahead and trademarked 'Danny & The Juniors'; it was about the best thing we ever did. Artie Singer had no part in the group trademark, although he tried — in fact the original contract had Artie Singer owning the name. Our manager was a guy called Nat Segal, who we took on as soon as the record started to move up on the charts, not Artie Singer.

Bandstand was local in Philadelphia until August 1957, and then Dick's show went national. It became a one-and-a-half hour broadcast which included a half-hour national show. Dick used established hit artists for the national slot, and we got our big break with *At The Hop* when he called us to replace Little Anthony & The Imperials, who were unable to appear. This was November-December 1957 and reaction was strong, with people phoning in from all over the country. After this appearance, *At The Hop* entered the Top 100, and we were very excited and knew that we had a career, particularly Dave White and I, as we were more into music — Dave playing piano and me the trumpet — than the other two who weren't as musical. Another reason for the record's rapid rise was a deejay called the 'Hound Dog' in Buffalo, New York, who played the heck out of it on his show, which covered the East Coast all the way down to Miami.

The record went to the top very quickly in a matter of weeks. That year, we did Alan Freed's Christmas show at New York's Paramount Theatre and the record was No.1 in New York at Christmas. By early January, it was a national No.1 in the States. When it went to No.1, the feeling was tremendous, but when it's happening it's like being in a whirlpool. You are real busy, everything is moving very fast and you are sucked along. Everything was going so quick.

Right from the start Danny Rapp had a tough time of being 'Danny'.

Chapter 11 – Joe Terranova / Danny & The Juniors

Dave White would do the talking onstage as Danny couldn't do it, but felt it was expected of him. It was the source of a lot of friction. He wasn't really the leader, that was Dave White. Danny was a quiet guy with only an Eighth Grade education, because he never paid much attention at school and his parents didn't push him. A lot of the times in TV interviews, his lack of skills would come to the fore — like the occasion when an interviewer said: 'You are booked in Australia, how are you going to get there?' and Danny seriously replied: 'By car.' And *meant* it! In our early days, there were a few fights and arguments; a few bruised egos and problems — mainly Danny's — but nothing to break us up and we all got along fairly well.

To promote *At the Hop* we did the likes of the Patti Page and Pat Boone shows. Pat Boone's brother, Nick Todd, covered *At the Hop* and, in fact, Frank Maffei tactlessly mentioned it to Pat Boone, but Pat was cool and we exchanged Christmas cards for years. We never did Ed Sullivan's show, as he cancelled all his rock'n'roll acts after a rock'n'roll riot occurred in Boston. After ten days at the Paramount Theatre Christmas show for Alan Freed, we then went out on tour for Irvin Feld, the big circus promoter, in his *Biggest Show Of Stars*. Headlining was Chuck Berry, and the other acts included: Paul Anka, the Everly Brothers, the Hollywood Flames and Margie Rayburn. Harold Cromer was the MC, and we used the Buddy Morrow Band. There was a tremendous camaraderie on these tours — like being in the services. One tour was for 44 days with Buddy Holly & The Crickets. Buddy didn't ride the bus, but the Crickets did. After that, we didn't see them again for thirty years, and when we did it was just like the party had never ended.

The tours were so much fun. Paul Anka and I used to double-date and go park in the girls' car as we didn't have one. I did the same with Glen Campbell when he toured with the Champs.

We were on one tour with Connie Francis and Dickie Doo & The Don'ts, and eight of us — four boys and four girls — went to the beach. Coming back at 2:00 am, I started to weave the car for a bit of fun. Anyway, a cop got us and locked us up. There was hell on, because the families had to come and get their daughters from the police station. We managed to keep it out of the papers, where it was heading: in those days you could have a friendly word with journalists — unlike today. Most times, however, we were smart and didn't get into trouble.

I learned how to shoot craps and jazz techniques and harmony from the band members — neat. There were tons of women everywhere we went, and that was the main thrust, I guess — that was the

134

Danny & The Juniors in *Let's Rock*, 1958.

fun. That and seeing the country we were born in. My first trip down in the South of the US was on tour and I saw segregation for the first time. At bus stops, they let off blacks to a different hotel; there were different water taps and different bathrooms. I didn't like what I saw. As artists, we had been thrown in without learning, so these tours were a great, great learning experience. My own favorite artist at that time was Bobby Darin — I was a big fan. I thought he was a consummate artist and loved his work, also Little Anthony, but, really, I like 'em all.

How did we deal with being celebrities at that age? Well, we were tough street kids from Philly. There was some booze, but not much in the way of drugs, thank God. The girls were great and always there — one of the perks of the job. *[laughs]* They'd rip your clothes off if they could catch you! We had a good road manager called Jerry Blavat, who wasn't much older than us, but handled us pretty good and set times for us to be in by. Jerry only gave us a certain amount of spending money and could handle any bother that we got into. I came from a very nice family who were respectful of people and, with that upbringing and Jerry, we kept out of trouble.

We were too busy to take stock of the effect this success was having on our private lives. In showbusiness, personal relationships take a back seat: there wasn't even time for a girlfriend. It's not easy to be married or have a girlfriend as you're away such a lot and this poses a lot of problems. Moneywise, we were looked after properly. Jerry would collect our money from the promoter and give it to Nat Segal. Then, it went to my mother, who looked after the group's business. She got the calls from the manager, then called all the other families, kept the tax records and generally looked after all of our wellbeing. She fought for our royalties, found us our first lawyer and, I would think — and I'm sure the other members would agree — we would have never seen a penny if it wasn't for mom.

ABC knew that we needed something similar for the follow-up record, and we had other songs. We had come off the 44-day tour, and the press had not been nice at all to the rock'n'roll acts and not kind to the music as a whole. Dave and I were telling my dad about this after dinner and dad pointed out the Little Richard song line *'rock'n'roll is here to stay'* and suggested we reply to these critics. So Dave said: 'What a good idea,' went home and wrote *Rock And Roll Is Here To Stay*. We had the first protest record!

ABC didn't assign an A&R man to us. Artie Singer was really in charge of our recordings so ABC left it up to him, and I guess that's what happened to our career. I wish that they *had* assigned somebody. *Dottie,* our third hit, was written by Artie Singer and John Medora, who obviously thought that it was a good idea to market their own songs. I never knew who *Dottie* was named after. In 1958 we were the biggest group, but other artists were more lucky because they had more choice over material. Ours was a sparkling success. If they had left Dave White alone, we could have had a long string of hits and that's where they stymied us.

Our lack of hits, and needing a change, led to our move from ABC to Swan in 1960. Really, we needed to leave Artie Singer. Our manager, Nat Segal, found the deal with Swan and negotiated the move, and at the same time Artie Singer released us from our contract with him. It wasn't amicable, but there was nothing he could do. We had recorded everything we had to in 1960 and then refused to do any more, so Artie told us we may as well go. We got *one* gold record between the four of us from ABC for *At The Hop*, but Artie Singer had it and somehow it disappeared.

We had a hit with *Twistin' USA* on Swan in 1960, and again with *Pony Express* in 1961. At the end of '61, we put out *Back To The Hop* — that was my idea! It was written by Dave and me and made the Hot 100. Dave White left the group in 1961, simply because he could make more money as a producer. He went into a production company with Johnny Medora: they wrote *You Don't Own Me* for Lesley Gore, *The Fly* for Chubby Checker and *1-2-3* for Len Barry. I think it came about because Johnny had a group called Carl & The Commanders, and Dave wrote material for them and gradually got into production. We never replaced Dave and continued as a trio.

In January 1962, we had a hit with *Twistin' All Night Long* with Freddy Cannon — a very nice guy, and the Four Seasons, who were then the Four Lovers, sang backing vocals. *Doin' The Continental Walk* was a hit for us in April of the same year. After that, we switched to Philadelphia's Guyden Records in 1963 and had a final hit with *Oo-La-La-Limbo*. Following that, the three of us — me, Frank and Danny — went on the road until 1966. In 1967, we had a remake on Lub Records with *Sometimes* b/w *Rock And Roll Is Here To Stay*, but it didn't do anything.

We did get sick of all our records being linked to dance hits, but that's the way we were perceived as artists by record label producers, who thought our records had to have that rockin' beat and wanted us to do *At The Hop* sideways. We did produce fresh material but it never got a chance. We even tried using different names with our fresh material: *'Together You And I'* by Joe Terry & Mystery *[Rollercoaster CD]*.

In the beginning we got paid our royalties, but had to fight for them with Singular. ABC paid Artie, but he didn't pay us. We sued Artie in 1981, after auditing his books, and got our money. Swan, who were notorious for not paying, didn't pay, but before we could sue they went bankrupt. Guyden paid very little.

Danny & The Juniors left the business in 1966. Danny drove a cab and worked in a toy store, and I went into record production with Frank Maffei. We produced five or six records, but nothing big. One of our records, *Oh Gee* by Anthony & The Sophomores was No.1 in five or six US cities. By 1969, we needed the money and had to go back on the road, and the revival circuit, and have been there ever since. There were three original members — Danny, Frank and I — for a few months until later in 1969, when Frank decided to leave because he didn't want to travel. Then we got Jimmy Testa from the Fabulous Four (the 'Four J's' at first). He stayed one and a half years. Bill Carlucci, from Billy & The Essentials, joined us in 1971-72 and stayed for seventeen years before returning to his earlier group.

Danny Rapp first left the group in 1975 and went out as 'Danny', and the rest of us worked as 'The Juniors'. When Danny left in 1975, Bill Carlucci and I worked as a duo for eight months before we were rejoined by Frank Maffei in September of the same year. We were fine as the Juniors, but after six months Danny decided to use the whole name as he was having a tough time getting work and so did we. He was back briefly with us in 1978-79, but was divorced by then and having a lot of alcohol problems. In 1980, he left the group for good. Over the years, the group members kept in touch from time to time. We saw Danny once in a while, but he was quiet and a loner. Showbusiness attracts extroverts and also people like Danny who are shy, but can have the outgoing personality they want when they go onstage. Sadly, Danny killed himself in 1983. Why? That's a good question. He was still performing at the time with a splinter group of a lounge band and girl singer doing the Holiday Inn circuit.

In 1975, I worked with Shirley Alston — formerly of the Shirelles — on *Sincerely*, a track from her album *'With A Little Help From My Friends'*. Her manager, Randy Irwin, and I were close and he invited us. It was a lot of fun to do. I don't know what the catalyst was for the success of our 1976 re-release of *At The Hop* and the subsequent career boost, but we got paid and finally got to Europe. Nat Segal received an offer for us to tour there in 1958, but Danny Rapp would never fly.

We never really had a problem from promoters who were reluctant to book Danny & The Juniors with no Danny in the line-up, as it was the group name and we always qualified the group members. It only happened once or twice where promoters said: 'We're not going to use you as you haven't got a 'Danny'.' About five years ago, Frank Maffei and I went to Washington to persuade Congress to pass a bill about the copyright of names and 'watering down the name', but we stopped our action as it was being misunderstood. Now the legal principle seems to be emerging that 'the continuing entity will retain copyright'. Today, Danny & The Juniors are Frank Maffei, his brother Bob and me.

Lack of success — that's the hard part. Sometimes you cope, sometimes you don't, and it still bothers us. You want your success to go on. Most have a limited success period and you hope that gives you longevity, and in that way we've been very lucky. We'd still like to have some more hits, but we have a great fan base which allows us to go out, work and develop our craft. It's a fun way of making a living and, as I am still interested in history and architecture, a good job for me as I can get around the world and see everything.

Do we value our place in pop music history? Absolutely! We are so lucky and so fortunate and do one hundred dates a year. Fifties' music fans are the best: fervent about the music and the time, and really nice people. I love our audiences. They range from eight to eighty, which gives us a lot of flexibility. It's really nice to know that most folks like *At The Hop* and Danny & The Juniors. It's a nice accomplishment to know you've spanned those generations.

With the revival and nostalgia circuit, the whole deal is that the public pay the money and you give them what they've come for — which is an emotional experience. You create an emotional magic, but it's not one-sided: it's a nice evening of give and take. I think that artists who please themselves do themselves a disservice, as they don't get that feedback from their audience. This 'give and take', and individual audience reaction, are what keeps *At The Hop* fresh. How you perform depends on the audience, and the 'give and take' refreshes you.

On the personal side of my life, I was married to Joyce for forty years, but we are now separated and getting a divorce. There are three children, two sons and a daughter, and five grandchildren. My youngest son, Ray, was a deejay and karaoke host.

There are two real high spots in my career. First, when USA schools, in conjunction with the RIAA, announced one hundred of the top songs of all time to be taught in schools and *At The Hop* was one of them. That was very, very exciting. The second one is when we worked the Catskills, where the audiences have seen everybody, and we got double and triple ovations. That's really a career high spot. In my private life, the highest spot is probably the birth of my children.

The lowest spot in my career was the first day I realized that we weren't on the radio or in the charts anymore. Panic! Also, somewhere in the Sixties, when we stopped for a while and I was trying to figure out how to jump-start it again. While you're figuring it out, that's a low spot. In my personal life, separating from my wife after forty years is positively the lowest.

Today, the music industry is in sad array and not making money. Back then music was controlled by producers, but they did listen to what kids were listening to and dancing to, and try to write something similar. Today they don't do that. They go write something and say: 'This is what you want, it is the latest thing.' I feel bad for the generation of kids getting some stuff thrown at them and not getting the chance to listen to good music that they might enjoy better. Somewhere along the line they have to go back and put some integrity into it, and when they do they'll make some money.

What would I like to have written or recorded? Well, I got to meet Perry Como and I loved his record of *It's Impossible*, and it would be very nice to have a record like that to close out your career. Jesus, that would be nice to have. I also liked Dean Martin's soft-and-easy singing and his *Innamorata*. I'll tell you a great story about Perry. In 1985, we were taking part in the *Rocky Mountain Italian Golf Tournament* in Denver, Colorado, as was Perry Como. Perry finished early and came over to our table and said: 'Hi! I never met you guys, I'm Perry Como. They're a bunch of old people up here. Us young folks should go downstairs and sing around the piano.' And we did — for two hours! Perry was singing rock'n'roll with us backing him, and then we sang and he backed us. We were ecstatic.

If I could go back and change anything, I'd like for us to have been better prepared and educated about our business before our early success. It was a bit scary because we weren't really ready. You needed the experience of the clubs to build it up, just like a college education is necessary for a corporate career. Also, we should have parted with Artie Singer earlier and demanded that they put out our stuff, which was more viable for the market. But, even with all the 'downs', it's been a great ride, because the 'ups' have been so great. We were there when rock'n'roll broke, and in that thrust which shook the States and the rest of the world: it was a brand new music. In 1988-89, Chicago University did a rock'n'roll survey, using *At The Hop* and *Rock And Roll Is Here To Stay* as yardsticks to project future tastes, and concluded that those records would still be played by the year 2030.

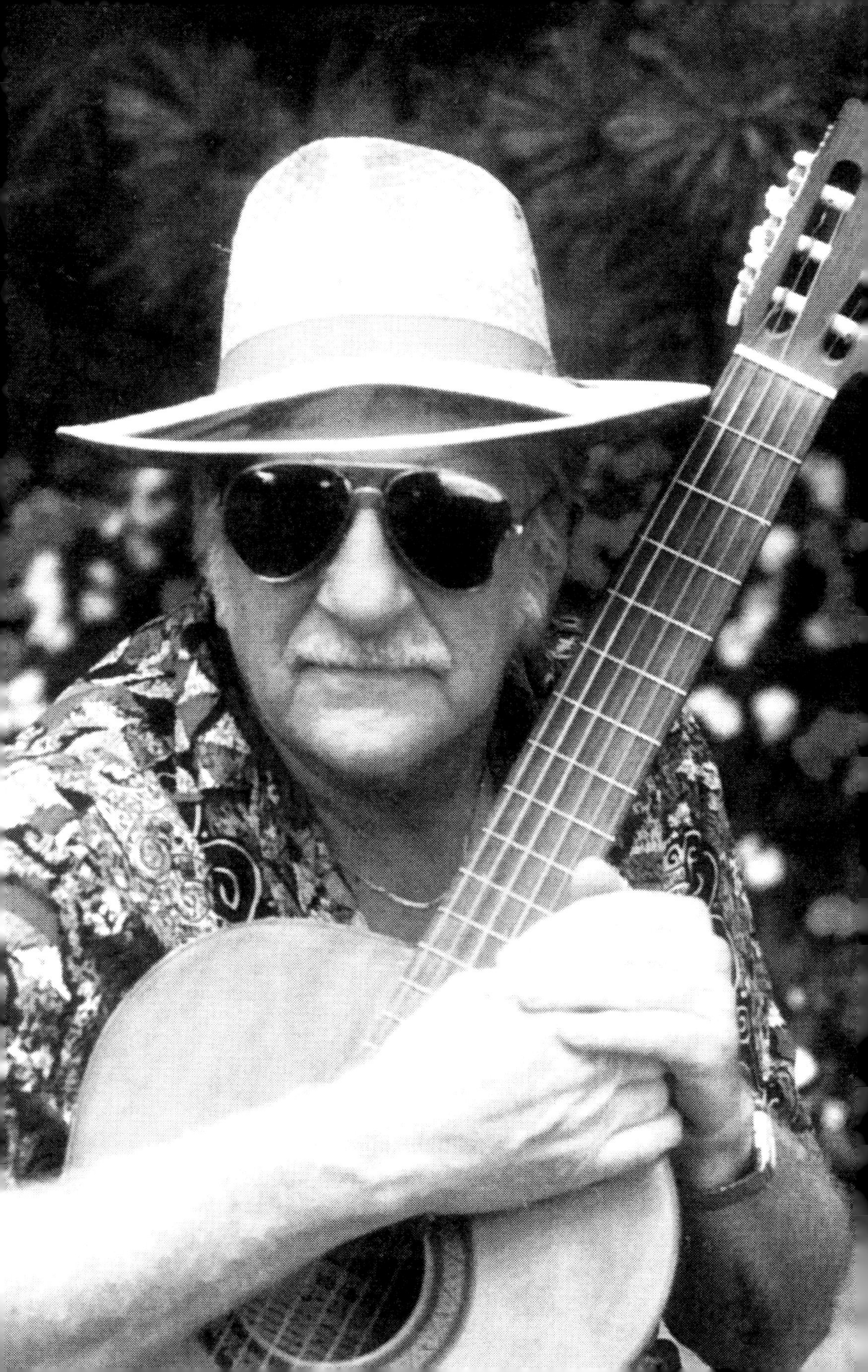

12

GREEN LIGHT, RED LIGHT
Mitchell Torok

College student Mitchell Torok shot to fame in 1953 when Jim Reeves' recording of his composition, *Mexican Joe*, went to No.1 on the *Billboard* C&W chart and was subsequently voted 'Country & Western Song of the Year' by *Cash Box* magazine. Within months, he'd also become a chart-topper in his own right with the self-penned *Caribbean*. He broke through in the UK in 1956 with the quirky *When Mexico Gave Up The Rhumba* — a Top Ten hit — and *Red Light, Green Light* but, starved of the successful career management and record company direction enjoyed by many lesser talents, quickly disappeared from view. A Fine Arts graduate, gifted painter and successful songwriter, he is still performing today.

I was born Mitchell Joseph Torok in Houston, Texas, on October 28, 1929. My musical talent apparently came from my father, Nick, who came from Hungary in the very early 1900s. He joined the army and learned to play all the brass instruments in the army band. His commander was the famous American general, John J. 'Blackjack' Pershing. My father fought in Mexico, France and the Philippines and became a first class musician in the army band. Mother's name is Irene, and they both came over from Hungary at different times, though they did know each other over there. Nick came over first, and then my mother's older sister and her father were already in Chicago and her father sent my mother the ticket for the boat trip. They both came through Ellis Island under strict rules and regulations, not like the illegals who come here today. They were both thrilled when they saw the Statue Of Liberty as they came to America to escape the harsh regime back home. My dad and mother both loved America, and had two sons, me and my brother Bill, who is older than me.

After my father served seven years in the United States Army and became a first class musician on his own, he got a job building railroad box cars in Gary, Indiana. Then he and my mother married near Chicago, where my mother's older sister, Helen, and their father lived. He then applied to become a postmaster in Wisconsin, but my mother couldn't take the cold winters and they moved to Florida, where they had five acres and were intent on building a house there. But a giant hurricane came and washed away much of the area in the early 1920s, so they left the land and moved to

Chapter 12 – Mitchell Torok

Houston, Texas, where I was eventually born in a clinic in Harrisburg on the outskirts of Houston, across from the famous Brown & Root Engineering Company. The land they left in Florida was in Orlando and right where Disney is today — how's that for a break? As an heir to that land, I could be emailing you this from the Bahamas!

My schooling started at Aldine Elementary on the outskirts of Houston; then John H. Reagan High School; then Wharton Junior College in Wharton, Texas, to 1950, and finished when I graduated at the Stephen F. Austin State College in Nacogdoches in June of 1953 with a degree in Fine Arts. Nacogdoches, which is 140 miles north of Houston, is the oldest town in Texas developed by famous early pioneer Stephen F. Austin, who helped develop the famous port of Galveston, Texas, which was destroyed by a hurricane in 1900 that killed six thousand people. At school, my grades were B's and C's and my favorite subject was History. I made one 'F' in high school and that was in Geometry, but I brought it up within the next six weeks. Texas History, American History and World History were my main interests, along with sports — American football and baseball, mainly.

We moved several times, but all in the Houston area: Aldine, Park Place, and finally Pasadena, Texas, where my mother and father both passed away some years back. My brother, Bill, is a fine guy. He graduated from Reagan High School before me, in 1941, and that's why I wanted to go there. He always helped me and pushed me along in everything. In the 1940s, out at Aldine, about twenty miles north of Houston, we both loved football. So he went to Aldine High School to the football coach and talked him into loaning him a complete football suit: pants, shoulder pads, jersey, old helmet and shoes that were too big. We had two acres, and we went out to the acre next door and I put on the outfit. The shoes were flopping around and we didn't have a ball. But Bill went inside, got a pair of jeans, rolled them up real tight and neat, tightened a belt around it, and that was our ball. And to tell you the truth, those were the good old days. He threw me that jean ball all afternoon, and I thought I was in the American Super Bowl. Later on, he helped me finance my first Martin guitar in Houston also. I remember it was a medium-size Martin guitar, too. It cost $65, and I paid out a little each week and that kinda got me started.

I had a good family life growing up. My mother's 'profession' was taking care of her family, which she did with a lot of kind advice and a lot of love — in the European Hungarian way — lots of chicken soup, paprikas chicken, pig-in-the-blankets and all kinds of Hungarian pastries. I miss 'em today. I'd come home from school and the house was always warm, with the smell of apples and oranges, which always seemed to be on the dining room table. My dad, being from the old country, always made white wine. We always had a gallon or two kept out of sight under the sink cabinet in the kitchen, and we always had a little wine. Did you know that it is the custom in Hungary to offer wine to any guest that comes into your house? But if it happened to be a *special* friend or guest, you would go and get your special home-made wine for them. What a friendly gesture.

My dad's profession in the greatest part of the last half of his life was working with wood as a carpenter, construction worker, home-builder and

Chapter 12 – Mitchell Torok

repairman. I worked with him, finishing trim-work in houses. We were working one summer, in 1948, out near the Houston Airport, when the great American baseball star Babe Ruth was coming in on a plane. We were working right across the street, and my dad let me go over there and join some three hundred people waiting for the plane to see 'The Babe' as he was called. He was in ill health, but he did come to the door, take off his cap and wave to all of us. He looked old and sick, and died a short time later, but I did get to see this gigantic hero.

My musical idol was Eddy Arnold, some Hank Snow, and of course Hank Williams — all of whom I heard on the radio. I began to play guitar at about ten years of age, when my older brother Bill brought home a big ol' brown guitar that cost him $5 and we both played around on it. He also brought some Jimmie Rodgers 78s and a songbook or two with Jimmie Rodgers songs in 'em. I learned to play *Waiting For A Train*, *Daddy And Home*. My family encouraged me, and my talent was first noticed at Aldine Elementary School, when I played songs in the classrooms in the second and third grades. I learnt to read music. Then, in high school, around 1948, I had my own little band called the Local Yokels in Houston. During 1948 I also served in the US Reserve of the Army National Guard. In 1950, there was another group, the Tex Sons, when I was on KFRD Radio in Rosenberg, Texas. In college, I was always a big hit with my guitar.

I had a radio show on three different radio stations at different times while attending college. One time in Rosenberg, Texas, the owner of Fort Bend Country Records, Mr. Schultz, heard me and my two-piece band on Station KFRD, there in the town, and cut my first two records with me and the Tex Sons: *Nacogdoches County Line* and *Piney Woods Boogie*. They are collectors' items today. The records played and sold a little up around the

Chapter 12 – Mitchell Torok

college. A promoter, Jimmy Franklin, got me some deals and I wrote a song for Conoco Oil celebrating their 50th anniversary, and then I cut some sides for him by myself and with a girl singer, Sally Lee. That was around 1950-51, a couple of years before *Mexican Joe*. After *Mexican Joe* and *Caribbean* hit, I think Franklin leased those masters to Imperial Records.

I married in 1951 to Gail Ramona Redd, who was my co-writer also. Ramona didn't do much singing except demos for female singers. And, in the same year, I won a talent contest on KTRE Radio out of Lufkin, Texas. I also spoke to some people who owned Macy Records around this time, in 1952, who expressed interest in me, but we never got together. Jim Reeves also came to Houston and cut some sides for them during this time, though we never met and our paths never crossed. We could have been on the same label at the same time, and who would have gotten *Mexican Joe?* — Interesting.

I played a quarterback on the football team and wrote *Mexican Joe* in the spring of 1953, while attending college and heading for my degree in Fine Arts in June of that year. In 1953, Fabor Robison, a record producer, came from California on a talent scouting trip sponsored by American Music Inc, and Tom Perryman suggested to him to go to Nacogdoches, where Stephen F. Austin College was located, to see if there was any talent among the kids there.

Fabor went to Mr. and Mrs. Johnson's record shop on the square in the town and asked if they knew of anyone who sang or wrote songs etc. I had a radio show at the time at 7:15 in the morning on KSFA Radio, and they knew all about me from football, playing and singing. They called for me out on campus and I went down to Stripling's Drug Store on the square to meet him.

I had written *Mexican Joe* about three weeks earlier and had tried to have the radio stations in the area help me to tape a demo with guitar to send to Hank Snow in Nashville. I offered four different engineers half-interest in the song if they would help me make this tape, and they were all too busy at the time! So, I went back home to college, and that's when Fabor appeared. We went out to the house. I played him *Mexican Joe.* He liked it. He had Jim Reeves over in Shreveport; he cut the record; he promoted the record, and there I was, No.1! Incidentally, Jim didn't want to record it. His wife, Mary, talked him into it. I have no regrets about giving Fabor the song. I was happy to have anyone cut it at the time. I think it was destined to have Fabor involved with it, and Jim too. It's all too unreal, really.

Tom Perryman knew Jim Reeves in East Texas, where they both played records on two different stations: Jim at Henderson and Tom at Gladewater. Tom set up the audition at the Reo Palm Isle Club in Gladewater for him to sing for Fabor, who signed him. Then, Tom moved to Murfreesboro when Jim hit, and they owned a radio station together in that town twenty miles outside Nashville. They did some other things together. Tom's wife, Billie, and Jim's wife, Mary, were good friends and played a lot of golf together. Tom is currently in Tyler, Texas, playing oldie records on a station there, and I understand the station is doing real well.

It was a wonderful year, 1953. As I was graduating, I had the No.1 country music song in America and followed that with my own No.1 recording of *Caribbean,* which I sat down and wrote in thirty minutes one cold January evening. I've always had a sense of humor, and the song just poured out and I have no idea about why. I always loved Hank Snow's Latin rhythms, like *Rhumba Boogie,* and I was into world history good in high school and college, and Columbus seemed like a natural to insert. The main thing people remembered of the song was the line *'The wide-eyed monkey on the limb'.* *Caribbean* was issued on Fabor Robison's Abbott Records label. There were no other record companies between Fort Bend Country Records and Abbott. *Caribbean* hit in September-October of 1953, and in the same year I joined the *Louisiana Hayride,* which is where I met Johnny Horton. I made my professional debut in 1954, when I headlined on Slim Willett's Saturday show, *The Midwest Texas Jubilee,* in Lubbock, Texas, and his band backed me. Slim wrote *Don't Let The Stars Get In Your Eyes.*

In late 1954 or '55, I was still living in Nacogdoches, Texas. I knew it would take management to continue my career, so I picked up the phone and called through to Colonel Tom Parker at his office in Madison, Tennessee. I bluntly told him who I was — he knew about me —

Chapter 12 – Mitchell Torok

and I asked him to manage me. He said he would love to, but he was managing Eddy Arnold and Hank Snow at the time, and wouldn't have time to do me right. He was very nice, and I thanked him for his time and hung up. He later picked up Elvis, and he and Hank Snow owned him together. It wasn't long before Parker talked Snow into selling him his share and, as they say, the rest is history. Later, on the *Louisiana Hayride*, I had a couple of people wanting to represent me, but I knew they couldn't do any more than I could do for myself concerning PR and bookings etc. So, I didn't sign any long-term thing with them. The only bill I played with Elvis was when he came to the *Louisiana Hayride* and I was there. He tore the place up and no-one wanted to go on after him. He liked my wife, Ramona, and held my oldest daughter, Michelle, backstage.

Fabor called one day in 1955 and said: 'I'm not gonna record any more of them damn Sylvester Cross songs.' I said: 'Hey, you signed me to American Music for five years and you're my producer, what the hell is this?' He said that he had a publishing company — Dandelion — and he would find me some songs. I said: 'I'm hot right now as a writer, and you want me to stop writing and record someone else's songs? You're stabbing everything we have built in the back with your greed, you sonofabitch; give me a release.' So, he called in a few days and said he had talked to Paul Cohen and Owen Bradley of Decca Records in Nashville, and they would be happy to have me. So, I went to

Nashville, signed with Decca in the old Andrew Jackson Hotel with Cohen and Bradley, and signed with BMI at the same time. When Fabor Robison dropped out, the Abbott Record airplay stopped.

There was no audition for Decca and they recorded my first session with all the 'A' Team pickers: Floyd Cramer, Grady Martin, Bob Moore, Buddy Harman, Harold Bradley, the Anita Kerr Singers, the Jordanaires, etc. You ready for this? On the stage of the empty Ryman Auditorium on a Sunday morning, they were trying to compete with and capture the bright sound Fabor had developed on his recordings! He had turned the c&w business on its ear with this particularly high-trebled and echoed sound. In fact, that's the first question they asked me in the hotel when I signed and we toasted with a drink: 'Mitchell, can you tell us how Fabor gets that bright sound on his records?' So, I lived and experienced that happening to prove what Fabor had done. He's not praised in any way in the business. He did a lot, but he was hard to work for and became greedy. Fabor claimed to everyone that *Mexican Joe* had generated four million dollars-worth of business.

My first record for Decca was *Roulette* in 1955. Owen Bradley did all of my Decca recordings, with Paul Cohen sitting in occasionally. Sometimes they leaned on me and forced a New York song, like *Red Light, Green Light* or *No Money Down*, on me. I needed to stay with the Latin things — which is what I had going for me — and some writers claim I was the king of ethnic songs in the early stages, with writing about all the different places in the world for my records: Mexico, China, Hawaii, the Caribbean, France, etc. To promote my records, I appeared on Dick Clark's *Bandstand* several times and local TV shows across the country.

After *When Mexico Gave Up The Rhumba* hit overseas, I was flying on American Airlines from Dallas to New York to London, over Central America at 3,500 feet, and I asked the stewardess for some notepad and a pen, and I proceeded to write a detailed letter to Dub Albritten, manager for Brenda Lee at the time. I told him about my *Mexican Joe* and *Caribbean*, and the hit overseas; that I was headed for this big tour; and that I had a hit, *Pledge Of Love,* in the can for Decca coming out when I got back. When I returned to the US, I called him about my letter and request for management. He also said that he wouldn't have time to devote to me, and that he was filled up with work on behalf of Brenda Lee. So, I tried the two top managers of the time and couldn't connect with either! Not having good management was a negative at the time and probably led to the bad situations which I later found myself in.

Pledge Of Love was written by my wife, Ramona. I recorded a demo in Dallas, felt like it was a hit, called Paul Cohen — the Decca A&R man in New York — played it for him over the phone on a Sunday night and told him that I thought I had one, meaning a hit. Right away he said: 'Well, guy, it sounds good, but we better come to Nashville and cut it over in the good studio.' 'Good' studio?!?!? They barely had an echo chamber in Bradley's Studio at the time! It was a room plastered on the wall for sound bounce, with a stool and a speaker on it, with the master mike in front of the speaker. That's a piece of info you didn't know, I'll bet! So, the demo master was held by the publisher Joe Leonard of Lin Music in Gainesville, Texas, who paid for

Chapter 12 – Mitchell Torok

four demos in return. He also had a label.

I fly off overseas, and my wife is in Dallas. While I'm gone, this Leonard fella is calling Paul Cohen in New York, pressing him to release the Nashville cut I did for Decca. I understand that he bugged Cohen over and over, and threatened to release the Dallas cut while I'm signed to Decca. Lo and behold, an eighteen year old kid named Ken Copeland walks into Leonard's office, I'm told, and asks if he can cut a record for his label and put one out, so he can get into Special Service — 'cause he was being drafted! Leonard goes: 'Hhhmmmm... let me see if I have something here for you young man,' and he pulls out the demo of *Pledge Of Love* with me on the vocals and says: 'Can you sing in this key?' Copeland mumbles around a bit, and they decide to wipe my voice off the three-track and put Copeland on there. My cut is sitting in New York waiting for release. Leonard masters the demo tape with Copeland on it, presses a few, takes it to a rock station in Fort Worth, Texas. They put it on the air and the phone falls off the hook! Keep in mind this is the *same* cut I played for Cohen and he demanded I re-cut it in Nashville — naturally 'cause he had a piece of the Bradley Studio action — get it?

Now, Copeland's record is kicking up dust in Dallas and Fort Worth. My wife learns about it and calls Cohen. They rush my cut out — second. Now there's ads in *Billboard* mag saying he's first, I'm first, etc. Leonard leases the master to Lew Chudd at Imperial, and here we go up the charts. Last I heard, Copeland was No.8 and I was No.10 in the *Billboard* pop charts in April of 1957. So, he perhaps ruined my chance for a No.5 — or better — pop record, if there had been only my record. That brings me round to my career again: I sold as much in the pop market as in the country. And, as I look back, someone should have made more of a pop star out of me, with supper clubs, concerts, etc... who knows now?

When I wrote *When Mexico Gave Up The Rhumba (To Do The Rock And Roll)*, 'Gale Jones' was a fake name we used to write the song because I was still tied to American Music. I wrote it mostly in the same manner as *Caribbean* — it's the same type of song. I came to record it because I knew it was a good song and a clever piece of material — the kind I like. I cut it and arranged it with Grady Martin, who was the backbone of the Nashville Sound and most of the early hits that came out here. He and Shot Jackson played the fiddles on the record, and the sudden ending came about from the three of us. We all liked it: it was unusual. *When Mexico Gave Up The Rhumba* was recorded in 1956 in

Chapter 12 – Mitchell Torok

Nashville at the Bradley Studios. It took two takes. It didn't make the US charts and did nothing over here — and it wasn't a hit in Mexico. I can't understand to this day why the British market went for the record. So, what would you call it? Any song becomes a hit with repeated radio airplay.

When Mexico Gave Up The Rhumba was a Top Ten hit for me in the UK in 1956, and as a result I arrived in London in February 1957 for a four-month tour. I remember Slim Whitman and his band, Hoot (steel guitar) and Curley (guitar), had their bags and guitar cases in the middle of the Dorchester Hotel lobby when I arrived to check in. We shook hands, and I registered and went upstairs to my room with Phil Solomon and the gang in big overcoats flopping along behind. I got checked in and we went to meet Tex Bromley, my conductor, and get on with the business at hand. In London, I appeared on the *Sunday Night At The London Palladium* TV show on February 17,1957. It was exciting to be at the Palladium, as I had heard so much about it beforehand. The following evening, I opened for two weeks at the Prince of Wales Theatre. After that, I toured UK theaters, some of which were very big and charming, until the end of May. On Sundays I was booked to play in Ireland as well, I remember. Two of the variety weeks were played at Edinburgh and Glasgow. Someone said: 'That's the Firth of Forth,' and I was humored by that. Everyone was nice, and I enjoyed those famous old vaudeville houses.

I used to watch the supporting acts, and was fascinated that these were old-time vaudeville acts that would probably be on their last time around in 1957. Of course, the tour over there was different with the pit orchestra and a music director; over here in the US it was a mess. Dickie Henderson was big at the time, and Shirley Bassey closed the first half at some of my shows. When we met, she kissed me backstage, and it was the first and only time I've been kissed by a black woman, star or singer, etc. At 27, from the USA for the first time, she did catch me off guard! I just went out and did my show the best I could and tried to be professional. Everything had written arrangements. It was the first time I sang with a pit orchestra, and I never missed a beat for the four months. I was not aware of any promotional help from Decca/Brunswick while I was in the UK.

A few reviews that I saw for that UK tour were mixed. I know it wasn't all roses — fourteen weeks was a long time. The only advice I asked for and received was from the promoter, Phil Solomon, and whoever else was with him, regarding the British public. They seemed to think what I had planned would work okay, and I was told by Phil that the tour was a success. I was paid $850 dollars a week for the tour, with some expenses paid. I've had a few feelers during the passing years, but never made it back.

My follow up record in the US was *True Love,* and in the UK I think it was *Red Light, Green Light* — a stupid rock'n'roll release written by some New York guys. I'm the type of guy who doesn't worry about the chart successes, because I had my art degree to work with and I painted all through the music successes anyway. I wasn't stupid enough to keep on trying for chart stuff after I saw the changes. Elvis almost destroyed the music scene in 1954.

Caribbean hit for the second time in 1959 or '60. I was on Decca

Chapter 12 – Mitchell Torok

Scotland, 1957.

when *Caribbean* showed up in the pop charts for the second time. It was the same master that hit before, and I'm told that it was one of the first times that had happened in the record business — it could have been the first. Anyway, I was in the state of Oklahoma promoting my latest Decca record, *The PTA Rock And Roll*, when I went into a distributor's office to meet him and thank him for his promo help on *PTA*. He showed a *Billboard* magazine in front of me on the front desk and said: 'How does it feel for *Caribbean* to be hitting again?' I said: 'Duh?' and then 'Huh?'

I looked at the *Billboard*, and there it was with a bullet on Jamie/Guyden Records. This had come about because Fabor Robison sold some masters and his music publishing to Jamie/Guyden.

My contract with Decca was about up, so I said: 'Hey, what do you want to do?' They gave me six months' extension on my contract and I did my last session for them in 1959. Who knows if I got my full royalties from Decca? I doubt it. When I came to Nashville, they say Charley Pride sued RCA for back royalties and found $800,000. They said they couldn't pay out to all the artists, or they'd have to go out of business — so that gives you some idea of what goes on, or went on. I guess it's different now, with all the managers and attorneys, etc.

I signed with Jamie/Guyden, got a $2,500 advance to let them have publishing on the new songs, and recorded some stuff for them at Bradley's Studio and one album with Fabor Robison out in California at Western Recorders. They were looking for the old magic, but it wasn't there. The album titled *'Caribbean'* is a mish-mash of stuff and is out of print. Jamie/Guyden lasted about a year and only *Pink Chiffon* got into the pop charts again. A lot of my stuff got into the pop charts back then, and I probably should have been promoted that way, and not country. Did I get paid properly by Jamie/Guyden? Probably not.

Very few people know of this detail of my career. Tillman Franks handled me for a few months after Johnny Horton was killed in 1960. He brought me to Nashville to record for Mercury Records and new A&R person Shelby Singleton. Shelby was working for Mercury in Chicago, and they wanted Damita Jo to cover *Save The Last Dance For Me*. They had no producer there, so they had Shelby produce it and it sold over 600,000 records, I learnt. So, they sent him to Nashville with a budget to cut some sides for Mercury. I was one of them, through Tillman. I recorded three sides, and one of them was a supposed movie song, *Comancheros*. Mercury released the first two songs as my first single — and it turned out to be my *only* single! Ya see, unknown to me, Tillman was also working with Claude King in Shreveport. Lo and behold, about three months after my session, I'm in Dallas listening to country music and hears Claude King's new record called *Comancheros*! I was on the phone immediately to both Shelby and Tillman, told them what I thought of them using my cut of the song as a demo, asked for my release from Mercury and kissed Tillman goodbye. Some artists I know would have killed both of them. What would you have done?

My last official long tour was a Johnny Cash tour in 1962. I never got paid enough to carry my own band. The headliner's band always backed the other acts on the shows: ie Hank Snow's band, Ernest Tubb's band, Carl

Chapter 12 – Mitchell Torok

Smith's band, etc. They were supposed to give you rehearsal time for the show, for which they were paid extra, but they were fairly arrogant and not desirous of helping the entire show along to be the best it could be. They usually sloughed us off and we did with very little rehearsal, sometimes just talking about the songs and telling them the chords backstage. For example: 'Okay fellas, when I do *Caribbean*, I start in C and then it goes to F and G7, and the bridge stays in C for a while, and then changes to the same two other chords — just follow my guitar.' *Mexican Joe* was handled the same way.

And if you had some new stuff, or cuts by a pop act they hadn't heard, they didn't know a damned thing that you were talking about! The headliners sounded great, 'cause they knew their stuff well and better get it right or they were out of a job, but the follow-up acts were absolutely in trouble with the bands when they were out on stage almost every night. That, the low pay and the travel conditions — with four people, a bass and baggage in one four-door Oldsmobile — was just too much. I had too much pride in my work to work under those conditions for long! Of course, I could turn to something else easily, but most of the others knew only to pick, drink and sing. I didn't fit into the smelly honk tonks either. It showed when I got up to perform: I wasn't one of them. Drunks! The smell of whiskey and beer; rowdy, outlandish and rude people back then — these two things combined told me I was not like them, and I turned to writing songs and to my art work. As an artist, what I got out of these tours was being in with a bunch of dopesters, hustlers, drunks, sex maniacs and very unprofessional promoters, etc.

I looked out for my own money and I never got into any bother on the road, because I didn't do drugs, or get drunk onstage, or throw things, or destroy hotel rooms, or shoot somebody, or leave my wife and kids, have affairs on the road, or provide money or drugs, etc. to important people. So, I didn't get that attention as a lot of others back then. You know the history of some of these people, I'm sure. This is the inside story of 'What happened to Mitchell Torok after his meteoric rise to fame in 1953?' That question has been asked in several books that are out on the market about country music and me. But to tell you the truth, nobody ever asked *me* what happened, and why I disappeared from the mainstream of country music after my return from a successful 1957 tour of England following my million-selling Decca record, *When Mexico Gave Up The Rhumba* over there.

So, I was on the road for a while but, as I said, I didn't like the atmosphere and thought I could do better — and I did. My success affected my family with my being gone in the early stages, and I'd rather have been home with my family, as I knew where my priorities were. I had a beautiful family at home, and I decided that it was more important to take care of them and be there to raise my two girls, Michelle and Ricci, as a complete man-and-wife and father-and-mother family, than chasing a fake and fleeting shooting star that I could live without. This is the main reason I quit touring, but continued to write and make a few records. I was there when my family needed me and I don't regret my decision for one minute. It's my opinion that if you're going to be an artist and tour, and be on the road day after day, don't get married! Its that simple, and it would save a lot of heartache in the world.

Arlie Duff was the closest person to me from the tours and country music days. We went to Stephen F. Austin College at the same time, and he played basketball while I played football. He was from Beaumont and I was from Houston. He wrote *Y'All Come* at the same time I did *Mexican Joe* and *Caribbean,* and we would be on some tours together and also on Decca at the same time. We visited back and forth, and he last visited me about five years ago and stayed in my apartment with me for a few days. We went to the *Opry,* and ate, and ran around Nashville. While he was on Decca, Arlie and I would go into a radio station while on tour to promote. He would say things to the deejays like: 'It sounds better if you take it out of the sleeve.' They would ask: 'How do you spell Duff?' He'd reply: 'D-U-F-F — and the 'P' is silent, as in swimming!' It wasn't long before he was back in Austin, Texas as a radio deejay. Bless his heart, he died on a golf course in Massachusetts on July 4, right after he visited me.

Some artists from the *Big D Jamboree* are still friends — like Lawton Williams, who wrote *Fraulein, Geisha Girl, Farewell*; and Frankie Miller, who wrote *Black Land Farmer, Too Hot To Handle,* etc. The very nature of the non-trusting business of country music lent itself to not many close relationships, because everyone is protecting their behinds and afraid you're gonna take their booking, or their songs, or their opportunities — so they look at you with a squinty eye, you understand, I'm sure. I know a bunch of the old stars like Carl Smith, but only when I see them at the *Opry* or the car wash. We used some of Carl Smith's band for one of my sessions, and I told him when I saw him that they came out sounding like Carl Smith records. He laughed and said: 'Hell, Mitchell, that's all they knew how to play.!!'

After the touring and recording faded out, I turned my attention to writing and painting to earn my living. That's when I got the cuts by Dean Martin (*Face In The Crowd* and *Open Up The Door And Let The Good Times In*), Glen Campbell (for the picture *Norwood,* I wrote three: *Norwood's Coming Home, Marie* and *Settlin' Down*), Clint Eastwood (*No Sweeter Cheater Than You* for the *Honky Tonk Man* movie) and Jerry Wallace (*This One's On The House).* There were also cuts by Sonny James, Jim Ed Brown, and others. I also produced some custom recording sessions here in Nashville, back when that was happening. I painted my Elvis mural in 1977, after his death; then the *Opry* mural around 1985; and other small murals in between of country stars and famous American football coaches, and I still received some royalties.

The huge Elvis mural, titled the 'Elvis-A Rama', is 110 feet long and 12 feet high with 16 panels on canvas and 8-foot figure studies of Elvis, with one face portrait that is 6 feet tall. It is currently on location in its special auditorium in Las Vegas, Nevada. I don't know what's going on with this mural; I don't have any ownership in it at this time as I was bought out by the investor. The *Opry* mural depicts a complete history of the *Grand Ole Opry.* I finished it in 1989, and it hung in the Ryman Auditorium for ten years before it was remodeled. This mural has five panels, four of which are 7 feet by 18 feet — starting with a humble beginning and going on through the 1980's with portraits and figure studies of over one hundred *Opry* stars. The middle panel, 'Hillbilly Heaven', 10 feet by 20 feet, and featuring the deceased members of the *Opry* at the time, fits into the middle of the five panels. It is currently down in a warehouse for touch-up, and we're looking for a new home for it either in

Chapter 12 – Mitchell Torok

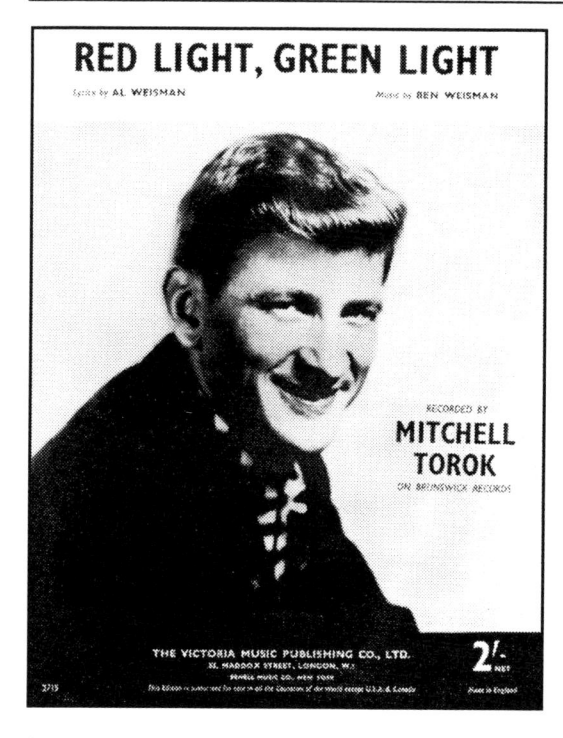

Nashville, Texas, or even overseas.

I don't consider any low spots in my career, and of course my highest had to be seeing *Mexican Joe* suddenly in the world charts along with *Caribbean*. There are others, like meeting Dean Martin and having him record two of my songs, working with Chet Atkins, Owen Bradley and Jimmy Bowen, and seeing my name at the top of the Prince of Wales Theatre when I arrived in London in 1957. Also, on the plane going over to England with movie star George Raft; letting him go down the ramp first with reporters and photographers all around — I was waiting for them to clear out when they began calling my name and they were there to shoot me mostly! We took a picture together on the ramp. I bet he was wondering: 'Who the hell is this guy?'

I don't place any value on my records or success. There were no gold records from anyone, but I consider myself — and everyone else who has accomplished anything in the music business — very lucky. You can hear story after story of how things happened when no one planned it or thought it would. Look at me and *Mexican Joe*. A man from Hollywood comes to a small unknown college town in East Texas among the tall pine trees, asks at the record store if any of the college kids sang, etc! Think: if Fabor Robison had never gotten the song, or came to Nacogdoches, or any of that, it could just as easily have *never* happened. So, what can I say? I consider myself very lucky — then look what happened to me on *Pledge Of Love*! Then look at my last conversation with Jim Reeves, when I played him my new song, *I Hate Me For Loving You*. He loved it, said he would record it next week, and crashed four days later. I now include that conversation in my stage act.

Writing my lyrics just came naturally. I don't know where it came from — I thought everybody did it. I didn't hold on to the publishing rights of my songs, except for a few last-minute Decca recordings in 1959-60, and there was no chance to own my masters.

I have five favorite songs that I pick on when I want to pick a little. If I had written them, I would be in the Bahamas: *Sunday Morning Coming Down*, *The Boxer*, *Mr. Bojangles*, *Taxi* and *I Don't Remember Loving You*. I don't mind nostalgia and played the *Louisiana Hayride Reunion* last June in Shreveport with many of the old stars who were there with me in the 1950s. I had fun and it was goosebump time.

I think my favorite artist was Waylon Jennings. I think that his arrogance and the big sound of his voice — when he wasn't snorting — to me was the epitome of a country artist. You'd have to include Johnny Cash's work too. You couldn't deny that three-piece beat and guitar work on his early records, and there was very good management and legend-building through the years. The thing about today's music is they should have named it something else and left 'country' out of it. It's bastardized and mechanical music. I'm told even the *Opry* management had said lately: 'Get the gray hairs out of the audience and off the stage!' Ah yes, one big happy family —*like hell!*

In looking back, I always feel I did what I thought was right at the time, given the unique set of circumstances at that particular time. In hindsight, I'm sure I would have done some things differently, of course. When Fabor called me to say he wasn't cutting any more American Music songs and I was signed for four more years or so, I went over to Decca. I have thought a lot lately that I should have called Mr. Cross at American Music in Hollywood, 'cause he had gotten some action on my songs, and he could have gotten me a record deal I'm sure, and maybe I would have wound up in the pop field. But there again, who knows? You can't look back, because now I'm in my seventies, and then I was in my twenties. It's all different now; you don't have the same wild spirit that you had back then. You know too much and you're not innocent any more. I believe what happened to me back then was that I had 'virgin mentality' not tainted at that time with reasons why 'it could never happen', but plowing straight ahead and *making* it happen. Back then, I just knew I was gonna do it, and my mouth still falls when I think back on it like a Hollywood movie.

My first wife, Ramona, and I had two daughters, Michelle and Ricci, and I now have one granddaughter, Donna. Ramona died in 1985, and currently I'm married to Maxine Nelson from Mississippi, also a songwriter with a Vernon Oxford cut on a song, *Have You Loved Your Woman Today?* Maxine is very religious, and I am somewhat. My wife and I just wrote and finished a sixty-minute CD titled *'Tennessee Heroes And Other Tall Tales'* for children of all ages, telling stories and singing songs about Tennessee history, and I wrote the Jim Reeves book, *Jim Reeves, Me And Mexican Joe,* which is packaged with a CD. We're just putting these two products in the East Texas record shops and in Gatlinburg gift shops. Also, we're making plans to help record and promote a little eleven year old girl singer down in Texas. I'm marketing paintings on the Internet and beginning to sell some — that's becoming fun. Currently, I am displaying my art on eBay at Trading Assistants 'Bookphair' — a red, white and blue series saluting American patriotism after 9/11. A new batch is going up in a few days, and I'm selling paintings and murals to many of the Mexican restaurants here in Nashville. Also, BMI royalties were good up until the last few years and still come in from overseas on all of my songs. Outside my interests of music and art, we travel and love to go to the casinos and play and win money. Sometimes it pays better than the music or the art!

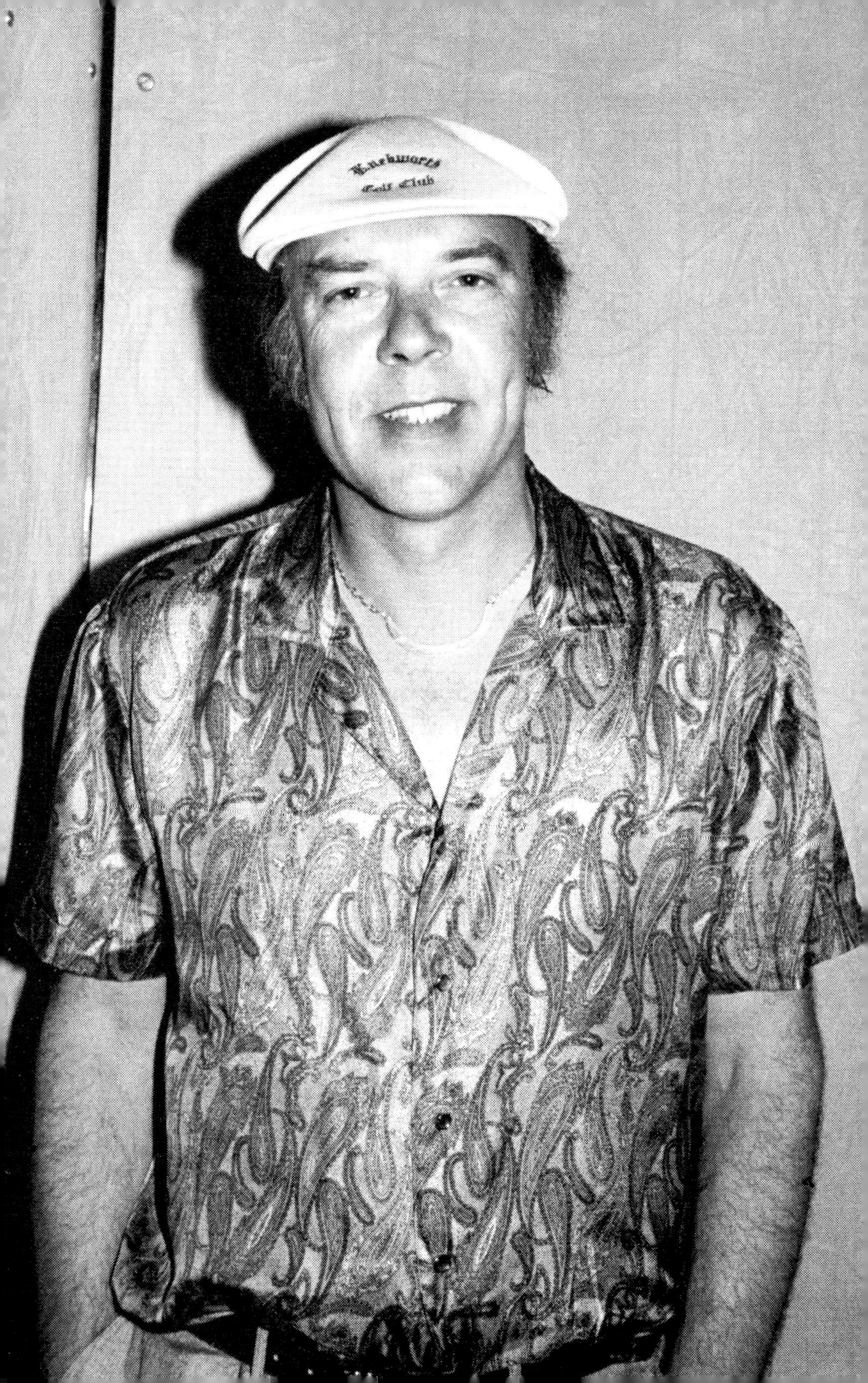

13

BAD BOY
Marty Wilde

Launched by Larry Parnes in 1957 in the wake of his success with Tommy Steele, Marty Wilde was one of the first British teen idols and even had a girls' story-paper named after him. A talented performer who could handle any material, his greatest successes came from covering US hits like *Endless Sleep, Donna, Teenager In Love* and *Sea Of Love*, while national TV exposure on pop shows *Oh Boy!* and *Boy Meets Girls* fuelled his domestic popularity. In 1960, his own composition, *Bad Boy*, made the UK Top Ten and dented the US Top Fifty. When his career cooled in the early Sixties, he moved into music production and management, subsequently masterminding the career of his daughter, Kim Wilde, in the Eighties. He continues to be a popular headliner on nostalgia shows in the UK.

My real name is Reginald Leonard Smith and I was born in Blackheath, London on 15 April 1939 to Reginald and Jessica Smith, who were living in Greenwich. I suppose that my earliest musical influences would be the songs that were coming out just after the war: big band stuff, Billy Cotton and the like. Later on, I loved Frankie Laine, Guy Mitchell and Johnnie Ray, but Frankie Laine was my favourite out of that era until rock'n'roll came along. My father was very musical. At weekends, instead of people sitting with no conversation watching mindless TV, we used to spend every other Sunday having a party, which would be thrown at someone's house. Out would come the brown ale, out would come the accordion and spoons, and I used to play ukelele which I learned to play when I was ten or eleven. So, we used to make our own music, our own fun, and there was definitely encouragement from the family. I just moved from ukelele on to guitar. It was very easy to do that as the chord structures are relatively similar. I don't play any other instruments, although sometimes I play a sort of crude kind of keyboard if I am trying to write something, but nothing serious.

I went to Halstow Road Primary School in Greenwich and eventually, when I grew up, moved on to a secondary modern, Charlton Central, which now no longer exists 'cause it's been knocked down. I didn't like school — I *loathed* it. Up until the age of leaving I really didn't know what I wanted to do, but when I was about sixteen I made up my mind I was going to be a singer, one way or the other. I think that with most singers it's the same. Like most people who get on and do things in life, most of them border on being very egotistical — and I was very ego-orientated. Obviously, I wouldn't have done it unless I felt that I could please people by singing. So, it was very much an 'ego' thing; I was very confident. Most things are done in life by people with quite big egos, which can make them rather boring. When they are not doing the job they are doing, you find they are quite self-centred. There again, we need egotistical people because things have to be done. My first public appearance was standing up in front of a load of people in an army barracks. I was about four then and I sang a little song.

The first record I ever cut was a song called *Wanted* and it was done out on a sea-front pier on one of those early things which produced an acetate-type demo. The thing was, I walked in and I thought I was great; I thought I was God. And I guess I was gonna go: *'Wanted, someone who...'* — you know, just singing it on my own. Anyway, I walked out thinking I had this fantastic voice. And, of course, they played the damn thing didn't they! Directly after it's finished they play it outside, and it was so dreadful I nearly *died!* That hurt.

If I hadn't gone into showbusiness, it's very difficult to say what I would have done. I was never happy in my environment; I wanted more of life. Dad was a bus driver and we weren't exactly wealthy. In fact, we were quite a poor family — very underpaid working class people — and I wanted more. I often look back on life as like being in a garden with a huge high wall that I could look over — at some point. Even as a young child I used to say to my parents that I would buy them a house and I would do all this. So, there was this kind of drive, there was this kind of motivation, but I don't know what I would have done if not singing. I just know that I was very, very keen to — maybe not so much change my *environment*, but to change my *affluence* in the world. I wanted money — like most young kids — and that was my big driving force.

I think my parents were caught along with my enthusiasm. The first time I heard rock'n'roll was an Elvis Presley album called *Elvis Presley,* which I've still got indoors. One of my treasured possessions — still my favourite album. When I heard this, I said to my father: 'Come in and listen to this, it's just mind-boggling.' And then, of course, at that time there wasn't just Elvis, obviously. As we all know, there was Buddy Holly, Little Richard, the Everlys... there was just so much excitement. And I loved all this, and my parents got caught up in that as well. They got caught up in my enthusiasm. They liked rock'n'roll; my mother still does and she is 74.

When I was about fourteen, we were on holiday and I went in for a competition. I think it was at Puckpool *[Isle of Wight].* I sang *Rock Island Line* and came first or second — it was one of the top prizes. Then we had a skiffle group which turned into rock'n'roll after I'd heard this Presley record. We went in for a major competition, which was at Hammersmith Palais in London, and when we got up there I thought: 'What's the point?' For, what was supposed to be an amateur contest, there was Basil Kirchin's Band in the competition, and there was Chas McDevitt and Nancy Whiskey, who were roaring up the charts with this record, *Freight Train.* We went in for the competition completely unknown and we came second — a very close second — to Chas McDevitt, with no hit record, no nothing. And that's when I knew I'd crack it, I knew I'd do it.

Before Larry Parnes managed me, there was a guy called Joe Brunnely, an American guy living over here who was into publishing, and he had connections. They did a *This Is Your Life* on him, so he was quite a personality. He was a very kindly man and he helped me initially. He heard about me through a friend who lived in Greenwich, wanted to see me, and felt that I had something to offer. He got me two weeks work in the West End; I was at the Blue Angel and the Condor Club in Soho. I did two weeks' work, and when I finished the second week Lionel Bart had seen me in the Condor Club and had told Larry. The next thing I knew was — I used to go to church — I came home from church and my parents said that this Larry Parnes had been at the door with a contract in his hand, and who was he and was he any good? I said: 'Well, he's Tommy Steele's manager, that sounds pretty good,' and off it went from there. It was really weird — especially for a guy to come all the way down, who hadn't seen me, with a contract in his hand and my name on it. I couldn't get over that. But I guess that's just being a really astute businessman, which he is.

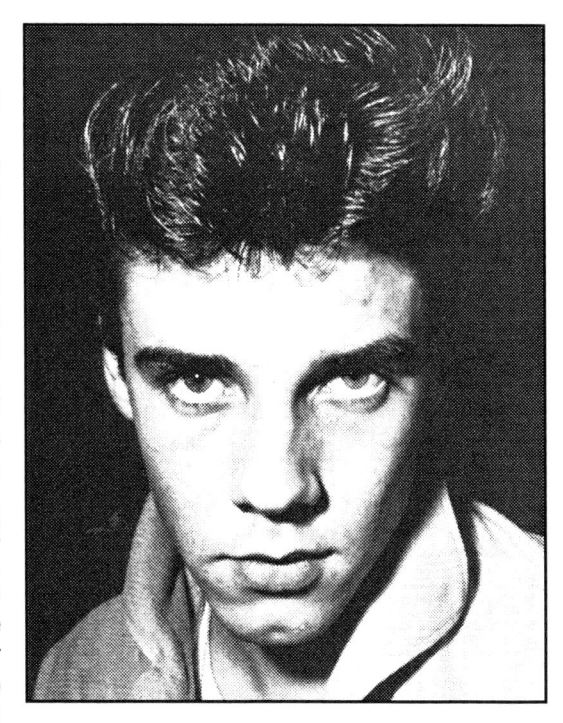

So much that happens in life always seems to me to be stranger than fiction. I had gone out as 'Reg Patterson'. In fact, when Lionel Bart saw me I was 'Reg Patterson' — 'Reg' being my first name, obviously. Patterson — I named myself after Floyd Patterson, 'cause he was my hero and I loved boxing. I love heavyweight boxing in particular. So, when I first went to Larry I was 'Reg Patterson'.

He said: 'I wanna change your name completely. I've seen this film with Ernest Borgnine in it, it was called *Marty* and this guy reminds me a lot of you, and I think Marty would be a great first name.'

I said: 'Oh, that's just an awful name.'

'Well, I'll tell you what I'll do,' he said — Larry was a colossal gambler — 'we'll flick a coin.'

So I said: 'Oh, all right.'

He flicks a coin; he won. So that was that. Now I'm called 'Marty Patterson'.

Then he said: 'And I think also, if you don't mind me saying so, Marty, that 'Patterson' doesn't look very good in print. I've got this idea... we've got Steele... I wanna call you 'Wilde', because of the other half of your nature. You're a two-sided person because there's a wild and tough side to your nature.'

I nearly fell though the floor! 'Marty Wilde' sounds like a bloody joke.

He said: 'Look, are you a gambling man or not?' *[laughs]* and he tossed the coin. Bastard won twice! *[laughs]* It sounds like a joke, but it wasn't. Knowing Larry, it was possibly double-headed, but it wasn't actually, as I did look at the coin.

He did me the greatest favour ever actually; I think it is a *fantastic* name, I've always said that. I think that entertainers should have names that really stand out. It just helps that much, it does. And also over the years, like with journalists — and also this has passed on to Kim, the 'Wilde' thing — just goes with the bloody puns. It's boring because they say the same old thing, but it does help, and I think her name looks great in print and I think mine does as well. The temptation has been there many times to change my name legally to 'Marty Wilde', but we're too proud because we were 'Smith'. It's a pretty basic name, but it keeps my sanity. I am a Smith and I'm proud of it, and there's no reason not to be. I wouldn't like to lose that. I wouldn't like to lose my identity, and I don't want the family to. I want the 'Smith'. If they wanna call themselves 'Wilde' and switch it over like Kim, well... Kim didn't — it was Mickie Most's idea — but it was a very natural thing to do. But hopefully the Smith name will be retained, as I hope indeed the Wilde side will be.

I went down and auditioned for *Six-Five Special* after Jo Douglas saw me at Winston's Club, and they turned me down. I failed the thing! And one of the times I went — the first time Jack Good ever saw me — I just had an acoustic guitar and I stood there, and they said: 'Okay, sing!' And I sang a song, and two of the strings went. I don't think they were over-impressed, but then Jack Good saw something in me and I was lucky. It was Jo who brought me to the attention of Jack Good and others, and it was Jo that pushed for me to be on the show as far as I remember. Nice lady, beautiful lady.

Six-Five Special was an unusual mixture, but funnily enough you look at some of the recordings of it now and it's still got that magic. It was very relaxed, and it was the only chance at that time for people in the country to see artists like Tommy Steele and hear bands play rock'n'roll. I'm not in touch with any of them now, we just meet in passing now and again and reminisce, talk about old times or whatever. Most of us now, we just go

Chapter 13 – Marty Wilde

our own way.

I signed with the Philips label because the others, frankly, weren't interested in me at all. I remember Decca weren't, and most of the other companies weren't, but we went to Philips Records and Johnny Franz liked me immediately. There wasn't any quibbling at all. It was: 'Yep, I like him. We'll sign him.' It was pretty fast. He was a great man — another one of the biggest influences in my career as well. Apart from teaching me an awful lot about music, he taught me a lot about manners, good food, good wine. Yeah, he was just a wonderful human being, a very wonderful man. The first record I ever made for Philips Records was *Honeycomb* b/w *Wild Cat [1957].*

The majority of songs I recorded were picked for me. Someone would say: 'Look, we want you to cut this, it's gonna be a big hit — *Donna.*' Sometimes it was Jack Good, who brought in *Endless Sleep* by Jody Reynolds, as far I remember. He was getting a lot of good stuff and had the original acetate. Johnny Franz heard it and said: 'Yeah, all right, we'll cut it.' But, you see, that wasn't the 'A' side. *Her Hair Was Yellow*, the other side, was gonna be the 'A' side, was the British approach. But thank God Jack did bring in that track.

Regarding my covering US records, I think that all is fair in love and war, although I don't think it's good necessarily from an artistic point of view. You see, I love the original version of *Donna* by Ritchie Valens; I think it's sensational — but, looking back after all those years, my version wasn't bad. It was completely different to his — it was so different. And obviously, being a home-grown product, I stood more of a chance, as Ritchie Valens was unknown — but I *love* Ritchie Valens' version. It was a travesty of justice that it wasn't in the charts. On the other hand, I *loved* Jody Reynolds' version of *Endless Sleep.* I loved it — it really, really, grabbed me. But, looking back on it now, and although it is very difficult for me to be impartial, I think my version walked it. And I think it would have walked it in America as well. It's a bit like Kim singing *You Keep Me Hangin' On*[*] — you can't continually do it, but there were great problems in those days in so much as there was no material. No-one was coming up with material *[in the UK]*: that's what started me writing

---

[*] Originally a hit in 1966 for the Supremes.

Chapter 13 – Marty Wilde

Marty and Cliff on *Oh Boy!* — 11 October 1958.

songs. I wrote *Bad Boy* out of sheer frustration. I was absolutely going mad: I couldn't get my hands on any songs. That also posed a problem for Cliff. Cliff was lucky to meet Ian 'Sammy' Samwell to get *Move It*, *High Class Baby* and stuff like that, which was great, fabulous stuff — real, true British rock'n'roll. But with me, I always had to write my own, which was an added problem. I was one of the first singer-songwriters, in some ways, of the early kind, but I was forced into it; I didn't want to do it.

    I think Larry Parnes could pick hits now and again, like the majority of people can, but his forte was definitely in the business sense. He could *smell* money! He was wonderful at making money. I was lucky with him: I was on a 60:40 deal — I got 60, he got 40. But some of the others were on £28 a week and as much as they could eat and drink, and most of them are still very bitter about it as well. I'm not bitter; I had a great deal, but I would never have settled for that anyway. That's their fault; that's their luck. It goes back to the question about business earlier on. I was never a good businessman. I'm well aware of that, and still fall asleep at meetings — but I wasn't a fool either. Larry wanted 50:50, I think it was, at one point when he first started, but we (mum and dad and me) wanted 60:40. Dad was concerned, as he had to sign for me, 'cause I was below the age of consent at the time. I think I was about seventeen or something like that. But I had a fair idea of what I wanted: I knew *exactly* what I wanted. That was the difference — that's why I had it over all the others —and an instinct for spotting talent in other people as well, especially musicians. I can still spot a good muso a mile off. I wanted to be in the business, saw myself as rock'n'roll when I started, and never saw it as a chance to make money and then get out. There's nothing else I've ever wanted to do. No way. No other business.

At that stage, I was very sharp and very confident. I wasn't sharp in a business sense, I never have been. But, although it sounds conceited, I didn't have to be, because things would happen. It's like a lot of people in the entertainment world, if you are reasonably successful, money comes to you. As long as you're not a complete and utter gibbering fool, then you're not gonna lose it. I was never fool enough to lose it, put it that way. But I was never intelligent as far as money goes; I'm still not. Larry Parnes was, without doubt, the best manager that this country ever produced. At that time, because he was breaking new ground, it was all pioneer stuff. He was miles better than the Beatles' manager, Epstein. Larry could have had the Beatles and 30% of their earnings, and he would have earned *millions*, and they argued over something like £75 a week with Epstein. But that's one thing which I loved about Epstein: he wouldn't sell the group for less than what he thought, even at that stage. It went down on Larry's headed notepaper: there was 'Tommy Steele', 'Marty Wilde', 'Joe Brown', 'Billy Fury', 'The Beatles' and then something else. And then a few weeks later 'The Beatles' was etched out, although you could still see 'The Beatles'. So, he was a pretty shrewd cookie — not shrewd enough maybe to get the Beatles, but you can't win 'em all.

I got the Wildcats round me by my own endeavours. I wanted my own band from day one — I'd always had my own band. I went to Philips Records and they would not allow me to use my own band. I went on and on about it. I think they felt that the kids just couldn't do it; they didn't have faith. They felt that the session musicians — solid, good drummers, etc — should do it. As it happened, on *Endless Sleep*, the drummer is playing brushes and is Phil Seaman, who is possibly this country's greatest drummer ever, in a general jazz sense. I had a big row with Phil Seaman over the way he used to play. I used to go mad with the guy, and he in turn said I didn't know a crotchet from a hatchet, which caused a few laughs — still does actually. And he was quite right. But what *he* didn't know, was that I knew the bloody field. I knew the field of rock'n'roll and he did not have that. Don't get me wrong, he was a brilliant jazz drummer and everything.

So, I had this fight right the way along. Cliff Richard came along, and of course that turned the whole thing. I had been using my own band. I hand-picked them all; I hand-picked Jim Sullivan. I've always been a great, great spotter of talent; I can smell talent from 600 yards, no matter who it is. Even now, I smell talent. And I knew those guys were good. They were one

Chapter 13 – Marty Wilde

of the best rock'n'roll bands ever. They never really got the chance to maybe do all the things that we should've done, which was a shame, but they were a brilliant band. And they're all still buddies of mine as well, which is lovely. When the Wildcats were loaned out to back Eddie Cochran and Gene Vincent on their UK tour *[in 1960]*, we'd been together for a while and it suited my purpose. I remember I was doing other things at the time. I can't remember exactly what I was doing, but I went to America for a while with Joy for about a month and things like that, and the guys couldn't be out of work. Also, I was approached by Eddie Cochran if he could use them, and of course I said yeah, and they backed Eddie right up on that very last fateful tour.

If I'd had my own way, my style would probably have been an exact copy of Presley because I adored the guy, but basically there was the influence of people like my manager, Larry Parnes, and more important possibly still, the man who changed my style — and indeed changed Cliff Richard — Jack Good. Cliff wanted to wear sideburns and do an Elvis thing, and he wouldn't have that. He wanted Cliff to cut his sideburns, and with me he wanted me to be more of an all-round entertainer. I wanted to be really just solid rock'n'roll, that was my driving force, but he put me on singing ballads and also a sort-of musical monologue, things like *'Gather round cats...'* in *All American Boy*, which pushed me into whole new different areas; it stretched me further. I think it was Jack Good that was the 'beacon of light'.

In a career sense, there was rivalry between me and Cliff Richard. I got on great with the guy, but my manager was obviously a little bit edgy about Cliff. Because Cliff came in with such a bang, it was obvious that it was gonna take some of the cream off my career. There was rivalry in the sense of obviously I wanted to be better than him and do better records, etc, but on a personal level I found him a very, very nice guy, a really nice person, and that has remained ever since. I've always got on great with him. If managers had been out of the way, possibly a lot of rivalry that did exist between us wouldn't have existed at all because we got on on a personal level.

When I started touring the Moss Empire theatres, I earned about £250, maybe £300 a week. That was nearly always clear. I never used to pay groups — my manager did.

I always remember the first time I heard that I had a hit record was when we were in digs, way up in the North-East — I think it was Newcastle. They came in and the guy threw the paper on the breakfast table and said: 'That's your name there.' I looked at it and couldn't believe it because *Her Hair Was Yellow* was supposed to be the 'A' side, but they'd turned the record over and *Endless Sleep* had got airplay. And the next week it really made a move as the airplay picked up. I would say that the highest point in my career has to be my first hit.

You didn't have radios in cars like you do now to follow how your record was doing. You could have portable radios — there were quite a few — but mostly I used to buy records. I read all the music papers, and as soon as I saw a new Buddy Holly, or there was gonna be a new Elvis, I'd go out and buy them. Also, I was quite lucky, as I had access to advance copies from America which a lot of people didn't. I had *I Beg Of You* b/w *Don't* by Elvis. I used to get loads of American records; I was *way up* in advance of everyone. It's a bit like somebody today hearing *Control* by Janet Jackson six months ahead of anyone else in England. You're gonna have that up your sleeve, so *[chuckles]* it was quite an advantage to have.

In fact, at Sunderland Empire — let me get this straight in my mind — I had an advance copy of *Jailhouse Rock* about three months ahead of this country. We stuck it on the local jukebox, and the kids didn't know who the hell it was! God, man, I always remember that. Brought the bloody place down, it did. I knew it was gonna be a No.1. Great days. We got the guy to turn the volume up, and the kids freaked out. Mind boggling.

There weren't any big pressures when I was touring: I just used to get very, very lonely. It was natural because, you see, I had a lot of buddies in Greenwich, and I can remember one night they asked me to do a TV ad, and it was our youth club's outing. And every year I'd been, every damn year I'd been. I can remember standing in this flat, watching the sun set, and I was really about as low as I could be — but I had a TV advert, and that's the life I'd chosen. But I used to get very lonely because I'm not the sort of guy who can give himself: I never let people know exactly what's going on. They'll know so much, but 99% they're never gonna know. I've always kept myself at arms length from most people and I'm still the same way today. I can be very friendly, and I love people and I love situations, but I'm very much at arm's length, which makes me almost like a voyeur — and voyeurs get lonely. *[laughs]*

I met some smashing kids, some smashing girls on the road. There was no code of conduct laid down. I mean, guys are guys and girls are girls; human instincts, physical instincts have never changed. Sex was an awesome hurdle to overcome. It could be embarrassing to most boys, whereas nowadays obviously it's thrust down your throat every second. In those days, it had a rather unique honour about it; it was romantic. Things were really exciting to meet a girl. It was more what you *didn't* see that was the turn-on, than seeing. Most of the liaisons on the road, speaking for myself, were very innocent by today's standards and I met some really nice people. Some of them were just really good fun. I was never into 'getting around'. Some of the guys were. There again, I come from quite a sheltered background. I was the only child in my family and I hadn't any experience of girls whatsoever, so I was quite shy in a way. Mind you, looking back on it, I'm damn glad I was. I think some of the worst things in my experience were artists that would abuse their position by dragging in some girl and using her, and then literally kicking her out, but that's life isn't it?

Sometimes you would hear a lamentable tale from another artist of what had gone wrong, and how the manager was screwing them and things, but most of the time I never used to get involved in that. I always felt, as I say, that I had a good deal; I had a great, great deal. I was a skint working class kid who had been literally yanked out of his environment and given a bloody good wage. I was extremely grateful. So, I couldn't have time for all that. Sometimes you couldn't help but get involved, because obviously you could feel a certain amount of compassion for someone who was being really badly handled. With most of the artists those types of conversations didn't take place. We used to swap notes quite a lot, and also you would just use your eyes and stand at the side of the stage and watch someone work. And, if they had anything good that you could utilise and take away with you, you used to steal it *[laughs]* — as we all did.

However, apart from the obvious Presley influences, I personally like to go my own way, and at that time liked to do my own things. In fact, some people used to copy me — even down to the point of singing my songs and dressing in the same way — which caused problems; and there were a few rows backstage with artists. I can remember you used to hear some hysterical arguments. One of the guys had jumped onto his amplifier and played his guitar in a solo, and the act that preceded it decided they would also jump on the next night, after they had seen this from the side of the stage. And there was the most furious row, like fisticuffs and everything — all over jumping on an amp and playing a guitar! *[laughs]* It was pretty funny at the time as well, come to think of it. But it was never my problem, thank God. I used to try and go my own way.

In those days, the weekly variety theatres that I played were trying to attract people of all ages with different acts: it was family entertainment. I look back on it and I think it was great, and that style may well come back. In fact, some of the shows now have fire-eaters, acrobats and things — and why not?

Some of the old-style variety artists resented me, definitely. Oh yeah, you felt the edge. And there was a kind of snobbery that existed; a kind of elitism that they felt they had, but they were the minority not the majority of people. I remember meeting Dickie Valentine, and he was lovely, he was really great. And I remember meeting Danny La Rue in his very, very early days — a most charming man: there was no malice, resentment or anything. As I say, thankfully, most of the artists were very kind to me.

But there was a lot of snobbery in the business side, like the moguls of showbusiness. You know: *[posh voice]* 'These boys, you know, get 'em off the street and bung 'em on there.' I was aware of it, though, and I used to feel it sometimes, but once my career started I couldn't give two hoots 'cause things changed then. They changed completely, and I couldn't give a damn what they thought then. But I was aware of it when I first started, yeah, very aware. People thought you didn't really have any talent whatsoever. It's a bit like today with some people watching the youngsters on the screen and saying: 'Oh, you know, they've got no talent.' A very dangerous thing to form an opinion that way, just because you don't like the style of music — because half of the youngsters have colossal talent, marvellous talent. The fact that you don't like the music and style and what they stand for is a different issue. People have got talent. And the rock'n'rollers had talent, loads of them did. Some of them were damn versatile as well, with very good voices. The fact that they chose to sing in rock'n'roll was a different thing, but some of them were extremely talented.

Basically, it wasn't necessarily that rock'n'roll was a better form of music or that the artists were better. I think there were great artists then and there are great artists now, but the thing that was on our side was just this complete breakthrough; this complete change. Once the style of music had been dance bands and so and so, and then suddenly the kid in the street stood a chance of doing it. He stood a chance of joining in all this damn thing.

British singers couldn't make a big impact on the States at that time

Chapter 13 – Marty Wilde

because they had fantastic home-grown product; there was no reason for us to crack it. I think records like *Move It* should've cracked it big in America. *Move It* should've been a huge No.1. But in those days, as I say, the Americans had such a lot of natural home-grown talent, and these people *lived* in that area. We were getting all our influences second-hand; they were getting their influences first-hand.

Presley had a colossal advantage: all he had to do was walk around the corner and go into a black church or a black nightclub and freak out. I couldn't. I was hearing what I could get from people like Muddy Waters, Howlin' Wolf — who I loved — and Willie Mae Thornton.

I didn't have any favourites among the British artists. I was mostly influenced by American acts anyway, although the British act that I enjoyed was Billy Fury. I worked with Billy on a summer season and I can honestly say I enjoyed his act every night. I thought it was sensational. I thought he was great. I think he was one of the best rock'n'roll acts I've ever seen — certainly the most exciting. He was aware of his heart condition in a minor way even in those days. I also enjoyed Cliff. I went to see Cliff down in Bournemouth, but that was later in his career, in the days of *Apache* and all those sort of times. Things had changed a little bit then.

I didn't meet Presley, but I had the chance to meet him. I could have gone over to Germany many times because all his buddies — people like Lamar Fike, all his henchmen — used to come over to the *Boy Meets Girls* shows over in Manchester and also some of the *Oh Boy!* shows. We got to be very good buddies, all of us. I used to send my records over to Elvis and things like that, and ask Lamar what he thought. Elvis heard *Bad Boy* before it was ever released here. I sent him over an acetate and I said to Lamar: 'What'd he think? What'd he think?'

He said: 'Great. He says a hit.'

I said: 'Oh, fantastic!' and stood about fifteen foot tall then. It was sad in a way — I do regret bitterly not going over there, just as I regret, for example, not going over to the Colston Hall in Bristol one night and seeing

Chapter 13 – Marty Wilde

Buddy Holly. Someone said: ' Do you wanna go?' and I said: 'Oh, I'd sooner listen to the record.' I've always been like that. I prefer records to concerts, but I wish I'd gone. I do wish that I'd seen him.

I was very fortunate whilst doing the *Oh Boy!* and *Boy Meets Girls* shows in meeting some really wonderful American acts. I met some marvellous people: Johnny Cash, the Browns — a brilliant country act, Brenda Lee, Sammy Turner, Freddy Cannon, Eddie Cochran, Gene Vincent — quite a few of the Americans. I was later to meet Bobby Rydell, but not here, in America. You got a chance to get know them pretty well, as they would stay over for about two or three weeks at a time. It wasn't like today, going down to do *Top Of The Pops* and meeting in a corridor and nodding. It was, like, in dressing rooms, sharing conversation, talking, drinking, going out together sometimes. It was great.

I met Joyce at the *Oh Boy!* show rehearsals. We used to rehearse in a church hall in the East side of London. I made up my mind that this was the girl! I told my manager and my parents. You see, I came from a very basic working class family with basic working class values, and also, I guess, in a funny kind of way, there was at that time a slight influence, possibly in a small way, by the church. I had been brought up to believe that if you found someone, you married them. It was put to me by Larry to take her on as a mistress, so that we could hush it up — at least, for a couple of years — and I said: 'No, I want to get married.' He said: 'Right, we'd better have a meeting.' We had a meeting and he laid the whole scenario out in front of me as to what would happen. He said: 'You will virtually destroy your career. You'll lose all the girls, but I think your career could continue, and I'm putting all these points to you before you make the final decision.' And I said: 'Well, I have to live my life. I cannot go on...'

I was very lonely, I was a lonely person. I was quite insular, introvert in some ways — an extrovert on stage, but quite introvertish off stage. I need somebody, and I was very much in love. And, as I say, I was always taught that you got married, you didn't... A load of other guys at that time used to have mistresses, but I didn't. I thought that would be an insult to her, and I didn't want people looking at her and saying: 'Oh, that's his bit of stuff,' or whatever people used to say in those days. So, we got married and I was

Chapter 13 – Marty Wilde

being very, very aware of what was gonna happen. I was *very* aware. We'd discussed it, we'd gone all through it, very cold bloodedly, and quite cynically said: 'Right, that's gonna happen' — and it did. But it's something that I have never, ever regretted.

1960 was a quiet time for me, but I was very fortunate I went to America. I'd been married about four months and we went as a kind-of late honeymoon combined with business. Philips paid for me to go, and I made some great records over there which were never subsequently released, which I've always thought was a shame, a great tragedy. Philips have still got the tapes as far as I know. Some of them were *really* good. I met Carole King, and she helped me. I chose the material: I went up to Hill & Range and places like that in New York, great big publishing houses, picked out the material: *Seventeenth Spring*, *Little Girl* and a lot of other tracks which, as I say, weren't released. Carole King organised a lot of the backing for me, and it was really exciting. That was the most electrifying session that I've ever been on in my life, to work with those American musicians — and it shows. It shows on *Seventeenth Spring*, maybe not so much on *Little Girl*, but also on *Angry*, which was cut there as well. There was a kind of buzz in the studio: real uppers the Yanks were — completely different to British style of recording. I was very, very excited by the whole thing. It was electric, but I didn't think of staying; that wasn't the purpose.

Following the US trip, there was a lot of adverse publicity, which was sad in a way, because there was an angle to that. What actually happened was that when we came back a certain person, who shall remain nameless, asked me if my wife was pregnant. I had strict instructions to say: 'No, she's not pregnant', because the story was going to be given to the papers on the Monday and one major paper was gonna break the story. It had been a deal that was struck that had nothing to do with me. The guy who asked me saw me lifting my wife down, because they asked for a photograph of us together, and it was almost getting really obvious she was pregnant. And this particular, very, very powerful journalist said: 'Is she pregnant?' and I said: 'No, she's not pregnant.' And he said: 'Are you sure?' I said: 'No.'

That was at the weekend. On the Monday, the story broke in the *Daily Mirror*. And then he had another five or six days to write this story and he tore me to pieces. He almost destroyed my career — he almost did it. Because it was *'Wilde Goes West'* — it was a real bad headline. It was about how I had said that American cars were better than this country's, I wanted to stay there, and blah-blah-blah. Well, yeah, I wanted to stay there *for a time*, but the very fact that I'd come home, the very fact that this is my home... And, as events have subsequently proved, I could live in America now if I wanted to. I could have done that many times over, but this is my home and I have no reason to do that.

It was done out of spite. Spite, no other reason. If I'd said: 'Yes, she's pregnant,' he would have built the whole thing around the pregnancy: it was major story, a major coup. But I'd been told to shut up. It wasn't my fault; I'd been given strict instructions. So, I had to lie to the man — which was not my fault. I think it was vicious because what he did was, the mean thing about it was, he'd asked me questions like, for example: 'What do you think of American cars?' And I said: 'Oh, I love American cars, I really do love 'em. I mean like Rolls Royce is a great car and all that, but American cars are really great.' And all he put was: 'American cars are really great.' So, the whole article was biased that way. He hurt my career, and he hurt it very badly. After the article appeared, I used to get booed driving along the road at odd times by people who really believed it — that I thought America was the be-all and end-all. After that article was definitely the lowest point in my career.

I'm wary of the press. In fact, I drummed it into Kim when she first began her career that I didn't want her to have bad relationships with the press. I wanted her to be honest, but cautious, and not to shoot her mouth off, as so many artists do, and to try and forge a good relationship with the press, which our office has always done. I think this is very important. I don't see why artists and press should fight, we need each other desperately. But you'll always get the odd article. Some guy in Australia recently — I could have wrung his bloody neck! It was one of these fan magazines. Kim went to Australia and she did a visit to a store, and in the article you read it's as though nobody turned up at the store. He wrote it that way and the picture he shows is just Kim standing on her own at this empty store. It was overflowing out in the street! It was outrageous. So, that kind of journalist that distorts is destructive journalism. I don't mind if someone says something really outrageous, like, if say for example an artist says: 'I'm a big supporter of the National Front.' They deserve everything they get. I mean, they should be *done*.

I'd like to have had a few more hit records, but there again, you see, rock'n'roll was dying at that stage, it was going fast. The tragedy of all artists is that they come in with very pure ideals and ambitions. They're fresh, they're natural, they come on there. And I've seen it so many times in my career. It happens all the time — it happens now. Look at Presley: from a little pink suit or a gangster-type image, within a couple of years he's walking around with bloody Tahitian garlands round his neck singing the most mundane songs. And for me it was a similar type situation. They changed me; they got to me. And they got to Cliff. Cliff, who was *really* exciting in his early days, was pointed into this... almost like a parody of what rock'n'roll was.

They changed us all. But it happens, I'm afraid folks. It's a fact of life, and life goes on. Cliff was at the most exciting time of his career during those first two years. But I think that goes for every artist in the world. I don't think anything ever follows that. I think that once an artist strikes it, like Presley, after two years things start to burn off a bit, no matter what success you have. That kind of 'something' goes. That's just my opinion.

They wanted me to be an actor, but I felt then — and I still feel now — that, with the exception of a few people, I think pop people should stick to their own. There's a lot of great actors and great actresses out of work. The only person I've seen in recent years who I thought was great was Madonna in *Desperately Seeking Susan.* I think she's an absolute natural and she's one of the few people I've ever seen that could do it. But not all the Marty Wildes and hundreds of names too numerous to mention — apart from maybe Doris Day who ended up a good actress, but again not as exciting as a real actress, as she hasn't got the benefit of real solid training like a good actress or an actor has.

If I could have recorded any song first, I don't know what my choice would've been. All the original songs I've heard over the years I've got so used to. I mean, I would dearly love to have recorded *Move It,* but there again I recently bought a Cliff Richard CD and I love it, I love it to death, because I love all the early stuff. I love *Summertime Blues* by Eddie Cochran, but there's no way in the world I would've tackled it, because nobody can beat him, and nobody can beat Cliff singing *Move It.* It's just one of those things the first time you hear it. But song-wise it's very difficult to say, as I love so many songs and the original artists do them so well that I wouldn't encroach on that.

I would've freaked if someone had given me some of the early Presley stuff. I had one Elvis song given to me. It's an interesting story: I was in England and Mort Shuman — there were two writers, Doc Pomus and Mort Shuman, I'd met them at the *Oh Boy!* show and we became buddies — went over to America and he came back and said: 'I've got this great song for Presley. I'm going over to Germany.' He stopped off in London prior to going and spent a few days with us. It was *It's Been Nice,* and I said: 'Oh God, I gotta have it! Mort, I've to gotta have it.' I know it sounds crazy, and again it sounds like one of these film things, but he was the sort of guy if he had the song in his pocket and you asked, he was such a lovely man, you'd get it. I mean, Billy J. Kramer got *Little Children* like that, as far as I know he did. I just freaked out. I said: 'I gotta have it! I gotta have it! I gotta have it!'

He said: 'I *can't.* My one chance to get... Presley will cut this, I know he will, and he'll murder it and I'll have a big hit.'

I said: '*Please*, come on, you can write another one.'

And I did get it. Of course, it never ended up an 'A' side, which is a *tragedy*, 'cause Presley *would've* murdered it; it would've been a monster No.1 for Presley. *[laughs]* Apologies to Mort, who I adore.

I keep performing rock'n'roll shows around the country at places like Ashington in Northumberland, where you saw me recently, because I think it's important to meet people. It keeps my feet on the ground. First and foremost, I love it. I've always considered my job to be a paid holiday. I could

Chapter 13 – Marty Wilde

never understand how I got paid such a high price for having an absolute *wonderful* time and showing off. Going onstage and getting *paid* for showing off! It's ludicrous. This year, there's a good chance I'm gonna be spending quite a lot of time in Bel Air. I've spent time in places all over the world; you name it, I've been there. And Ashington is as important to me; I mean it's a basic as that. I'm a basic man. I still have — I don't think I've lost the common touch. I love people, and I love going on stage, and if Ashington wants me, then I'm more than happy and more than honoured to go there. I know it sounds cornball, but it's true. I mean, unless an audience start throwing things at you — well, that's a different kind of feeling obviously. We go on there, and for us it's the most wonderful feeling in the world. An old 48 year old man still showing off, and people still coming backstage saying: 'Oh, you brought me back so many happy memories.' That is a kick, and that's my role in life. My role in life for those people in Ashington, at that little small moment in time, is to make them happy. It's part of life's chain. We all need each other and we all have to do our best. I believe that sincerely, even though I'm no longer religious.

    A lot of artists in my position would not have done the Ashington show. What happened was, I had a keyboard player — who has since been fired — who, at the last minute said he couldn't do the show. I had a guitarist, who, at the last minute, had to go Germany, which again infuriated me. We got a guitarist up *that day*, and that guy had to learn those numbers on the way up and do that show. Since then, that man has joined my band, and the band are pretty good. So, Ashington weren't really seeing me at my best. The first band on the show were absolutely spot-on. Imagine how I felt. I was so upset about the whole situation, but it was either that or not doing the show. I could have easily walked away and, as I say, I think a lot of other artists would've done, but I thought: 'No, no, to hell with it! I'm gonna go on there and do my best.' To get things straight on that subject, the pianist and the guitarist pulled out the morning of leaving for that show, so I was left with a bass player and a drummer!

What happens is that someone will ring our office here at the studio, and they'll say there is an offer for a gig, blah-blah-blah. Do you wanna do it? Last year, I wouldn't do anything outside of, I think it was, a 140 mile radius. We literally drew a circle round the map and I said: 'I'm not going outside of that area. I get too tired,' or whatever. That was last year; this year I thought, 'I'm in the twilight of my life and my career — certainly in the sense that I won't be able to sing like this forever. At some point, I'm gonna start getting old like Sinatra and Crosby and I won't be able to sing these songs.' So, I said: 'Oh damn it, I'm gonna go out this year and I'll go anywhere — Land's End, John O'Groats.' And also it's a chance to catch up and get that feel again. That's a great advantage of travelling around the country — keep your eyes open and you're aware. You get a feel of people, and you *know* what they feel. And you get to know about life that way. I was always very lucky that way. I've been everywhere in this country, almost *everywhere.* And I've always got to know the people, and that's why I suppose I love it so much. That's why I am very proud of my country. Extremely proud.

It is hard to know who is still performing. Sometimes other guys will say : 'Oh, we would've loved to book you, but we just didn't know.' But I've got more than enough things to do and I'm virtually semi-retired now. Because I'm relaxed about performing, I think I'm working better now than I've ever worked in my entire life, basically because of that reason. I don't have to prove anything, whereas in the early days I was always trying to prove that I could do this or do that, which is obviously important to the ego, but now I don't. I don't have any ego. I don't think I'm the world's best singer. I don't think I'm particularly good-looking. I don't think I'm a sex symbol or anything. I just feel I'm Marty, and just wanna have some fun on the stage.

It used to really bore me singing the same material. It used to really get to me when I was doing week after week after week. In the Sixties, when I went into cabaret, that really used to get to me. I used to *hate* singing some of the songs. I used to be almost to the point of yawning. And that happens to every artist throughout the world. But these days it doesn't happen that way, because I can't work that often because of commitments here, and commitments to Kim and to her career. I don't want to keep charging all over the place. I haven't got the energy, and I've got two children growing up and I like to be close to them.

In September, I will have five children in total. The way I look at it in life is I consider myself to be a lucky man. I come in the studio and I'll wash up if there's things to be done — I'll wash up. If I'm out on the road and someone needs a hand I'll pull in the gear, because — I don't know — it's just:

Chapter 13 – Marty Wilde

'Why not?' I'm a real snob as far as food is concerned and I *adore* high class French cuisine, but equally I enjoy bread and dripping, and I had some last night. So, I've got the best of all worlds.

I didn't want my kids in the business; not at all. Certainly not on the stage. That's the last thing I wanted for Kim and I didn't encourage her at all. On the other hand, there's not a way in the world I would stand in any of my children's way if they wanted to do things. My youngest daughter at the moment is mad keen on horse-riding. She's seven and she rides round this bloody corral and I sort-of sit there in the Shogun *petrified*, but there's no way in the world I'm gonna stop that girl from doing it. And it's exactly the same for Kim — because it's a very punishing business and it's so ego-orientated. You have to have that ingredient of ego that you are fairly good, pretty good, and you can get out there and do it. But also because you've got that, you are also very vulnerable to when things go wrong. It's like my love for heavyweight boxing, which has never changed or diminished through the years. Like anybody, one day you meet someone who's better than you. And it's a bit of a rude shock. Later on, you can look back on it, rather like Cassius Clay I suppose, and say: 'Well, so what the hell, I did my best.' I think the important thing is going out and going for it. The fact that you get beaten by people, that people are better singers than you, doesn't matter.

I think the saddest thing is like Presley. For somebody who could give so much happiness to so many people in the world — and still does, and still will do for thousands of years to come I would think, hopefully anyway — it's a shame that they have to end up so sad and so lonely; lonely figures. As I say, I started in this industry and I was lonely, and now I'm not. I'm quite the reverse. There's so much love around me and so many lovely people around me, genuine people. And it's a shame that Presley couldn't — I think that's *tragic,* that a person like that had to end up with such a sad death because they lose touch with reality. The success brings the goldfish bowl syndrome where they can't go to the pictures, can't play golf. I've always thought: 'Damn it,' you know.

I've always been frightened to be, in some ways, too ambitious. I can remember *Abergavenny [1969]* was going in the American charts[*] and I had this idea to go over there, and then I thought: 'No.' And I said to Joyce: 'What the hell, why should I go over and bash my head against the wall and do all those things?' I just didn't want to do it; I stayed home. I was offered trips over there, but I thought: 'To hell with it.' I'd sooner play golf and keep my feet on the ground, 'cause it's easy to lose your identity, and to lose yourself in this business. I've seen too many people do it, and they *lose*. They lose that contact, they lose their humanity — it's very destructive. It's not just showbusiness, it happens to a lot of people who get into the limelight. It's a very destructive thing, and it doesn't *have* to be that way. You are obviously gonna go through your traumas and touch-and-go situations, but if you come through them, you're that much stronger and that much happier.

I've seen a lot of people in our industry run towards things. They run to try and find success, and they do anything to get into the limelight. I

---

[*] In the USA, the record was released under the pseudonym 'Shannon'.

Chapter 13 – Marty Wilde

stopped that years and years and years ago. I was never like that. I felt, if they want to take my picture, or they want to do something, they'll do it. I never push. That's why I do very little TV. I get offered TV, but I don't wanna do it. I don't wanna go on there. I don't feel that I have to push and I don't want to. It's not a priority, and never was in my life. I would love to work with Cliff, I'd love to do a show, but I think it's too late. I don't think it will happen unless it was on a one-night basis or something like that.

About a year and a half ago, there was Cliff, Joe Brown, myself, Denis Lotis, Lita Roza, Rolf Harris, Lonnie Donegan, Don Lang, loads of people — we did a show for royalty, and that was lovely as well. It was very strange to meet all again; talking with Joe and talking with Cliff all at the same time was really weird. And seeing Denis Lotis again was weird And Lita Roza, who looked fantastic. The funniest thing, or the thing that struck me as funny, was this security around the theatre, which was in the West End. Because of the size of the cast, which was colossal, they kept us all together, and we had to catch a coach. There we were and, because of the traffic, which was packed, the coach driver had to drive halfway around London to get to the silly theatre, which was only about half a mile away. And it was just really funny, it was just really strange. Sitting in that coach with Donegan and Joe and all these people.

You say that Lonnie Donegan didn't think much of rock'n'roll. I don't regard Lonnie Donegan's career very favourably once he dropped what he was, which was a brilliant, brilliant, genius bluesman. The minute he wanted to become an entertainer, he lost — for me — the very essence of what he was all about. That's my own personal opinion. I loved Donegan — tracks like *Rock Island Line*, which is a *classic* track. But even more than *Rock Island Line* — much more — was *Frankie And Johnny.* That sums up what a brilliant, brilliant singer he was. He was a brilliant talent, and he got caught up in what I mentioned earlier. The commercial industry gets in, and on goes the suit, the haircut changes, and on comes soft shoe shuffles and shiny shoes, and the whole *guts* and the *balls* just blow right through the window.

If I had come into this business now, I would've made it. There's not a shadow of doubt in my mind, because I'm a very single minded, ambitious, person. When I want something, I go out and I get it, and I don't let anything defeat me — nothing will defeat me. If I want something, that is it. I will get it, through hell or high water. I think things have changed — some a lot for the better — but a lot of the spontaneity has been lost in our industry. These days, there's an expert in every different region of our business, but the great thing is the expanding market, obviously. The market is colossal: it's virtually a world market, and one day, who knows, it may even get into Russia.

Those days were, more from an emotional point of view, the most exciting times. *Nothing — but nothing —* has ever come near the impact that rock'n'roll had. The second-closest thing was the rise of the Beatles in those early Beatle years. That was an exciting time as well, but not in the same class as rock'n'roll. And nothing has happened since the Beatles that has come anywhere near that kind of excitement and euphoria. I mean, you have all these bands, and being in America you see all the films on them and all that, but no way can you ever compare these days to those days for pure excitement.

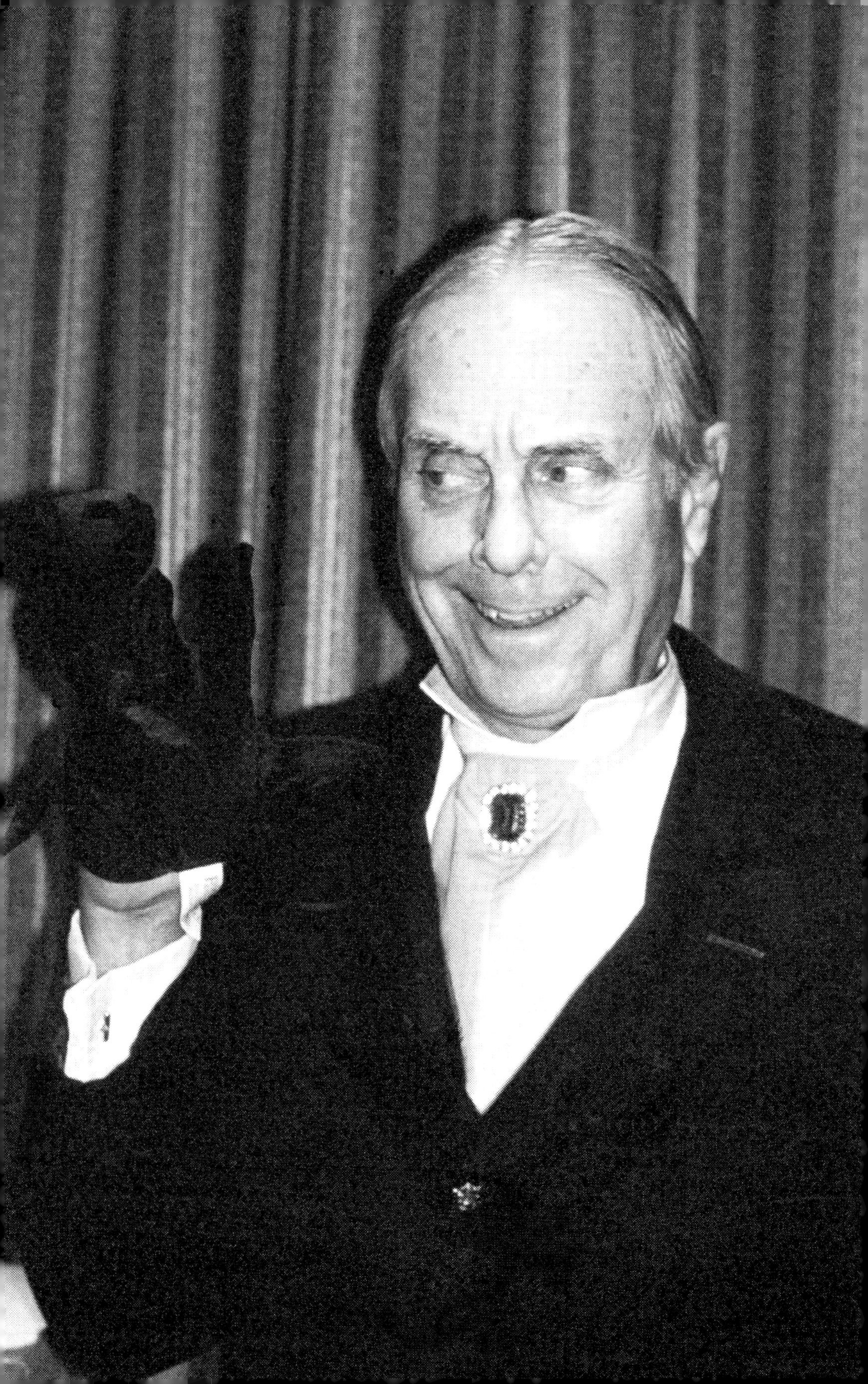

14

THE COOL GHOUL
John Zacherle

Nicknamed 'The Cool Ghoul' by Dick Clark, actor/presenter/recording artist John Zacherle was responsible for the unforgettable 'horror rock' classic, *Dinner With Drac* — No.6 in the US in 1958 — and numerous outings in the same vein, including *Lunch With Mother Goose, I Was A Teenage Caveman* and *Hurry, Bury Baby*. A legend, thanks to his characterisation of alter ego 'Roland' from US TV's *Shock Theatre*, he continues to host conventions for horror film fans. A definite one-off.

My date of birth was September 26, 1918 — *l-o-n-g* time ago! I was born John Karsten Zacherle in German Town, Philadelphia. Zacherle, pronounced 'Zachearl', is Bavarian and 'Karsten' is from the Netherlands. My mother was Anna Bruce (*née* Henderson), and she was a mother and housekeeper. Father was George Henry Zacherle, and he worked in a trust department of the Fidelity Philadelphia Trust Company. You may have seen that in a movie called *Trading Places*. They used the bank interior as the place where all the scheming was going on, and that palace — as it seemed to me whenever I saw it — is on Broad Street, south of City Hall, in Philadelphia. It looks like a pretty fancy place to work in, and I think my father felt that way. He stayed there all his life!

I had two older brothers and a sister. I was four years younger than the rest. Let's see: oldest brother was born, and two years later my sister was born. Two years later, my next brother was born, and then they thought that was it, but four years later — whoah-oh! — here comes John! Top brother was George Henry Jr, a veterinarian who joined the army in about 1940 and retired many, many years later as a colonel in the Veterinary Corps. Sister, Laura Wight, came next — she was a secretary and then a housewife, married a doctor who lived in Worcester, Massachusetts. Second brother is Bruce Henderson, an electrical engineer who graduated from the University of Pennsylvania in 1936.

I got on well with my parents and siblings. Childhood was a lot of fun times and we had several dogs. We had a good time, it was great. I lived in what was called a row house, a lot of kids were around and we had a great public playground behind our house, which was very convenient. I hung out a great deal with my cousins, who were twins and about the same age as I.

Chapter 14 – John Zacherle

Their name was Lamberton, and at one time was the Mayor of Philadelphia. One of the twins was killed some weeks after the European invasion in World War II. He came in with an armoured division and was in a tank when they gave the orders to button up. As he closed the lid, he was last one in. A shell struck and he was killed instantly. Very Sad.

As a child and youth, my interests were just running around playing touch-football and tennis, I guess, stuff like that. And swimming — never learned to swim real well, though. I never did have a musical education although I did sing in the Presbyterian church choir! I played the piano for about three weeks. My sister was trying to teach me — she learnt from my mother, though I think she had lessons too, to tell the truth. We had a great upright piano, wonderful old thing, and I was sorry that we lost that in many moves. So, I played the piano under her instruction for about three weeks, and when she introduced me to the black keys, I said to myself: 'I can't... this is ridiculous,' and I gave it up. Too bad, never should have done that. Everybody should know how to play some kind of an instrument. My second brother, Bruce, played the trumpet and he took lessons — I recall a music teacher came to the house. One day, a man two blocks away from us said to my father: 'Say, your son's coming along pretty good with that trumpet' — he could hear him playing out the back window. *[laughs]* Oh, dear!

I was not interested in drama when I was a child, though at church we were always putting on little pageants or something when Christmas and Easter came — that kind of nonsense. My brother would blow a trumpet like he was a herald, you know: 'Jesus is born, Jesus is born!' *[sings]*, but I wasn't excited about any of these at all. They were really silly. Oh boy!

I think my father took me to see a Shakespeare play once, downtown in Philadelphia, which was pretty impressive because we sat in the extreme top balcony where you kept hanging on to your seat for fear that you would fall off into the people below — without as much as a 'howdy-doo'. As I got older, I never had any involvement in amateur dramatics.

Were my parents very strict and conventional? Yes!!! They were Presbyterians for Lord's sake! What do *you* think? *[laughs]* Well, Presbyterians of course you think in terms of very dour and not very fun-loving, but they had a great sense of humor and everything. The only thing they didn't let me do when I was younger was dance. My older brothers and sister would have dances and I would crank the Victrola. I guess the others thought that I got away with murder because I was the baby, but I don't know what murder they were talking about! I had a little room, my sister had a larger room and the two other boys shared a room. Without my appearing on the scene there would have been rooms for all three of them, but they had to double up when I arrived.

When did I become aware of horror movies? Ah! Well, you see, there you are, the Presbyterians! They had little magazines come to the house and tell parents what kind of shows were decent for children and so on. I guess this was during the Thirties, when there were signs of censorship. The Hays Office and the Breen Office and all kinds of things sprang up because they thought Hollywood was going a little *too far*. Women were not wearing bras and things like that. Jean Harlow, I think, and Mae West were vilified in the press as being unfit, but everybody loved them. *[laughs]* I didn't see 'em. But the horror movies — I never saw one until I was maybe thirty-five years old. And I saw them, like a lot of other people did, younger than myself, for the first time on TV. All the movies I introduced on TV, I never saw them in movie houses, because, on Saturday afternoon, when other kids went to the movies, if it was a horror movie I didn't go. I stayed home and played outdoors. So, the cinema was no influence on me as far as horror was concerned. I did go to see *Robin Hood*, with Errol Flynn, and things like that which were very big in those days.

The Cool Ghoul in New York, 1973.

I lived in German Town, Philadelphia until I went to college at the University of Pennsylvania in about 1936. I graduated in 1940, and by that time we had moved to another upscale little area in Philadelphia known as Chestnut Hill. My education was at grammar school, then what they call junior high school, high school and then the University of Pennsylvania, where I majored in English. I had started out majoring in Pre-Med, but gave that up because I hated it. I wasn't a good student then, not a good student now. What was I? Probably 75 out of 100. *[laughs]* I guess History and English were the favorite subjects.

At the university I was the manager of the band! I loved that! My brother was a senior when I got in there as a freshman. I always loved the football games and the family always went to them every Saturday. The band was a big deal and we would see my brother marching down the field: dump-de-dump-de-dump-de-pomp-pomp. He was pretty good at that type of music and he told me that they were looking for 'heelers', as they called them, which meant that you heel around and stand up and do what you're told, and go get this and that for the conductor. So, I did that, and eventually I became the manager of the band in my senior year and I had a great time there. In fact, we have a reunion coming up this year which will be... phew... wow... Jesus, some sixty-plus years! I think they must all be dead, though I'm still alive, I'm

Chapter 14 – John Zacherle

still here. But they had a paper come out saying that, if you're interested and used to play in the band, you are invited to come down and sit with the band, have lunch with them, and then go into the stadium for the ceremonies of Alumni Day. May happen, may happen.

I went right from university into the armed forces as a second lieutenant — probably as dumb as any second lieutenant ever to be in the army. I ended up in something I knew nothing about — and to this day don't like to even *think* about — and that was keeping records in warehouses, and unloading ships and moving food and stuff around. My regiment was the 240 Quartermaster Battalion and I served in England, North Africa and Italy. The guys who were under me, the sergeants and those people, knew what they were doing. They had been people who worked in those situations in private life, so they knew just how to do it. I never learned, and I'm still not interested in it. I ended up as a captain, and eventually, after the war, became a major in the Reserves. But when they started shooting in Korea, me and the rest of the guys said: 'Hey! time to get out.' So we got out. We would have been no good anyway.

After the war, I didn't see my career going anywhere. I just horsed around awhile and got interested in a little theater group my cousin was in — a really nice little group. They had a barn in Chestnut Hill, where I lived, and it was called 'The Stagecrafters' and they had a great cast of characters to take part in their shows. I was just saving some money from the army and I just hung on. My parents were kind enough to let me hang around the house and live there and keep the house going until I finally settled down. I met some people at that theater group who worked for the Board of Education, and they were doing radio shows to be played in the classrooms. This was before television — *before* television, you know — and the kids would listen to a radio show about the history of George Washington or something like that. I took part in that, and at one time Dick Clark was in one and I played his father one time in one of these little episodes! He was just starting on the radio in Philadelphia and hadn't started his TV shows at that time. By the way, The Stagecrafters still exists — nice place, and they do great work.

Now, this is *really* interesting! In 1955, before the invention of tape, they did a live cowboy show on afternoon TV called *Action In The Afternoon*. We had live horses, of course, and we ran indoors and outdoors. The studio was of the WCAU, a part of the CBS network. There were no real networks in those days, not coast-to-coast anyway, I don't think. At any rate, there was a sort of Eastern hook-up and this show was on every day for an hour, five days a week. There was an assembly of regulars: the sheriff, his wife, the guy who owned the newspaper, the blacksmith of course, the sheriff's deputy who sang us songs when he played his guitar, and all that stuff. I think that there had been some cowboy shows on television — old movies a lot of them. Roy Rogers, Gene Autry and people like that were steady fare on TV, so they thought that they would do one live.

I got involved when one of the ladies at The Stagecrafters said: 'Hey, you should go out to Channel 10, they're starting a cowboy series and they had auditions about two weeks ago.' When I finally went, it turned out that they'd had so many people show up to try to be on television who could

Chapter 14 – John Zacherle

neither ride a horse nor shoot a gun. I could shoot a gun of course. I was in the army and knew how to shoot on a firing range! *[laughs]* Anyway, I think they'd had so many resumés that they must have thrown them all out — because, when I showed up four weeks later, they said: 'Sure, sure, go get into a costume.' So, I got dressed up as a cowboy and I was holding horses. No speaking lines, but I was there! And one day, one of the ladies who was in charge of the costume department was up in the control room and reportedly said to one of the directors: 'That guy over there holding the horse, he look so lonesome. Why don't you give him something to say?' *[laughs]* So, that's how I started. Her name was Pennebaker. (Pennebakers made that great film *Monterey Pop*. Did you ever see that? I hope you did. I don't know that she was connected to the Pennebaker family, but she's the only other person I know with that name. It's a very rare name, but perhaps there are many of them in England — I don't know.)

We all took turns at playing characters who would come to town on a Monday, and by Friday we'd either been shot, hung, run out of town, or we married the preacher's daughter, or joined the little community. And the next week, another stranger would come to town. Well, the show was very confusing to do — especially for the actors, who came down from New York to take these parts of the strangers with problems. As a result, they often missed their cues and wandered around in the outdoors when they were supposed to be running indoors to get to the interior set of the building that they were standing in front of, having come in on horseback, hitched up and said: 'Howdy, howdy, how are you doin'? I think I'll go in and have a drink here.' And you go inside and there's nothing behind it, just a false front. Then you run around it and get indoors to the studio where the set was already fixed up for the day's shoot. Certain sets were left there all the time because they were regularly in use. For example, the name of the local bar was the 'The Copper Copper' or something like that, and the lady who ran the bar she was a regular and so on. The show lasted for one year before it folded. It did very well in the ratings but they never got a sponsor, which is what they were after. They wanted to get a breakfast cereal sponsor to do it, but it didn't happen.

I never tried for a film career — never did, never did! But we made a little film between the time the cowboy show went off the air and the beginning of the horror movie job. One of the guys who used to watch the cowboy show called everybody out there who had been on the show. He thought that we were like a little touring group of actors, I guess. He had written a movie script. It was like a cop show, but no shooting as I recall, and he made this film out in the suburbs of Philadelphia for about $6,000. In those days $6,000 was a nice piece of change. It was called *A Key To Murder* and I played a detective. Somebody said that they saw it years ago on TV, but I haven't. But I did see it once, and it was pretty embarrassing.

For about two years after the cowboy show died, I was bumming around doing still photography. There were a lot of drug companies in Philadelphia and they did a lot of advertising to get doctors excited about their new discoveries. About that time they were coming out with tranquilizers, and I remember doing one tranquilizer series of still pictures where I was a guy who was a manic depressive or something like that. Anyway, they took a picture of me as if I was chasing my wife with a carving knife; then they took another picture of me sitting quietly reading a book after I took the pill — whatever that pill was! *[laughs]* It's true, that's what they did. I did a lot of

Chapter 14 – John Zacherle

stuff like that.

In the cowboy show I had played an undertaker one week, and about two years after the show folded they called me up from WCAU - Channel 10 and said: 'Do you want to be the MC for this horror show, where we just get a whole bunch of horror movies and we're the only ones allowed to play them in this town? We signed a contract and we can play all these movies all year long.' So I said: 'Okay.' I had no idea what they were talking about, never having seen a horror movie! But that's how I got into it, and my interest in horror films therefore started in 1957, when I got the job of MC for this show

I guess, maybe seventy movies were in this thing called *Shock Theatre*, which started in September 1957. It was a package of films that the people in Hollywood had gotten together, and they made deals with one television station in every city to allow them to play these films — for a fee, of course. My character was called Roland (Ro-LAND), a name dreamed up by Ed White, the producer, and Roland would be a sort of vampirish, crazy, looney, sometimes scary, mostly funny character who introduced the horror movie. I would say: 'Good evening, this is Roland. This evening's movie is a great old friend of mine, Count Dracula -ha -ha -ha.-ha.' And I would do some crazy experiments and so on in the intermissions. We had a lot of commercials here in this country — you didn't do that. I remember going to England many years ago. There were no commercials on the TV, which was shut down in the early evening hours so you could put the children to bed! But now, eventually, I think it's all become commercial.

The horror films appealed to me because I thought that some of them were really very good, very well done — the Dracula films with Bela Lugosi, and what Boris Karloff did. My favourite actors were Lugosi and Karloff, and the ladies — whose names I can't recall — who played with them in those old movies. Lon Chaney Jr. did *The Wolfman* and that was a big thing, but some of the other films he did were not too great.

We created such a *sensation* in Philadelphia! WCAU had an open house one time to see how many people were listening, so that they could try to get a key sponsor who would take over the whole show. The cops said it was 12,000 people; the station said there were 20,000 people. I would be happy if there was 2,000 people, but somewhere in there it was a whole mob of people! My sister was excited because I stopped traffic, and it was broadcast on the radio, and TV too, I guess, that you should avoid City Line, where the station was, because there was a big back-up of cars there. I think my father had died by the time I was appearing as Roland, but my mother enjoyed it. In fact, kids in her neighbourhood would come around and ask her if I was funny around the house like I was on TV, and all that kind of thing.

We used to open up that *Shock Theatre* show when I would come down a circular steel stairway that went up to a catwalk. It was a very big studio in Philadelphia, very high — must have been forty feet or more. Anyway, up at the top was the catwalk, so that the engineers could go up there and maneuver their lights and so on. So, I used that. They made the wall look like a dungeon and I would come down the stairs with a wicker basket in my arm, and it appeared to be dripping blood and that kind of thing. I would say: 'Good evening, my name is Roland.' Then I would recite a limerick that someone had sent in. Some people sent me limericks and some sent lyrics. They were all about ghouls and things like that. Nothing terribly dirty, but some of them were crazy:

There once was a girl named Irene
Whose hair was a dark shade of green.
When asked how she dyed it,
She simply confided:
'I just use the juice from my spleen.'

I came to record *Dinner With Drac* in 1958 because Bernie Lowe, the guy who ran Cameo-Parkway, used to sit home with his little daughter and watch the show and he got on to this business of reading these limericks. He called me up and said: 'Hey, we can make a record! Come on in.' So, his idea was to make a record of me reciting these crazy limericks, and his group of musicians, called Dave Appell and The Applejacks, would play, as he put it, some 'funky' music behind. I had never heard the word 'funky' before, and this was my introduction to pop music. *Dinner With Drac* didn't need many takes. They recorded at night — they had their offices and studio in a business building so they couldn't play music during the day. If they needed an echo effect, they used to put speakers out in the hallway.

So we made that song and it was 'a big smaash'. *[laughs]* I can hear him saying it: 'big smaash' — that's the way they say it up in New England — 'a big smaash theyre'. I didn't think anything at all about Bernie Lowe's idea to make a record. I just did it, and enjoyed doing it. No, siree, I had never been in a recording studio before then. Anyway, he made the 45, and it was a big hit and we made several others after that. The writers of *Dinner With Drac* were credited on the record as 'Sheldon–Land', but I think these were made-up names. The writer was Kal Mann and the music by Dave Appell; the players were the Applejacks. Kal Mann wrote 90% of all the Cameo-Parkway hits for Chubby Checker, Bobby Rydell, etc.

The original *Dinner With Drac* record label showed 'John Zacherle – "The Cool Ghoul" – who plays Roland'. Dick Clark coined 'The Cool Ghoul', but he didn't play any instruments on *Dinner With Drac* or attend the session. He was a good friend, and still is, but I haven't seen him in years. My girlfriend out in California used to work for him, and I saw him more often then than lately. I remember we were both commiserating many years ago: I lost a girlfriend and he was getting divorced from his wife.

I recorded for Cameo-Parkway. Dick was very close to Cameo-Parkway: they were in Philadelphia and so was he when he first started. So, they would just call him on the phone and say: 'Hey, do you want Chubby Checker to come out? Or the Orlons, or the Dovells, or Bobby Rydell? Do you want them out and get them on the air right away?' Whenever they had a new single, they'd call him up right away and see what he thought and so on. He had me on his show — usually at Halloween — which was a natural!

Igor was the original flip side of *Dinner With Drac*. It was dropped because of Dick Clark. He said that the original *Dinner With Drac* side was too gruesome, as he thought the lyrics too 'distasteful' or something. Well, it certainly wasn't gruesome by today's standards, or even then. So, we changed some of the lyrics — I honestly don't remember which ones or why; maybe... I don't know... I can't tell you.... — and came up with *Dinner With Drac (Part 1)* as the airplay side b/w *Dinner With Drac (Part 2)*, which was the original top side. The original record, with *Igor* as the 'B' side, is now a valuable record if you can find it. The record was never banned in the US, but it was banned and withdrawn in the UK. I have no idea if it was a hit in other countries... but maybe.

Did Dick Clark help to promote the record and did I appear on his *American Bandstand*? That's a good question. I suppose I must have. I know I never appeared on his *Caravan of Stars*, as that didn't really exist back in those days.

I did a tour of movie houses in Philadelphia when *Dinner With Drac* became a hit, with Frankie Avalon, Bobby Rydell, Chubby Checker, Fabian and Jerry Granahan — these are names of people you've probably heard of, or some of 'em. They were all people who had hits on the radio in those days. We'd do little stage shows and then they'd show some film. We had a good time. I remember Bobby Rydell saying to me: 'I'm going to make a million bucks by the time I'm thirty.' And he did better than that! But he was a nice guy, a very pleasant guy, a New York kid.

Did I forge any lasting friendships from this time? Mmmm, w-e-l-l... no! But I do know that I went back to Philadelphia about ten years ago, when they had a ceremony. They put people's names on the sidewalk: Dick Clark and so on. I was asked to be there, and share in that and give out awards. So, I was able to say: 'Hey! how are you doing!' *[laughs]* They were all very friendly because they all remembered me as Roland down there. It was a big deal, and they were all upset when I left town after just one year

I guess I followed *Dinner With Drac*'s progress into the Top Ten, but I don't really remember it. I didn't get a gold disc for one million sales, but it was on the chart for quite a few weeks and in the Top Ten. I remember that I had a lawyer who drew up the contract, and I think the guy gave me $10,000. He disappeared in the other room and said: 'I'll go see what...' So, you never know how many they sold — they could have kept two or three different kinds of books for all I know. But that sounded like a lot of money, and it was to me. And I honestly have no idea how many they sold, nobody ever knows. With regard to the other records — including the LPs I made after *Dinner With Drac* — I have no idea how they did either, nor do I remember how much they paid me.

Did *Dinner With Drac* change my life? Well, once you've made a lot of money from something like that original *Dinner With Drac*, you can't help but think: 'Maybe I made even more than I ever imagined, but I never, ever got it.' You'd have to *demand*; bring in lawyers and all that stuff to see — and they could hand you a set of books that meant nothing. You have no idea what goes on in the record business... or maybe you do!

Who was the guy who played the saxophone on *Dinner With Drac*? Everybody asks me about that! I don't remember. He was great. Oddly

Chapter 14 – John Zacherle

enough, I have re-recorded that. I have a CD out called *'The Dead Man's Ball'*. They re-recorded the whole thing and found a saxophone player on Long Island whose name was Paul something — I think his name is on the credits — and he had never heard the song! I must say, I think he's just as good as the other guy, but the nice thing about it is that they let him wail on much longer at the end of the song; they didn't just cut it. Because it was not to be a 45 any longer, you could just spend the time, so he just went wailing along. I often wanted to get him to come out and do conventions, which I do twice a year for people who like horror films. We have a party every Saturday night of the convention and the house band and do our best with *Dinner With Drac* and the Bobby Pickett song, *Monster Mash*.

In 1960, I recorded my first LP, *Spook Along With Zacherley* — a take-off of the *Sing Along With Mitch* television show — for Elektra Records. The guy who arranged the music had done Broadway shows and was a very competent guy. I was amazed when I walked into this big studio, which was over in Bayside, Queens, I think, where a lot of big bands used to record. I walked in and, my Lord, there were six or seven people and a nice little orchestra with violins, trumpets, keyboard and all this sort of stuff. We did the record, and I remember losing my voice after the first song because I really wasn't a trained singer, so they fed me hot tea all night till we got through it. I think we did the whole thing in one night, but I'm not sure. Is that possible?

Anyway, that didn't really take off. I forget what happened. I was on the air and I went to another station. I don't remember ever using this LP on the air... I *must* have — but I don't remember. It didn't catch on, but it is being re-released. They discovered not long ago that the actual master tapes had been in the closet somewhere. Elektra was sold, as all these companies get sold, back and forth. It became Geffen Records at one time, then it became something else. Eventually, Allen Klein — no, he got Cameo-Parkway label: he had the Beatles all wrapped up in a miserable contract here for a long time in New York City. But it is being released on what they call Collectors' Choice label along with a lot of other stuff that was produced back in the Fifties,

Chapter 14 – John Zacherle

Sixties and so on.

A few years later, I think I did two albums for Bernie Lowe back at Cameo-Parkway. One was called *Scary Tales* and the other was called *Monster Mash*. After Bobby Pickett made the song *Monster Mash [1962]*, they decided they would cover that and make an album, and they did it in just two days! They took all the hits they had in the Cameo-Parkway library, put earphones on me, and played back the musical tracks and changed the words to make parodies of their own songs. So, it cost them, like, nothing to make this thing and they had it out on the market as an LP before the Bobby Pickett boys knew what happened. The songs were written by Kal Mann, who wrote songs for the other people in the Cameo stable, and they were all hit songs. So, the *Hully Gully* became *Hurry, Bury Baby*, *The Cha Cha Cha* became *The Ha-Ha-Ha*. After that, there were no more albums until my recent CD *'Dead Man's Ball'*, which I mentioned before.

Normally, in those days, you'd make a single and then you'd make another single. If you made a big noise with those, then they would make an album. Nowadays, you have to come into the studio with enough for a full CD. It's been that way for a while, a long time, actually — back in the days of 33⅓rds.

After *Dinner With Drac* in 1958, it was time to move on to the big city, and I left WCAU and came to WABC - Channel 7 in New York City and did the same kind of show here from September of that year. We changed the name of my MC character from Roland to 'Zacherley' because, broadcasting from New York and Philadelphia, there are people in the middle who could get both stations. The people in New York were concerned that if I used the name Roland, which I used in Philadelphia, that the people who ran the station down there would object that I had stolen this name. So they said: 'Well, your name's kinda funny. Do you want to use your name?' I said: 'Sure, that's okay,' so that's how 'Zacherley' became the name in New York, and I did it here for about four years.

I went from one station to another using all the scary movies that they had, and then I ran into a guy, name of Barry Landers, who was a floor manager at the last television station and he said: 'Hey! They're opening a new television station over in New Jersey in Newark. I have suggested to them that they do a dancing show.' They had to do counter-programming because they couldn't get any films, as all the stations in New York had signed up every kind of a film. This was done by agreeing to have a dancing show, as nothing like that was going on in New York City. Dick Clark was going of course, but there was no local show going on. They also had bullfights from Mexico — nobody was doing that of course — and they had some interview shows that nobody was duplicating. Also, various language shows (Spanish, German, Italian, etc) and the English-speaking programmes. I was part of that scene with *Disc-O-Teen* around 1965.

Every afternoon we had an hour of dancing. We didn't have any scenery — we just made it look dark and mysterious. They had painted the whole walls a kind of dark color. It had been a Shriners' Temple at one time: a big place, a *huge* auditorium. At one time, while our show was on the air, the Rolling Stones came through there and played, and we got to introduce them. It was very exciting. Nobody could hear us though, as the kids were screaming so hard.

I did the dancing show in New Jersey for about two and a half years until it closed. A friend of mine, Vaughn Meader, used to watch the show on TV and, after I came back from the studio, I often went to his place for dinner, and we'd talk about the show and all the new music that was coming out. He did an album years ago called *The First Family*, which was a take-off on the Kennedys. Vaughn mimicked the voice of J.F.K. and it was produced by Earle Doud. It was a *huge* success. He made lots of money and then he just spent it. Unfortunately, he didn't save it the way he should have. He made other versions of that — whoever became president he would do a comedy album on them — but they did not sell as well as the very first one which was 'a big smash hit' as they used to say in the record business here.

I got into music because of that dancing show. Everything was on little 45 rpm records. Remember them, with the big hole in the middle? When it ended, this friend of mine, over dinner, said: 'Why don't you go down to the radio station WNEW-FM, they're changing their format.' Up to that point, they had been playing big band music, Frank Sinatra and things like that. The Government said if you own an AM and a FM station, you will not be allowed just to play identical programming, you have to get separate programming. So, they decided they would go in for the LPs that were coming out: the Beatles, the Doors, the Kinks and all those things. I went down and told a guy what my history of music was: I had been doing the dancing show for nearly

Chapter 14 – John Zacherle

Zach with monster and unknown stage hand.

three years. It turned out that the guy I spoke to went home and asked his son if he thought it was a good idea to hire Zacherley, and the kid said: 'Yeah!' I guess that Zacherley was something that the kid remembered from the early Sixties, and here it was 1967 and the kid is now a little older and listening to good music and all this stuff — 'the new music' as we called it.

So, that's how I got into FM radio, and I did that for seven or eight years. The best part was the very first station I went to, when we were able to play anything we wanted to — much like John Peel. Back in the old days, he was famous for that also: playing the best that he could find and making up his own shows each night. I left that station and went to another station that was more 'far out', as we used to say. They were playing jazz and all kinds of things, but in the end the management decided that they would have to go to a playlist, and they did that and that was not awfully enjoyable. It was just like an easy job, but it was painful because we were playing the same thing. I suppose everywhere around the world the same things happen: management takes over and you get a playlist and that's where everything ends up.

I am meandering here — but I'm old enough to meander without anybody arguing with me!

At one time I was in two plays. One was called *Memo For A Green Thumb*, the other one was *La Belle Hélène*, which was like an early Andrew

Chapter 14 – John Zacherle

Lloyd-Webber type of show. They used all the melodies from Offenbach and put their own words to them. It was a story about Helen of Troy and King Menelaus and all that kind of stuff. One guy who was in it was interesting enough. He was George Segal, who became a Hollywood star. He was taking the part of the guy who was supposed to be romancing Helen of Troy. Actually, the part was to be taken by an opera singer who was out on the road and would not be available until two weeks before the show. So, we were rehearsing all along here and George is taking this guy's part, but George couldn't sing. But George did such a good job reading and doing these lines that they decided, by the time that the guy came back who was supposed to do the singing and talking, that they would pay him off and keep George. That meant that they had to have somebody to sing, so it turned out that they figured out a plan — a *bad* plan.

Whenever it came time for George to sing, he had a servant who would appear in the background, or at an open window, or he would come walking along and stand and sing songs to her. What a silly idea, really! Anyway, the show died in Philadelphia as I recall. But that was an experience for me, and I realized that being on the stage was not something I really wanted to do. I couldn't see being in a successful play and coming in and doing the same thing every night forever — although that rarely happens. But right now, actually, I live in a building here where there's a lady who's been head of the costume department in *Les Misérables.* That's been going on for *years.* Years! Unheard of! She even bought a house, she's doing so well. But there's talk now that the show is finally going to close. At any rate, I was not encouraged to stay in it. The two plays I was in were more or less comedies, and I enjoyed that, but I couldn't see doing it forever. I never liked learning lines anyway. I was always scared that I would say the wrong thing, and I did on occasions.

So, life, life, life! I'm retired now. This is a big area here, you know — New York, New Jersey and Connecticut — l-o-t of civilization here, lot of people, and we have a convention every Halloween and one right after Easter, just across the river. It's in the area where the professional football players play, maybe a half hour from here; I'm in Manhattan. Thousands of people show up and they just keep coming back. We wondered how many people would show up after the bombing of the World Trade Center. More people showed up than ever before! It was incredible.

I never got married. I thought I'll never be able to support myself and a family and I had no intention of having 'a day job', as they say if you're an actor. So there are no children. I have enjoyed, and do enjoy the company of some very nice ladies, and one of them just went back to California after New Year.

Am I like my character? I like kidding around. I kid around all the time. But no, no, I don't dress as the Roland/Zacherley character on the street, I don't do that! *[laughs]* In fact, I just got a new coat: I had somebody make me a new black coat — a Prince Albert coat is what I wore. I had two original ones from the 1890s — true, really true. That theater group I belonged to in Philadelphia had a great wardrobe department where people would unload their old clothes. A lot of the rich people in that area dumped off

Chapter 14 – John Zacherle

a lot of really classy old clothes, and that's where I got my first Prince Albert coat. I wore that one out, I wore another one out, and just about six months ago I had to make a new one because it was getting too ratty.

Interests outside of showbusiness? I like nature a lot and, in my old age, I like going for drives. We have a great place here: we have a great highway that goes up right up along the river up into the mountains which are about fifty minutes away. I'm anxious to go up there and see how it looks with the snow and the ice on them. There are a lot of lakes up there and it's a beautiful spot.

Looking back, would I change anything? *Yes*, in all seriousness. I was not a very good businessman and there were things I could have done — but I'm just not into self-promotion. I should have hitched up with somebody, I guess. A good friend of mine, who I met at one of the radio stations, he did that. He knew how to do it, and he's now living out in Hollywood Hills and still working occasionally. He did a lot of voices for cartoons — Hanna-Barbera people and all that — and also he did some nice small parts in films, but I never, ever got into that. What does the future hold? *Oh my God!* You'll have to ask George Bush. I have no idea! But what he has to say, I'm afraid, wouldn't interest me too much.

How would I like to be remembered? Oh, that life is worth living and you gotta enjoy it. This is it. I think that this is really *it!* I don't really believe that you're going to go to some other place and find all your — I had a friend who was so sure that he was going to meet his mother and father *in the flesh!* I said: 'Come on, come on.' But, at any rate, if people believe that, that's okay, but I think this is a one-trip deal, and it's pretty wonderful. So, you do the best you can and be nice to each other.

This is the end of the broadcast here; we're not gonna broadcast anymore. I'm gonna send this to you and maybe in place of 8x10's for illustrations I'll send you a picture-book that one of the guys that comes to the conventions put together. Actually, he's a State Trooper in the state of Pennsylvania — which is a good two hours away from here — and a big fan. I think there's every picture in the world in there you can copy from. So, David, my boy, thank you, thank you. And as we used to say at the end of the show: 'Bye-bye, whatever you are! Ha-ha-ha-ha...'

The Interviews

1. **Freddie Bell**
   By letter and tape, 2004.

2. **Martin Denny**
   By email, 2003.

3. **Johnny Farina**
   By email, 2003.

4. **Kalin Twins**
   By email, 2003.

5. **Robin Luke**
   By email and tape, 2002 and 2003.

6. **Chas McDevitt**
   By telephone, 2004.

7. **Phil Phillips**
   By email, 2003.

8. **Marvin Rainwater**
   By email and tape, 2003.

9. **Herb Reed**
   By telephone, 2003.

10. **Tommy Sands**
    By telephone and letter, 2004.

11. **Joe Terranova**
    By telephone and email, 2003.

12. **Mitchell Torok**
    By email, 2004.

13. **Marty Wilde**
    7 May 1987, Knebworth, Herts.

14. **John Zacherle**
    By letter and tape, 2003.

Index

1-2-3 136
Abergavenny 174
Absolute Monster Gentlemen 91
Across The Bridge 85
Action In The Afternoon (TV show) 180
Acuff, Roy 101
Adelman, Ben 102
Adler, Buddy 127
A Key To Murder (film) 181
Albino Stallion 102
Albritten, Dub 147
All American Boy 164
Allen, Steve 127
All I Have To Do Is Dream 59
Allison, Joe & Audrey 127
Alpert, Herb 25
Alston, Shirley 138
Ambrose 80
American Bandstand (TV show)
    17, 19, 33, 46, 95, 104, 132, 133, 185
    See also *Bandstand*
American Eagle 47
Ames, Lauri 83, 84
Andrews, Paul 86
Angry 169
Anka, Paul 83, 95, 134
Anthony & The Sophomores 137
Apache 167
Appell, Dave, & The Applejacks 184
Armstrong, Louis 89
Arnold, Eddy 56, 64, 125, 143, 146
As Time Goes By 51
Atkins, Chet 126, 154
At The Hop 131, 132, 133, 134, 136, 138, 139
Autry, Gene 101, 180
Avalon, Frankie 42, 62, 128, 185
Back To The Hop 136
Bad Boy 68, 157, 162, 167
Bain, Bob 127
Baja Marimba Band 25
Baked Alaska (CD) 29
Baker, LaVern 83, 95
Ballard Jr, Clint 38, 39, 40, 41, 43, 46
Banana Boat Song (Day-O) 84
Bandstand (TV show) 133, 147
Bare, Bobby 107
Barry, Len 136
Bart, Lionel 159
Bass, Ralph 114
Bassey, Shirley 149
Baverstock, Jack 84, 85
Baxter, Les 26, 29

Beatles 47, 54, 69, 131, 163, 175, 187, 189
Beautiful Brown Eyes 64
Because I'm A Dreamer 106
Bechtel, Perry 54, 55
Beggar of Love, The 38, 39
Bell, Freddie, & The Bellboys **15-23**, 87, 88
Bell Notes 33
Be Mindful What You Do 97
Bennett, Jean 116-7
Bennett, Les 87
Bennett, Tony 37, 51
Benny, Jack 127
Benson, Gerry 85
Benton, Brook 121
Berry, Chuck 42, 71, 83, 134
Bertram, Bob 57, 58, 61
Big D Jamboree (radio show) 153
Biggest Show of Stars (package tour) 120, 134
Billy & The Essentials 137
Bishop, Dickie 85, 89
Bishop, Stephen 70
Black Land Farmer 153
Blavat, Jerry 135
Block, Sandy 83
Blocker, David 28
Blue Hawaii (film) 53, 62
Bogart, Humphrey 16
Boo Hoo 103, 105, 106
Boone, Pat 68, 134
Borgnine, Ernest 159
Bouquet Of Roses 56
Bowen, Jimmy 154
Boxer, The 154
Boy Meets Girls (TV show) 157, 167, 168
Bradley, Harold 104, 147
Bradley, Owen 146-7, 154
Bramwell, Bill 84, 87
Brando, Marlon 82
Branker, Rupert 117
Breakfast Of Champions (film) 28
Brent, Frankie 17, 21
Brewer, Teresa 102
Bromley, Tex 149
Brown, Jim Ed 153
Brown, Joe 89, 163, 175
Brown, Ruth 83
Browns 168
Brunnely, Joe 159
Burgess, Dave 72
Burton, Ed 34
Bury Me Beneath The Willow 101
Bush, George W. (President) 192

Index

Bush, Ray, & The Avon Cities Jazz Band 85, 89
Butterfly 65
Bye Bye Love 83
Cadillacs 83
Cagney, James 16
Calton Weaver, The 80
Calvert, Eddie 43, 44
Campbell, Glen 72-3, 134, 153
Cannon, Freddy 136, 168
Caravan Of Stars (package tour) 95, 185
Caribbean 141, 144, 145, 147, 148, 149-151, 152, 153, 154
Caribbean (LP) 151
Carl & The Commanders 136
Carlucci, Bill 137
Carson, Johnny 19, 27
Carter, Dennis 82, 84
Cash, Johnny 63-4, 71, 103, 107, 124, 151, 155, 168
Cha Cha Cha, The 188
Champs 134
Chaney Jr, Lon 183
Charles Singers, Ray 40
Checker, Chubby 136, 184, 185
Chicka Chicka Honey 68
Chopin, Frédéric 29
Chudd, Lew 148
City Ramblers 78
Clanton, Jimmy 33
Clapton, Eric 51
Clark, Dick 42, 46, 60, 61, 62, 68, 95, 104, 120, 132, 147, 177, 186, 190-1, 194
Clark, Roy 108
Clay, Cassius 174
Cleary, John 91
Coasters 95, 112, 113
Cobb, Arnett 16
Cochran, Eddie 164, 168, 171
Cohen, Paul 146-7, 147-8
Cole, Buddy 38
Cole, Nat 'King' 37, 129
Colgate Comedy Hour (TV show) 19
Collie, Biff 125
Collins, Joan 80
Collins, Joe 80
Colon, Augie 25, 26
Columbus, Christopher 145
Colyer, Ken 81, 89
Comancheros 151
Como, Perry 16, 31, 33, 61, 71, 127, 139
Confessions Of A Dangerous Mind (film) 28
Conti, Russ 17
Control 165
Cooke, Sam 65
Cookie & The Cupcakes 94
Cool And Crazy 17
Copeland, Ken 148
Corsin, Amel 132

Cort, Bob 79
Costa, Fred 17
Cotton, Billy 157
Cotton Song, The 80, 85
Cramer, Floyd 46-7, 104, 147
Crane River Jazz Band 76, 78
Creedence Clearwater Revival 108
Crests 33
Crickets - *See* Holly, Buddy
Cromer, Harold 134
Crosby, Bing 31
Crosby, Bob 27
Cross, Sylvester 146, 155
Daddy And Home 143
Daddy's Footprints 108
Daddy's Glad You Came Home 102
Danny & The Juniors **131-9**
Darin, Bobby 38, 135
Dark Town Strutters' Ball 76
Davidson, Harold 20
Davis Jr, Sammy 31
Day, Bobby 61
Day, Doris 171
Dead Man's Ball (CD) 187, 188
Dean, Don 25
Dean, James 125
Dene, Terry 83
Denny, Martin **25-9**
Desperately Seeking Susan (film) 171
Dickens, Little Jimmy 107, 124
Diddley, Bo 42
Dining With Martin Denny (CD) 29
Dinner With Drac 177, 183-185, 186-7, 188
Disc-O-Teen (TV show) 188
Disney, Walt 54, 55
Dr. John 91
Doin' The Continental Walk 136
Domino, Fats 38, 42, 89
Donegan, Lonnie 42, 75, 78, 79, 83, 87, 89, 175
Donna 157, 161
Don't 164
Don't Drop It 126
Don't Let The Stars Get In Your Eyes 145
Doo, Dickie, & The Don'ts 134
Doors 189
Dottie 136
Doud, Earle 189
Dougherty, Marion 126
Douglas, Jo 160
Douglas, Shirley 85, 86, 87, 89, 91
Dovells 185
Draper, Rusty 83
Drifters (USA) 95
Drifters (UK) - *See* Shadows
Duff, Arlie 152-3
Duncan, Johnny 85, 105
Eager, Vince 91
Eaglin, Snooks 89
Eastwood, Clint 153

Index

Ebb Tide 35, 113
Echols, Pop 124, 125
Eddy, Duane 34
Ednie, Dick 57, 59
Ednie, George 59
Edwards, Tommy 106
Edwards, Webley 26
Electric Light Yellow Magic Orchestra 28
Elvis Presley (LP) 158
Enchanted Sea, The 25, 27
Endless Sleep 157, 161, 163, 164
Entwhistle, John 89
Epstein, Brian 163
Evans, Paul 40
Everlovin' 68
Everly Bros. 34, 38, 42, 59, 83, 89, 134, 158
Exotica (LP) 26, 27, 28
Fabian 42, 185
Fabulous Four 137
Fabulous Johnny Cash, The (LP) 64
Face In The Crowd 153
Face In The Rain 85
Fame, Georgie 87
Farewell 153
Farina, Ann 31, 32
Farina, Johnny **31-5**
Feld, Irvin 19, 134
Festival of Britain 76
Fike, Lamar 167
Finch, Earl 59
Firecrackers 28
First Family, The (LP) 189
Five Minutes More 61
Fly, The 136
Flynn, Errol 179
Foley, Red 102
Ford, Tennessee Ernie 127
Forget Me Not 37, 42, 45, 51
Formby, George 75
Four Aces 38
Four J's 137
Four Lads 38
Four Lovers 136
Four Preps 132
Four Seasons 136
Four Tops 121
Francis, Connie 42, 99, 103, 134
Frankie And Johnny 175
Franklin, Jimmy 144
Franks, Tillman 124, 151
Franz, Johnny 161
Fraulein 153
Freed, Alan 19, 83, 95, 133, 134
Freeman, Art & Dottie 58
Freight Train 75, 79, 80-1, 82-3, 84, 85, 91, 158
Funicello, Annette 95
Fury, Billy 91, 163, 167
Gamblin' Man 106
Garland, Hank 83

Gateway Quartet 93
Geisha Girl 153
Gershwin, George 29
Get Yourself A College Girl (film) 21
Ghost Of St. Maria, The 96
Gibson, Steve, & The Redcaps 131
Giddy-Up-A Ding Dong 15, 18, 19, 20, 22, 79
Giveaway, The 47
Give Thanks 115
Glaser, Joe 17
Godfrey, Arthur 16, 54, 102
Golden Gate Quartet 93, 111
Gonna Find Me A Bluebird 99, 102, 103
Good, Jack 91, 160, 161, 164
Gordon, Lee 19, 63, 128
Gore, Lesley 136
Gorn, Isadore 25
Grammer, Billy 47
Granahan, Jerry 185
Grand Ole Opry (radio show) 101, 153, 155
Grayson, Larry 80
Great Pretender, The 111
Green Back Dollar 85
Grofe, Ferdie 26, 29
Guess, Bill 107
Guitar, Bonnie 63, 64
Gunter, Cornell 111, 112, 113
Gunter, Shirley, & The Queens 115
Ha-Ha-Ha, The 188
Haley, Bill, & His Comets 19, 21, 42, 120
Half-Breed 106
Hamilton, Roy 93
Hamilton, Russ 89
Hanna–Barbera 192
Hardy, Rick 90
Harlem Globetrotters 89
Harlow, Jean 178-9
Harman, Buddy 147
Harris, Jet 90
Harris, Rolf 175
Harris, Wynonie 16
Harrison, Lennie 84
Hart, Freddie 107
Have You Loved Your Woman Today? 155
Hawaii Calls (TV show) 26, 27
Hawaii Five-O (TV show) 129
Hawkins, Hawkshaw 107
Hawkins, Screamin' Jay 83
Henderson, Dickie 149
Henderson, Joe 80
Hep Dee Hootie (Cutie Wootie) 127
Her Hair Was Yellow 161, 164
Hey! Now 115
High Class Baby 162
High Curley Stompers 76-7
Ho, Don 129
Hodge, Alex 111, 112, 115
Hoedown Corner (radio show) 125
Holland, Jools 90
Holliday, Michael 43, 86-7

Index

Holly, Buddy/Crickets
    56, 71, 89, 134, 158, 164, 168
Hollywood Flames 134
Holzman, Marv 40
Hometown Jamboree (TV show) 126
Honeycomb 161
Honeydrippers 96
Honky Tonk Man (film) 153
Honolulu Symphony Orchestra 61
Horn, Bob 19
Horowitz, Vladimir 29
Horton, Johnny 124, 145, 151
Hot And Cold 103, 105, 106, 108
Hound Dog 17, 18
House of The Rising Sun 76
    See also *New Orleans*
Howland, Chris 69
Howlin' Wolf 167
Hully Gully 188
Hurry, Bury Baby 177, 188
I Beg Of You 164
I Dig You Baby 106
I Don't Remember Loving You 154
Igor 185
I Gotta Go Get My Baby 102
I Hate Me For Loving You 154
I'm Satisfied 85
Ink Spots 111
Innamorata 139
Intimate Martin Denny, The (CD) 29
Irwin, Randy 138
I Still Get Jealous 61
It's Been Nice 171
It's Impossible 139
It's Only The Beginning 37, 45, 51
I Walk The Line 64
I Was A Teenage Caveman 177
Jackson, Janet 165
Jackson, Mahalia 93
Jackson, Shot 148
Jailhouse Rock 165
James, Etta 41, 51
James, Sonny 153
James Brothers 24
Jefferson, Joe 112
Jennings, Waylon 155
Jets 90
Jewel, Jimmy 43
Jewel & Warris 43
*Jim Reeves, Me
    And Mexican Joe* (book/CD) 155
Jo, Damita 151
Joe's Apartment (film) 28
Johnnie & Jack 124
Johnny B. Goode 71
Johnny Cash Show (package tour) 63
Johnny-O 85
Jones, Gale 148
Jones, John Paul 89
Jones, Spike 83

Jordanaires 127, 147
Joye, Col 63, 66-7
Jubalaires 93
Juella 94
Jumpin' Jack 39, 41
Juvenairs 132
Kalin, Jack 37
Kalin Twins **37-51**, 83
Kane, Jackie 17
Karloff, Boris 183
Kassel, Art 123
Kaye, Danny 16
Keeney, Chick 17
Keep, Ted 27
Kelly, Bobby 81
Kennedy, John 79
Kennedy, John F. (President) 189
Kent, Tommy 69
Kerr Singers, Anita 147
Khoury, George 94, 95-6, 97
Kidd, Johnny 90
Kim, Frank 26
King, Carole 169
King, Claude 151
Kinks 189
Kirchin, Basil 158
Klein, Allen 187
Kohn, Tony 84, 87
Kraft Theater (TV show) 126
Kramer, Billy J. 171
Kramer, John 25
La Belle Hélène (stage musical) 190
Lady Of The Mountain (TV show) 124
Laine, Frankie 31, 37, 51, 157
Landers, Barry 188
Lang, Bob 27
Lang, Don 175
La Rue, Danny 166
Lattanzi, Peppino 18
Laurie, Cy 78
Lawrence, Nick 79
Lee, Brenda 147, 168
Lee, Sally 144
Leonard, Joe 147-8
Le Sacre du Sauvage (LP) 26
Les Misérables (play) 191
Lewis, George 89
Lewis, Jerry 19
Lewis, Jerry Lee 46, 87, 128
Lewis, Vic 77
Little Anthony & The Imperials 133, 135
Little Children 171
Little Girl 169
Little Richard 136, 158
Little Walter 89
Lloyd, A.L. 86
Lloyd-Webber, Andrew 190-1
Local Yokels 143
Lodge, John 89
Logan, Horace 124

Index

Londonaires 43
Lopez, Jennifer 28
Lorenz, George 'Hound Dog' 133
Lotis, Denis 175
Louisiana Hayride (radio show) 124, 145, 146
Louisiana Hayride Reunion 154
Louvin, Charlie 107
Love Me Baby 106
Love Pains 125, 126
Lowe, Bernie 184, 188
Lugosi, Bela 183
Luke, Robin **53-73**
Lunch With Mother Goose 177
Lyman, Arthur 25, 26, 27
Lymon, Frankie, & The Teenagers 120, 132
Lynch, David 112, 113, 114, 120, 121
MacGregor, Jimmie 81, 84
Mack, Ted 16
Madara/Medera, Johnny - See Medora, Johnny
Maddox, Rose 102
Madonna 171
Maestro, Johnny 33
Maffei, Bob 138
Maffei, Frank 131-2, 134, 136, 137, 138
Magic Fallacy, The (play) 125
Mahal, Taj 91
Majesty Of Love, The 99, 103
Mann, Kal 184, 188
Marie 153
Mariza 90
Marsh, Tony 43
Martin, Dean 19, 31, 139, 153, 154
Martin, Grady 104, 147, 148
Martino, Al 121
Marty (film) 159
Marvin, Hank 86, 90
May, Brian 89
Mayo, Jerry 17
McCall, Bill 102
McDevitt, Chas 20, 21, **75-91**, 158, 159
McKuen, Rod 127
McVay, Kimo 57
Meader, Vaughn 189
Medora, Johnny 132, 136
Melody Ranch (radio show) 124
Memo For A Green Thumb (play) 190
Metis, Frank 27
Mexican Joe 141, 144, 147,152, 153, 154
Michener, James A. 26
Midwest Texas Jubilee (radio show) 145
Mighty Clouds Of Joy 111
Miller, Frankie 153
Miss Otis Regrets 76
Mr. Bojangles 154
Mitchell, Guy 157
Moffatt, Tom 58, 59
Molly Darling 56, 64
Monash, Paul 126
Monster Mash 187, 188
Monster Mash (LP) 188

Monterey Pop (film) 181
Moody Blues 89
Moonglows 83
Moore, Bob 147
Moore, Merrill E. 127
Morris, Sonny 78
Morris & Mitch 79
Morrison, Jimmy 63
Morrow, Buddy 134
Most, Mickie 160
Most Brothers 43
Mount, Peggy 91
Move It 162, 167, 171
Move Me Baby, Move Me 17
Mud 89
Muddy Waters 89, 167
Mudlarks 43
Mure, Bill 83
Music Hall Week 91
Musselwhite, Charlie 70
My Buddy 101
Myers, Gerry 82
My Love Song 128
*My Mommy Bought Me
    An Ice Cream Cone* 124
My Old Man 87
My Prayer 111, 117, 119
Nacogdoches County Line 143
Nancy Whiskey (The Calton Weaver) 80
Nelson, Ken 126, 127, 128
Nelson, Maxine 155
Nelson, Rick(y) 56, 68
New Orleans (House Of The Rising Sun) 79, 84
New Orleans Jazz Festival 91
Nina & Frederik 87
Nolte, Nick 28
No Money Down 147
None But The Brave (film) 128
Norwood (film) 153
Norwood's Coming Home 153
No Sweeter Cheater Than You 153
Now, The Hop Fields (TV show) 86
Offenbach, Jacques 191
Oh Boy! (TV show) 91, 157, 167, 168, 171
Oh Gee 137
Oklahoma Hills 124
Old Time Rock'n'Roll 108
One More Time 46
Only You 111
Oo-La-La-Limbo 136
*Open Up The Door
    And Let The Good Times In* 153
Orioles 17
Orlons 185
Owens, Buck 127
Oxford, Vernon 155
Ozark Jubilee (TV show) 102
Pacino, Al 96
Page, Patti 42, 127, 134

199

Index

Parker, Colonel Tom 18, 59, 123, 125-6, 129, 145
Parnes, Larry 79, 157, 159-160, 162, 163, 168-9
Parsons, Louella 26
Patterson, Floyd 159
Paul, John 79, 81, 84
Peabody, Eddie 55
Peel, John 190
Penguins 17
Pennebaker, D.A. 181
Perryman, Tom 144
Phillips, Phil **93-7**
Pickett, Bobby 'Boris' 187, 188
Pierce, Webb 101, 107
Piney Woods Boogie 143
Pink Chiffon 151
Pinnochio (show) 15
Platters 19, 21, 42, **111-121**, 128
Playmates 63
Pledge Of Love 147-8, 154
Pleis, Jack 39, 40, 41, 50
Pogues 80
Pomus, Doc 171
Pony Express 136
Porter, Cole 29
Potter, Bob 77
Powell, Roy 87
Precious Jewel, The 101
Presley, Elvis 18, 53, 56, 59, 62, 71, 103, 123, 124, 125, 126, 128, 129, 146, 149, 153, 158, 164, 166, 167, 170, 171, 174
Pride, Charley 151
Prima, Louis 131
Proud Mary 108
PTA Rock And Roll 151
Pure Steel (Volume 1) (CD) 34
Quiet Village 25, 26, 27
Raft, George 154
Ragsdale, Harvey 25, 26
Rags To Riches 51
Railroaders 86
Rainwater, Bob 99
Rainwater, Cedric 99
Rainwater, Marvin **99-109**
Rainwater, Patti 99, 106
Rainwater, Ray 99, 101, 102, 103, 104, 107
Raitt, Bonnie 91
Ram, Buck 115, 116-7, 119, 120
Randazzo, Teddy 83
Randolph, Boots 46
Rapp, Danny 132, 133-4, 136, 137-8
Ravens 111, 116
Ray, Johnnie 37, 38, 45, 49, 50, 51, 157
Rayburn, Margie 134
Redd, Gail Ramona 144, 147
Red Light, Green Light 141, 147, 149
Reece, Red 87
Reed, B. Mitchell 127

Reed, Herb **111-121**
Reeves, Jim 124, 141, 144, 145, 154, 155
Remember This 81
Reynolds, Jody 161
Rhumba Boogie 145
Richard, Cliff 42, 44, 49-50, 90, 162, 163, 164, 167, 170-1, 175
Richards, Rick 90
Ricks, Jimmy 116
Righteous Brothers 129
Riley, Norm 103
Ring-A-Ding-A-Ding 126, 128
Robeson, Paul 43
Robi, Paul 115-6, 117, 120, 121
Robin Hood (film) 179
Robins 113
Robison, Fabor 144, 145, 146, 147, 151, 154, 155
Rockabilly Wildman (CD) 108
Rock And Roll Is Here To Stay 131, 136, 139
Rock Around The Clock (film) 15, 21
Rockin' The Polonaise 21
Rock Island Line 158, 175
Rodgers, Jimmie 101, 143
Rodgers & Hammerstein 25-6, 29
Roe, Tommy 69
Rogers, Barbara Ellen 124
Rogers, Roy 101, 180
Rolling Stones 51, 71, 188
Roulette 147
Roza, Lita 175
Rubinstein, Arthur 29
Rumble On The Docks (film) 21
Ruth, Babe 143
Rydell, Bobby 168, 184, 185
St. Louis Trio 78
Salvo, Richie 17
Samwell, Ian 'Sammy' 162
Sands, Ben 123
Sands, Tommy **123-9**
Santo & Johnny **31-5**
Save The Last Dance For Me 151
Scary Tales (LP) 188
Scottise, Artie 132
Seals, Jimmy 72
Seals & Crofts 72
Seaman, Phil 163
Sea Of Love 93, 94-6, 97, 157
Sea Of Love (film) 96
Sears, Al 83
Seat, Don 46
Segal, George 191
Segal, Nat 133, 135, 136, 138
Seger, Bob 108
Settlin' Down 153
Seventeenth Spring 169
Shad, Bob 18, 19
Shadows/Drifters 44, 90
Shake A Hand 19
Shakin' All Over 90

Index

Shannon [Marty Wilde] 174
Shannon, Del 96
Sharratt, Marc 78, 79, 81, 82, 88, 91
Shepherd, Jeannie 107
Sheridan, Tony 90
Shirelles 138
Shock Theatre (TV show) 177, 183
Shore, Dinah 27, 127
Show Of Stars (package tour) 59, 65
Shuler, Eddie 94, 97
Shuman, Mort 171
Silver Seagull 47
Sinatra, Frank 16, 27, 31, 68, 128, 129, 189
Sinatra, Nancy 123, 128, 129
Sincerely 138
Sing Along With Mitch (TV show) 187
Sing Boy Sing (film) 127
Singer, Artie 132, 133, 136, 137, 139
Singin' Idol, The (TV play) 123, 126, 127, 129
Singleton, Shelby 151
Six-Five Special (TV show) 160
Skylark 96
Sleeping At The Foot Of The Bed 124
Sleep Walk 31, 32-3, 34, 35
Smith, Carl 151-2, 153
Smith, Harmie 124
Smoke Gets In Your Eyes 111, 119
Snow, Hank 143, 145, 146, 151
Solomon, Phil 149
Someone's Watching Over Me 109
Sometimes 132, 136
Sometimes It Comes 47
South Pacific (musical) 26
Spider And The Fly, The 38, 39
Spitz, Lester 25
Spook Along With Zacherley (LP) 187
Sporting Life 87
Stagecrafters 180
Starr, Kay 51
Starr, Randy 27
Stars of Jazz (TV show) 27
Steele, Tommy
        20-1, 79, 85, 157, 159, 160, 163
Stevenson, Augustus 106
Stone, Cliffie 126, 127
Stormy Weather 96
Sturges, John 26
Styne, Jule 61
Sullivan, Big Jim 163
Sullivan, Ed 19, 33, 42, 82, 83, 84, 91, 103, 127, 134
Summer Festival (package tour) 83
Summertime Blues 171
Sunday Morning Coming Down 154
*Sunday Night At
    The London Palladium* (TV show) 105, 149
Sunshine Ruby 126
Supremes 161
Susie Darlin' 53, 56-9, 60-1, 68, 69, 70-1
Swamp Pop Ponderosa Stomp (festival) 96

Sweet Slumber 93
Sweet Sugar Lips 37, 45, 51
Syrup Soppin' Blues 125
Tag-A-Long 40
Tales Of The South Pacific (book) 26
Tapps, Georgie 18
Tarzan 25
Taxi 154
Taylor, Sam 'The Man' 83
Taylor, Zola 115, 120, 121
Tear Drop 34
Teen-Age Crush 123, 126, 127, 128, 129
Teenage Letter 87
Teenager In Love 157
Temptations 121
*Tennessee Heroes
    And Other Tall Tales* (CD) 155
Tennessee Mountain Boys 124
Tequila 72
Terranova, Joe **131-9**
Terry, Joe - *See* Terranova, Joe
Testa, Jimmy 137
Tex Sons 143
Thinkin' About You Baby 47
This Is Your Life (TV show) 127, 159
This One's On The House 153
Thompson, Chic 82, 84
Thompson, Hank 124
Thornton, Willie Mae (Big Mama) 167
Three Men of Rhythm 16
Three O'Clock Thrill 40
Timlett, Pete 78
Todd, Nick 134
Together You And I (CD) 137
Tommy Steele Story (film) 85
Too Hot To Handle 153
Top Of The Pops (TV show) 168
Torok, Mitchell **141-155**
Toups, Wayne 91
Trading Places (film) 177
Trees 113
Treniers 18, 87, 89, 90, 131
Trouble 46
True Love 149
Tubb, Ernest 151
Tubb, Justin 102
Tucker, Gabe 125
Turner, Joe 83
Turner, Sammy 168
Tuvey, Roy 79
Twilight Time 111, 119
Twistin' All Night Long 136
Twistin' USA 136
Twitty, Conway 46, 106
Two Fools In Love 106
Valens, Ritchie 161
Valente, Caterina 33
Valentine, Dickie 166
Vance, Nina 125
Varley, Bill 79, 80, 82, 85, 86

Index

Vee, Bobby 69
Ventura, Charlie 17
Ventura, Ernie 17
Vienneau, Jim 103
Vincent, Gene 63-4, 164, 168
Vipers 79
Waiting For A Train 143
Wake Up Little Susie 59
Walker, Frank 102, 106
Walker, Jimmy 108
Walkin' To School 39, 40
Wallace, Jerry 153
Wanted 158
Ward, Oliver 85
Warner, Sandy 25, 27
Waronker, Si 26, 27
Warris, Ben 43
Washington, George (President) 180
Wayward Angel 106
Wechter, Julius 25, 26
Weeping Willow 96
Welch, Bruce 86
Wells, Kitty 107, 124
Werner Brothers 79
West, Mae 178-9
When 37, 40, 41, 42, 45, 51
When (Disco Version) 47
When Mexico Gave Up The Rhumba 141, 147, 148-9, 152
Whiskey, Nancy
  20, 75, 79, 80, 81, 82, 84-6, 88, 158
White, Dave 132, 133, 134, 136
White, Ed 183
White, Josh 75-6, 78
Whitehouse, Alex 82, 84
Whitman, Slim 124, 149
Whole Lotta Woman 99, 103-4, 106, 108, 109
Wick, Ted 127
Wild Cat 161
Wildcats 163, 164
Wilde, Kim 157, 160, 161, 170, 174
Wilde, Marty 68, 86, 96-7, **157-175**
Willett, Slim 145
Williams, Andy 65
Williams, Hank 101, 102, 106, 124, 125, 143
Williams, Lawton 153
Williams, Tex 125
Williams, Tony 112, 113, 118, 120, 121
Williams Brothers 65
Willis, Bruce 28
Winchell, Walter 26
With A Little Help From My Friends (LP) 138
Wolfe, Digby 80
Wolfman, The (film) 183
Wood, Randy 58, 68
Wood Stix 22
Worried Man 84
Wright, Geoff 79
Wright, Johnny 107
Write Me A Letter 111, 114

Y'All Come 153
Yancey, Jimmy 81
Yellow Bird 27
Yempuku, Ralph 59
You Don't Own Me 136
You Keep Me Hangin' On 161
You'll Never Walk Alone 97
You, My Darlin', You 103
Zabach, Florian 43
Zacherle, John **177-192**

ILLUSTRATIONS AND PHOTO CREDITS

Ad on page 48 courtesy Gary Sneyd; ad on page 81 courtesy Terry Kay; ads on pages 83, 85, 105 and 118 courtesy Lee Fuller; ad on page 87 from author's collection; ads on pages 84 and 88 courtesy Chas McDevitt; ad on page 96 courtesy Bill Millar; ad on page 137 courtesy George R. White.

Business card on page 70 courtesy Robin Luke.

EP sleeve shot on page 22 courtesy Terry Kay; EP sleeve shot on page 34 courtesy Tony Wilkinson.

Label shot on page 18 courtesy Showtime Music Archives, Toronto; label shot on page 33 courtesy Tony Wilkinson; label shots on pages 43, 80, 148, 184 and 185 courtesy George R. White; label shot on page 60 courtesy Andy Mérey; label shots on pages 94, 106 and 134 courtesy Roy Rydland; label shots on pages 103 and 126 courtesy Lee Fuller; label shot on page 145 courtesy Bill Millar; label shot on page 160 courtesy Terry Kay.

LP sleeve shot on page 27 courtesy George R. White.

Newspaper cover on page 173 courtesy Lee Fuller.

Photographs on pages 14 and 23 courtesy Freddie Bell; photo on page 16 from author's collection/courtesy Mercury Records; photo on page 21 courtesy Showtime Music Archives, Toronto/Columbia Pictures; photo on page 24 by Christina Denny © 2003/courtesy Martin Denny; photo on page 26 courtesy Martin Denny; photos on pages 30, 32 and 35 courtesy Johnny Farina; photos on pages 36 and 50 courtesy Kalin Twins; photo on page 39 courtesy George R. White/Decca Records; photo on page 41 courtesy Gary Sneyd; photos on pages 52, 57. 58, 61, 67 and 73 courtesy Robin Luke; photo on page 65 courtesy Robin Luke/Dot Records; photo on page 74 courtesy Chas McDevitt; photos on pages 92 and 95 courtesy Phil Phillips; photos on pages 98, 100 and 109 by Paul Harris © 2003, 1987 and 1989; photo on page 102 courtesy Marvin Rainwater/MGM Records; photo on page 107 courtesy Marvin Rainwater/Okie Records; photo on page 110 courtesy Herb Reed; photo on page 114 courtesy Terry Kay/Mercury Records; photos on pages 116, 159, 186 and 187 courtesy George R. White; photo on page 122 courtesy Tommy Sands; photo on page 127 courtesy Tommy Sands/20th Century Fox; photo on page 130 courtesy Joe Terranova; photo page 135 courtesy George R. White/Columbia Pictures; photos on pages 140, 143, 144, 146 and 150 courtesy Mitchell Torok; photos on pages 156 and 172 by Dave Nicolson © 1987 and 1986; photo on page 162 courtesy George R. White/ABC-TV; photos on pages 176, 179, 180, 189, 190 and 192 courtesy John Zacherle.

Programme on page 20 courtesy Brian Smith; programmes on pages 44 and 120 from author's collection.

Sheet music covers on pages 19, 42, 46, 47, 66, 104, 128, 129, 168 and 169 courtesy Terry Kay; sheet music covers on pages 40, 82, 117, 119, 133 and 161 from author's collection; sheet music cover on page 154 courtesy Bill Millar.

OTHER TITLES FROM MUSIC MENTOR BOOKS

(35 Years of) British Hit EPs
George R. White
ISBN 0-9519888-1-6 *(pbk, 256 pages)* 2001   RRP £16.99

At last, a chart book dedicated to British hit EPs! Includes a history of the format, an artist-by-artist listing of every 7-inch EP hit from 1955 to 1989 (with full track details for each record), analyses of chart performance, and — for the first time ever — the official UK EP charts reproduced in their entirety. Profusely illustrated with *over 600* sleeve shots. A collector's dream!

Long Distance Information: Chuck Berry's Recorded Legacy
Fred Rothwell
ISBN 0-9519888-2-4 *(pbk, 352 pages)* 2001   RRP £18.99

Detailed analysis of every recording Chuck Berry has ever made. Includes an overview of his life and career, his influences, the stories behind his most famous compositions, full session details, listings of all his key US/UK vinyl and CD releases (including track details), TV and film appearances, and much, much more. Over 100 illustrations including label shots, vintage ads and previously unpublished photos.

Elvis & Buddy — Linked Lives
Alan Mann
ISBN 0-9519888-5-9 *(pbk, 160 pages)* 2002   RRP £12.99

The achievements of Elvis Presley and Buddy Holly have been extensively documented, but until now little if anything has been known about the many ways in which their lives were interconnected. For the first time anywhere, rock & roll expert Alan Mann, author of *The A–Z Of Buddy Holly*, takes a detailed look at each artist's early years, comparing their backgrounds and influences, chronicling all their meetings and examining the many amazing parallels in their lives, careers and tragic deaths. Over 50 illustrations including many rare/previously unpublished.

American Rock'n'Roll: The UK Tours 1956-72
Ian Wallis
ISBN 0-9519888-6-7 *(pbk, 424 pages)* 2003   RRP £21.99

The first-ever detailed overview of every visit to these shores by American (and Canadian!) rock'n'rollers. Includes full tour itineraries, supporting acts, show reports, TV appearances and other items of interest. Illustrated with vintage ads, original tour programmes and atmospheric live shots. A fascinating and nostalgic insight into a bygone era.

Elvis: A Musical Inventory 1939-55
Richard Boussiron
ISBN 0-9519888-7-5 *(pbk, 264 pages)* 2004   RRP £17.99

An extraordinarily detailed listing of the King's earliest musical influences – songs he learned at school, spirituals he sang at church, numbers he performed on the radio, etc. The product of over 30 years' original research including interviews with a host of people who knew him including his teacher, church ministers and neighbours. And, for the first time anywhere, complete details of all the historic Sun sessions — taken directly from the personal files of Marion Keisker. A 'must have' for anyone with an interest in early Elvis.

Let The Good Times ROCK!
A Fan's Notes on Post-War American Roots Music
Bill Millar
ISBN 0-9519888-8-3 *(pbk, 362 pages)* 2004   RRP £18.99

For almost four decades, the name 'Bill Millar' has been synonymous with the very best in British music writing — from his pioneering books on the Drifters and the Coasters, to his long-running 'Echoes' column in *Record Mirror*, *Let It Rock* and *Melody Maker*, to the authoritative sleevenotes he has penned for dozens of albums. This book contains 49 of his best pieces — some previously unpublished — in a thematic compilation covering hillbilly, rockabilly, R&B, rock'n'roll, doo-wop, swamp pop and soul. Includes essays on acappella, the doo-wop renaissance and blue-eyed soul, as well as detailed profiles of some of the most fascinating and influential personalities of each era. Passionate and knowledgable, music journalism rarely comes much better than this.

Music Mentor books
are available from all good bookshops
or by mail order from:

Music Mentor Books
69 Station Road
Upper Poppleton
YORK YO26 6PZ
England

Telephone/Fax: 01904 330308
International Telephone/Fax: +44 1904 330308
Email: music.mentor@lineone.net
Website: http://musicmentor0.tripod.com